THE CONSTITUTIONAL SYSTEM OF THE HONG KONG SAR

This book explores the legal, judicial and constitutional framework of the Hong Kong Special Administrative Region. As with other volumes in the classic Constitutional Systems of the World series, it offers a rigorous overview, looking at general constitutional themes such as law-making and adjudication, before exploring themes specific to the Hong Kong legal order.

Pictorial Narrative

The composition is formed from two pyramidal shapes in red reflecting each other, symbolising Hong Kong's parallel structure as 'One country, two systems'.

The inverted pyramid at the top displays the five golden stars of the Republic of China's national flag, and, to the left a roaring dragon stands for the authority of the Chinese central government.

To the left penetrating the dark blue is a shining pearl representing Hong Kong as the 'Pearl of the Orient'.

Within the red pyramid below iconic skyscrapers represent the economically vibrant Hong Kong itself which functions as a Special Administrative Region (indicated by the letters SAR picked out bottom left). Gazing back an enrobed lion is a reminder of the British colonial past. At the base the ripple pattern of the Hong Kong SAR Legislative Council is placed above the façade of Hong Kong's Final Court of Appeal.

To the right there is a modern sea container ship juxtaposed with the distinctive traditional sails of a Chinese junk in order to form a link between Hong Kong's historic and contemporary role as a great port.

Putachad
Artist

Constitutional Systems of the World
General Editors: Benjamin L Berger, Rosalind Dixon, Andrew Harding, Heinz Klug, and Peter Leyland

In the era of globalisation, issues of constitutional law and good governance are being seen increasingly as vital issues in all types of society. Since the end of the Cold War, there have been dramatic developments in democratic and legal reform, and post-conflict societies are also in the throes of reconstructing their governance systems. Even societies already firmly based on constitutional governance and the rule of law have undergone constitutional change and experimentation with new forms of governance; and their constitutional systems are increasingly subjected to comparative analysis and transplantation. Constitutional texts for practically every country in the world are now easily available on the internet. However, texts which enable one to understand the true context, purposes, interpretation and incidents of a constitutional system are much harder to locate, and are often extremely detailed and descriptive. This series seeks to provide scholars and students with accessible introductions to the constitutional systems of the world, supplying both a road map for the novice and, at the same time, a deeper understanding of the key historical, political and legal events which have shaped the constitutional landscape of each country. Each book in this series deals with a single country, or a group of countries with a common constitutional history, and each author is an expert in their field.

Published volumes

The Constitution of the United Kingdom; The Constitution of the United States; The Constitution of Vietnam; The Constitution of South Africa; The Constitution of Japan; The Constitution of Germany; The Constitution of Finland; The Constitution of Australia; The Constitution of the Republic of Austria; The Constitution of the Russian Federation; The Constitutional System of Thailand; The Constitution of Malaysia; The Constitution of China; The Constitution of Indonesia; The Constitution of France; The Constitution of Spain; The Constitution of Mexico; The Constitution of Israel; The Constitutional Systems of the Commonwealth Caribbean; The Constitution of Canada; The Constitution of Singapore; The Constitution of Belgium; The Constitution of Taiwan; The Constitution of Romania; The Constitutional Systems of the Independent Central Asian States; The Constitution of India; The Constitution of Pakistan; The Constitution of Ireland; The Constitution of Brazil; The Constitution of Myanmar; The Constitution of Czechia; The Constitution of New Zealand; The Constitution of Italy; The Constitutional System of the Hong Kong SAR

Link to series website

www.bloomsbury.com/uk/series/constitutional-systems-of-the-world/

The Constitutional System of the Hong Kong SAR

A Contextual Analysis

Albert Hung-yee Chen
and
Po Jen Yap

•HART•
OXFORD • LONDON • NEW YORK • NEW DELHI • SYDNEY

HART PUBLISHING

Bloomsbury Publishing Plc

Kemp House, Chawley Park, Cumnor Hill, Oxford, OX2 9PH, UK

1385 Broadway, New York, NY 10018, USA

29 Earlsfort Terrace, Dublin 2, Ireland

HART PUBLISHING, the Hart/Stag logo, BLOOMSBURY and the Diana logo are trademarks of Bloomsbury Publishing Plc

First published in Great Britain 2023

A catalogue record for this book is available from the British Library.

A catalogue record for this book is available from the Library of Congress.

Library of Congress Control Number: 2023938226

ISBN: HB: 978-1-50995-629-6
ePDF: 978-1-50995-631-9
ePub: 978-1-50995-630-2

Typeset by Compuscript Ltd, Shannon

Preface

Hong Kong is an international financial centre and a cosmopolitan city with a population of over seven million, and its GDP per capita for 2021 was higher than that of Britain, its former colonial master. Since 1997, Hong Kong has been governed as a Special Administrative Region (SAR) of the People's Republic of China (PRC) in accordance with a constitutional framework known as 'One Country, Two Systems' (OCTS). This arrangement for Hong Kong's autonomy under Chinese sovereignty has been enshrined in the Basic Law of the Hong Kong SAR, which was enacted by China's legislature after China and Britain signed the Sino-British Joint Declaration in 1984.

The implementation of the Basic Law over the last 25 years has not been plain sailing. Hong Kong has been in the international headlines from time to time, such as when half a million people demonstrated against a proposed national security law in 2003, and during the months-long 'Occupy Central' or 'Umbrella' movement in 2014, and the Anti-Extradition movement in 2019. Hong Kong was once again in the global spotlight in 2020 when the Chinese legislature enacted a national security law for Hong Kong and applied it to the SAR. The reaction of the Western world to this development has been generally negative, especially with the United States imposing sanctions on senior Chinese and Hong Kong officials for their role in the law's passage and enforcement.

OCTS constitutes the foundation of the Hong Kong SAR's unique constitutional system. As originally conceived by the Chinese authorities, this constitutional arrangement entails the coexistence of the socialist system in mainland China and a capitalist system in Hong Kong. However, the political instability and occasional crises that Hong Kong experienced after the handover in 1997 were largely not attributable to any inherent conflict between the socialist and capitalist economic systems, but to the tension between China's authoritarian mode of rule and the aspirations for liberal democracy on the part of the majority of Hong Kong's population. This book explores the constitutional system of the Hong Kong SAR in the context of its complex and difficult relationship with the political, legal and constitutional system that operates in mainland China. The book also highlights the role of Hong Kong's judiciary in managing this relationship, and the SAR courts' efforts to protect fundamental rights in Hong Kong.

With the proliferation of constitutional arrangements around the world that empower regional or local autonomous territories, an analysis of the distinctive features of the Hong Kong SAR's autonomy under OCTS can contribute to the comparative study of federalism and devolution. As many countries in the world face unprecedented democratic regression, the constitutional crises engendered by the ultimately unsuccessful social movements in Hong Kong, which sought greater democratisation for the autonomous polity, reflect this global trend. And at a time when constitutions and rights globally are judicialised, the Hong Kong SAR judiciary's performance under OCTS has also come under the global spotlight.

This book is divided into eight chapters. Chapter one provides a brief review of Hong Kong's constitutional history from colonial times to 2022, which marked 25 years of Hong Kong's governance as an SAR of the PRC. The chapter also provides the context for the discussion in the subsequent chapters on various aspects of the constitutional system of the Hong Kong SAR and its relationship with the central authorities in Beijing.

Chapter two investigates the nature of the Hong Kong SAR as an autonomous regional entity within the PRC, focusing in particular on the powers of the central authorities over Hong Kong and those of the Hong Kong SAR government. The chapter includes a discussion of the national security law enacted by the Chinese legislature for Hong Kong in 2020, which is perhaps the central authorities' single most significant act vis-à-vis Hong Kong since the Basic Law came into force in 1997.

Chapter three moves from our analysis of the constitutional relationship between the Hong Kong SAR and the central authorities to a study of Hong Kong's internal political system, particularly the office of the Chief Executive, the executive branch of government and the legislature. In chapter four, we continue our study of Hong Kong's political system by examining its electoral system, the pattern of political polarisation in Hong Kong, and the continuous struggles between the 'pro-democracy' forces and the 'pro-China' forces in Hong Kong politics. The chapter also tracks the Hong Kong SAR's constitutional reforms and political crises over the past 25 years, which culminated in the anti-extradition bill movement of 2019 and the Chinese government's complete overhaul of Hong Kong's electoral system in 2021.

Chapter five examines the role of the judiciary in the Hong Kong SAR. It introduces the structure of the Hong Kong judiciary and discusses major issues relating to its constitutional jurisdiction and its relationship with the central authorities in Beijing. The chapter also explores the inter-branch relationship between the Hong Kong judiciary and other branches of the Hong Kong SAR government, both from the perspectives of the 'separation of powers' principle and the China-led discourse on 'executive-led government'.

Chapter six moves on to study the protection of constitutional rights in Hong Kong. The protection of fundamental rights and civil liberties is a fundamental pillar of constitutional governance. We explore in this chapter the unique features of Hong Kong's system of rights protection, and its practice under the tenure of each Chief Justice.

Chapter seven proceeds by looking at how constitutional rights are enforced in Hong Kong through the use of constitutional remedies. It is axiomatic that abstract declarations of rights are in themselves inadequate, unless courts can grant concrete and effective remedies when rights are violated. Chapter seven features the efforts and innovations of the Hong Kong judiciary in this regard. Finally, chapter eight sets out our concluding reflections on the constitutional project of OCTS as practised in the Hong Kong SAR.

We gratefully acknowledge the support for the research for this book project by the Research Grants Council of Hong Kong, GRF Project No 17611318. We are also grateful to Professor Andrew Harding for inviting us to contribute this Hong Kong volume to the Hart Series on *Constitutional Systems of the World*, and to both Professor Andrew Harding and Professor Peter Leyland for their helpful comments on our manuscript. It is an honour and privilege for us to be part of this grand project. At the time of writing, the project of OCTS is facing more challenges than ever before. We hope that the constitutional practice of OCTS will endure, and that the constitutional jurisprudence of the Basic Law of the Hong Kong SAR will continue to evolve and meet the aspirations of the people of Hong Kong.

Albert HY Chen and Po Jen Yap
Faculty of Law
The University of Hong Kong
12 February 2023

Contents

Table of Cases

Table of Legislation

Hong Kong/PRC

United Kingdom

United States

International

1

Hong Kong's Constitutional Journey

Constitutional History – Colonialism – Sino-British Joint Declaration – Basic Law Drafting – Democratisation – Extradition

MANY COLONIES AND constituent parts of the British Empire became independent states over the course of the twentieth century. Despite the change in sovereignty, there usually exists a considerable degree of continuity in the laws and legal institutions of these jurisdictions after independence. Therefore, for these jurisdictions, a study of their colonial legal systems is often essential for the purpose of understanding their post-colonial legal, constitutional and political orders.

Hong Kong differs from the general pattern of decolonisation that took place in other parts of the British Empire. Decolonisation of the British colony of Hong Kong in 1997 did not result in the creation of an independent state. Instead, the British colony was incorporated into the People's Republic of China (PRC) as a Special Administrative Region (SAR) governed under a Basic Law drafted on the basis of the Sino-British Joint Declaration of 1984, which guaranteed a 'high degree of autonomy'[1] for the city under Chinese rule and the continuation of its existing economic, social and legal systems in accordance with the policy of 'One Country, Two Systems' (OCTS). This continuity means that, as is the case for post-colonial independent states, the study of the laws and legal institutions of colonial Hong Kong is also highly relevant to the understanding of its post-colonial constitutional, legal and political history.

This book therefore begins with an overview of Hong Kong's colonial history, the negotiation of the Sino-British Joint Declaration on Hong Kong's return to the PRC, the drafting of the Basic Law of the

[1] Joint Declaration, para 3(2); Basic Law, Art 2.

Hong Kong Special Administrative Region (HKSAR) – Hong Kong's new constitutional instrument – and Hong Kong's transition from a colony to the HKSAR. This chapter will also chronicle the major episodes in Hong Kong's post-colonial constitutional history.

I. HONG KONG BEFORE THE 1980s

The present territory demarcated by the HKSAR was an integral part of the Chinese empire over successive dynasties in the last two millennia. It became a British colony as a result of three treaties signed between the Qing Empire in China and the British Empire in the nineteenth century. By virtue of the Treaty of Nanking, signed by China in 1842 after its defeat in the Opium War, the island of Hong Kong was ceded to the British. A subsequent war leading to the Anglo-French invasion of Beijing ended with another treaty, signed in 1860, under which Kowloon Peninsula was added to the colony of Hong Kong. In 1898, a third treaty provided for a 99-year lease by the Qing Empire to Britain over the 'New Territories' (north of Kowloon Peninsula).[2]

Colonial Hong Kong was ruled on the basis of a rudimentary constitution enshrined in the Letters Patent and Royal Instructions issued by the British monarch.[3] Power was concentrated in the hands of the Governor, who ruled with the assistance of an Executive Council (a cabinet-like body) and a Legislative Council appointed by him. Leading members of the local business and professional elite were co-opted onto these councils as 'unofficial members' (as distinguished from 'official members', who were government officials). There was no popular election except for a municipal council. This took the form of the Urban Council, which originated from the Sanitary Board established in the nineteenth century, vested with responsibilities over public health, environmental hygiene and recreational facilities. Apart from appointed members, the Urban Council also had members elected on the basis of a limited franchise. The English legal system, based on the common law and corresponding traditions relating to the rule of law and judicial independence, was transplanted into Hong Kong.[4] Also transplanted

[2] See P Wesley-Smith, *Unequal Treaty 1898–1997*, revised edn (Oxford University Press, 1998).

[3] See generally P Wesley-Smith, *Constitutional and Administrative Law in Hong Kong*, vol 1 (China and Hong Kong Law Studies, 1987) ch 4.

[4] See P Wesley-Smith, *An Introduction to the Hong Kong Legal System* (Oxford University Press, 1987).

was the English bifurcation of legal professionals as solicitors and barristers. There was no bill of rights in the colonial constitution, and laws enacted by the colonial regime placed considerable restrictions on freedoms of speech, publication, assembly and association.[5]

Located on the southern coast of China, Hong Kong had long been a place of refuge for migrants from the mainland.[6] More than one million people fled to the British colony as civil war between the Chinese Communists and the Chinese Nationalist Party (Kuomintang) raged in the late 1940s. In the 1960s, the Cultural Revolution in China had a spill-over effect in Hong Kong, which took the form of riots against colonial rule in 1967, but the overwhelming majority of the population of Hong Kong stood by the colonial government at the time.[7] Since then, and particularly after the introduction of new social policies by Governor MacLehose in the 1970s, it was apparent that Hong Kong people supported the continuation of British rule, for they realised that the only alternative to colonial rule would be Hong Kong's integration into Communist China. Thus, there was no independence movement in colonial Hong Kong, despite the development of a local identity (as 'Hongkongers') among the new generation born in Hong Kong after the Second World War.[8] Unlike their parents, who were mostly refugees from mainland China, the new generation of Hongkongers never lived elsewhere in China, and considered Hong Kong their home.

In the 1970s, colonial Hong Kong was relatively well governed in terms of indicators such as the rule of law and efficient governance, when compared with its neighbours in East and Southeast Asia. Controls on civil liberties in Hong Kong in the 1970s were more relaxed than those practised by the other three of the 'Four Little Dragons' of East Asia – Singapore, Taiwan and South Korea. Social stability and economic prosperity in Hong Kong under colonial rule and popular support for its continuation[9] meant that the colonial government could afford to rule without the severe repression of civil liberties.

[5] See R Wacks (ed), *Civil Liberties in Hong Kong* (Oxford University Press, 1988); N Jayawickrama, 'Public Law' in R Wacks (ed), *The Law in Hong Kong, 1969–1989* (Oxford University Press, 1989) ch 2.

[6] See generally AHY Chen, 'The Development of Immigration Law and Policy: The Hong Kong Experience' (1988) *McGill Law Journal* 631.

[7] S Tsang, *A Modern History of Hong Kong* (Hong Kong University Press, 2004) 183–90.

[8] ibid 190–96; D Faure, 'Reflections on Being Chinese in Hong Kong' in JM Brown and R Foot (eds), *Hong Kong's Transitions, 1842–1997* (Macmillan Press, 1997) ch 5.

[9] See generally Lau Siu-kai, *Society and Politics in Hong Kong* (Chinese University of Hong Kong Press, 1982).

Hong Kong's economic development had been spectacular, particularly after the establishment of the PRC in 1949, which resulted in a capital flight from Shanghai and other Chinese cities to Hong Kong and massive migration from the mainland. By the 1970s, Hong Kong had risen to become one of the 'Four Little Dragons' of East Asia. By 1982 – the year when Britain and China began negotiations over Hong Kong's future, Hong Kong, with its population of 5.2 million (in contrast to the population of approximately 1 billion in mainland China at that time) and a geographical size of 1000 square kilometres, had a GDP, which was 15 per cent of that of mainland China's.[10]

II. NEGOTIATION OF THE SINO-BRITISH JOINT DECLARATION

With the death of Mao Zedong in 1976 and the rise to power of Deng Xiaoping in the late 1970s, a new era of 'reform and opening' began in China. A new policy towards Taiwan was also adopted, which subsequently became highly relevant to Hong Kong. Instead of calling for the 'liberation' of Taiwan, which implied the extension of communism to Taiwan, a new concept was developed for the purpose of reunifying Taiwan with mainland China. This was the OCTS model, which would allow for the peaceful coexistence of capitalism (in Taiwan) and socialism (on the mainland), a 'high degree of autonomy' for Taiwan under the PRC's sovereignty, and the preservation of the existing social and economic systems in Taiwan after reunification. Article 31 of the new (fourth) Constitution of the PRC, enacted by the National People's Congress (NPC) in December 1982, authorises the establishment of SARs in the PRC that practise social and economic systems different from those on the mainland.

In September 1982, Britain and China began negotiations over the future of Hong Kong. The negotiations were initiated by the UK because by the early 1980s, the British government was concerned that there was no legal basis for its continued governance of the New Territories after 1997, and it wanted to secure the Chinese government's consent to the continued British administration of the whole of Hong Kong after 1997.

[10] In 1997 – the year of Hong Kong's handover to the PRC, Hong Kong's GDP was 18% that of mainland China. However, due to the continued rapid economic growth in mainland China since then, by 2020, Hong Kong's GDP was only 3% that of the mainland (and the population figures of the mainland and of Hong Kong in 2020 were estimated to be 1.4 billion and 7.5 million, respectively).

The Chinese government considered the issue of Hong Kong's future a subject to be discussed exclusively between the Chinese and British governments, and emphatically rejected the idea that the people of Hong Kong or their representatives should also be involved.[11] From the Chinese government's point of view, the interests of the people of Hong Kong were to be represented and taken care of solely by the Chinese government. At the same time, the British government also purported to speak for the interests of the Hong Kong people.

The PRC considered all the three treaties constituting the legal basis for British rule in Hong Kong to be 'unequal treaties' and not binding on the PRC. As there was, in China's view, no valid legal basis for British colonial rule in Hong Kong, the PRC, upon joining the United Nations (UN) in 1971, requested the removal of Hong Kong (and Macau) from the UN's list of 'non-self-governing territories' or colonies; this request was acceded to in 1972.[12] China perceived the cession of Hong Kong to the British as a result of the Opium War as an episode of humiliation and shame for the Chinese people that was imposed by Western imperialists. Being fervent nationalists, the Chinese Communists absolutely ruled out the option of allowing continued British administration of Hong Kong after 1997. The concept of OCTS, though originally conceived for Taiwan, was at hand and was thus offered to Britain as the solution for Hong Kong's constitutional future.

It was proposed that the whole of Hong Kong would be returned to the PRC in July 1997, and it would become an SAR of the PRC that exercises a 'high degree of autonomy'. Its existing social and economic systems and laws would be preserved, as would the lifestyle and liberties of its people. The principle of 'Hong Kong people ruling Hong Kong' would be applied in accordance with a 'Basic Law', in which China's promises for post-1997 Hong Kong would be codified in a constitutional instrument.

After protracted negotiations, the British realised that they had no choice but to accept the Chinese proposal. The result was the Sino-British Joint Declaration on the Question of Hong Kong (JD), signed in late 1984, in which the details of the Chinese plan for the post-1997 governance of the HKSAR were solemnly set out. The JD expressly stipulated

[11] P Cradock, *Experiences of China* (John Murray, 1994) 187 and 211.

[12] List of Former Trust and Non-Self-Governing Territories', www.un.org/dppa/decolonization/en/history/former-trust-and-nsgts; N Jayawickrama, 'Hong Kong: The Gathering Storm' (1991) 22(2) *Bulletin of Peace Proposal* 157; PA Dagati, 'Hong Kong's Lost Right to Self-Determination' (1992) 13(1) *New York Law School Journal of International and Comparative Law* 153.

that the policies set out within it regarding post-1997 Hong Kong would be provided for in a Basic Law.[13]

III. DRAFTING OF THE BASIC LAW

After the JD was concluded, China began drafting the Basic Law. Its official policy was to welcome the participation and input of Hong Kong people in this drafting process. In 1985, a 59-member Basic Law Drafting Committee (BLDC) was appointed; 23 of its members were from Hong Kong, mainly from the business and professional elite, but also included a few individuals from the labour and religious sectors. Nine of the Hong Kong members were serving or former members of the Executive Council or Legislative Council (LegCo) of colonial Hong Kong.[14]

The Chinese government never acknowledged publicly that the British or the colonial Hong Kong government had any role in drafting the Basic Law. The Chinese government viewed the enactment of the Basic Law as a purely domestic affair of the PRC. However, both British and Chinese sources published subsequently reveal that the British did provide significant inputs during the drafting process behind the scenes.[15]

The BLDC held its inaugural meeting in Beijing in July 1985. The meeting decided the timetable for the drafting of the Basic Law. The first draft of the Basic Law would be completed and released for public consultation in early 1988. After the consultation exercise, a second draft would be prepared and submitted to the NPC Standing Committee in early 1989. There would be a second round of consultation. The final version of the Basic Law would be submitted to the NPC for enactment in early 1990. This timetable was strictly followed in the years that followed.

[13] Approximately half of the provisions of the Basic Law that were subsequently enacted in 1990 were largely reproduced from the JD. This estimate is based on the authors' article-by-article comparison of the text of the Basic Law with that of the JD.

[14] See generally E Lau, 'The Early History of the Drafting Process' in P Wesley-Smith and AHY Chen (eds), *The Basic Law and Hong Kong's Future* (Butterworths, 1988) ch 6.

[15] See generally AHY Chen and M Ng, 'The Making of the Constitutional Order of the Hong Kong SAR' in KYL Tan and M Ng (eds), *Constitutional Foundings in Northeast Asia* (Hart Publishing, 2022) ch 3. The following discussion draws on AHY Chen, 'The History of the Drafting and Implementation of the Basic Law of the Hong Kong Special Administrative Region' in NS Bui, S Hargreaves and R Mitchell (eds), *Routledge Handbook of Constitutional Law in Greater China* (2023) ch 3.

At the inaugural meeting of the BLDC, it was also decided that research work in preparation for the drafting of the Basic Law would commence immediately. The plan was for the second plenary session of the BLDC to be held in the first half of 1986, when the topics to be covered in the Basic Law would be decided, and the drafting work would then begin. It was also decided that a Basic Law Consultative Committee (BLCC) would be established in Hong Kong to collect the views of Hong Kong people and provide input to the BLDC. In December 1985, the 180-member BLCC, consisting of Hong Kong people from different walks of life – largely nominated by business, professional and social bodies – held its inaugural meeting.

In April 1986, the second plenary session of the BLDC was held in Beijing. The structural outline of the Basic Law was adopted. At the meeting, it was decided that five sub-groups of the BLDC, specialising in different Basic Law topics, would be set up. Initial drafts of various chapters in the Basic Law would be prepared by the relevant sub-groups for consideration by the BLDC at its plenary sessions.

Over the course of the Basic Law's drafting, which concluded in early 1990, the BLDC held a total of nine plenary sessions, and its five sub-groups held a total of 73 meetings in Beijing and other Chinese cities. Each sub-group was led by two co-conveners, one from the mainland and one from Hong Kong. There was a fairly high degree of transparency in the meetings of the BLDC and its sub-groups. The usual practice was that journalists from Hong Kong were notified of these meetings, and representatives of the BLDC or its sub-group met with journalists after the meetings were held. With regard to the BLCC, it initially formed eight sub-groups, which were reorganised into six in 1987. The BLCC held a total of eight plenary meetings, and produced a huge volume of research papers and consultation reports.

The most controversial issues arising from the drafting of the Basic Law concerned how democratic the political system of the HKSAR would be and how much power the central government in Beijing could exercise over Hong Kong. The Basic Law was drafted in tandem with and alongside the political and constitutional reforms launched by the colonial Hong Kong government in the 1980s. These changes proceeded in several stages, as follows.[16]

[16] See, eg K Cheek-Milby, *A Legislature Comes of Age: Hong Kong's Search for Influence and Identity* (Oxford University Press, 1995); Lo Shiu-hing, *The Politics of Democratization in Hong Kong* (Macmillan, 1997); AY So, *Hong Kong's Embattled Democracy* (John Hopkins University Press, 1999).

In 1982, 18 new District Boards – advisory bodies at local levels – were established, consisting of members appointed by the government as well as members elected by universal suffrage. At the same time, the franchise for the members of the Urban Council, which included both elected and appointed members, was broadened to allow for universal suffrage.

In 1985, some of the seats in the LegCo – hitherto an entirely appointed body – were opened up for election for the first time in the colony's history.[17] Electoral colleges, comprising the District Boards, the Urban Council and the newly created Regional Council (for the New Territories), elected 12 seats. Another 12 seats were elected by members of 'functional constituencies' consisting of business and professional groupings (such as chambers of commerce, industrialists' federations, banks and trade unions) and members of professions (such as lawyers, doctors, engineers and teachers). The original rationale for having functional constituencies, as explained by the colonial government, was that they represented sectors of society from which appointed unofficial members of LegCo were formerly drawn, and in the course of Hong Kong's democratisation, it was appropriate for the corporate bodies or individuals in these sectors to elect their own representatives into LegCo.[18]

The discussion and debates on issues arising from the drafting of the Basic Law in the Hong Kong community and among politicians, political groups, business and professional elites, social activists and civil society organisations began with the consultative activities launched by the BLCC in 1986. The constitutional discourse gained further momentum with the launch of the Hong Kong government's Green Paper on the '1987 review of developments in representative government'.

The '1987 review' was introduced for the purpose of deciding whether 'direct election' (by universal suffrage) to a portion of LegCo seats should be introduced in 1988. The Chinese government had opposed the introduction of such direct election in 1988 on the ground that constitutional change in colonial Hong Kong should 'converge' with the model of the HKSAR's political system as prescribed by the Basic Law. Therefore, before the Basic Law was finalised, no significant constitutional change should be introduced unilaterally by the British in

[17] *White Paper: The Further Development of Representative Government in Hong Kong* (Hong Kong Government, November 1984).

[18] See generally C Loh and Civic Exchange (eds), *Functional Constituencies: A Unique Feature of the Hong Kong Legislative Council* (Hong Kong University Press, 2006).

Hong Kong. By late 1985, the British had come to accept in principle this concept of 'convergence'.[19]

The political elite and public opinion in Hong Kong were divided on certain fundamental issues arising from the drafting of the Basic Law, particularly with regard to the degree of Hong Kong's democratisation that should be codified in the Basic Law.[20] The conservative political forces were led by the 'Business and Professional Group' (BPG or 'Group of 89 persons') of the BLCC. The establishment of the BPG in August 1986 was followed by the formation in October 1986 of a pro-democracy alliance of 91 civil society organisations and more than 300 individuals (including 19 BLCC members) known as the 'Joint Committee on the Promotion of Democratic Government' (JCPDG), which stood at the other end of the political spectrum. The JCPDG represented Hong Kong's nascent democracy movement and advocated for the introduction of Western-style liberal democracy in Hong Kong. Within the BLDC, only two Hong Kong members advocated for this position: Szeto Wah and Martin Lee, who were elected into LegCo in 1985 by the functional constituencies for teachers and lawyers respectively.

In 1986–87, initial drafts of various chapters of the Basic Law were produced and discussed at meetings of the relevant BLDC sub-groups, followed by discussion at plenary sessions of the BLDC itself. At the seventh plenary session of the BLDC in April 1988, the first consultative draft of the Basic Law was adopted. It was then published for consultation. There was a five-month consultation period, ending on 30 September 1988. In this period, the fervour generated by the discussion and debates in the Hong Kong community on issues arising from the draft Basic Law reached a new high.

During the consultation period, the first draft of the Basic Law was discussed in considerable detail both in Hong Kong's LegCo and the British Parliament. LegCo's debate on the draft Basic Law took place on 13–14 July 1988. The British House of Lords' debate on the subject took place even earlier, on 10 June 1988, followed by the House of Commons' debate on the draft Basic Law on 15 July 1988.[21]

After the end of the consultation period, sub-groups of the BLDC held several meetings to consider revisions to the first draft of the Basic Law. For example, the sub-group on the political system met twice in

[19] Chen and Ng (n 15) 53–54.

[20] See generally So (n 16); Lo (n 16); M Sing, *Hong Kong's Tortuous Democratization* (RoutledgeCurzon, 2004).

[21] For extracts of the speeches, see MK Chan and DJ Clark (eds), *The Hong Kong Basic Law* (Hong Kong University Press, 1991) 92–144.

Guangzhou in November and December 1988 and adopted a controversial electoral plan for the HKSAR known as the 'Cha-Cha model' (named after Cha Leung-yung Louis and Cha Chi-min, two influential Hong Kong members of the BLDC).[22] The revisions proposed by the sub-groups were finalised and voted upon at the eighth plenary session of the BLDC in January 1989; the procedure required each article of the draft to be endorsed by a two-thirds majority vote. This second draft of the Basic Law was submitted to the NPC Standing Committee in February 1989 and then published for a second round of public consultation. The improvements (particularly from Hong Kong's perspective) to the first draft – evidenced in the second draft – were substantial,[23] although the provisions on the electoral model and the pace of democratisation were still controversial.

The following are some key examples of the significant improvements made in the second draft vis-à-vis the first draft. First, as regards the application of mainland Chinese law to the HKSAR, Article 17 of the first draft had provided that the State Council may issue a directive to the HKSAR government to apply in Hong Kong any specified mainland law that relates to defence, foreign affairs or other matters of national unity and territorial integrity that are not within the SAR's autonomy. But under Article 18 of the second draft (which is the equivalent of Article 17 of the first draft), mainland laws that are applicable in the HKSAR shall be listed in Annex III to the Basic Law and are limited to matters of defence, foreign affairs and other matters not within the SAR's autonomy.

Secondly, as regards the power of the central authorities to veto laws made by the HKSAR legislature, Article 16 of the first draft had provided that this veto power is applicable to any law that is considered

[22] The model was concerned with the mode of election of the Chief Executive (CE) and the Legislative Council (LegCo) of the HKSAR. It proposed that the 2nd-term and 3rd-term CEs would be elected by an 800-member election committee. The number of directly elected LegCo members would progressively increase during the first few terms of LegCo, so that half of the members of the 4th-term LegCo would be directly elected by universal suffrage. The model also proposed that during the term of office of the 3rd-term CE, a referendum may be held (if LegCo, the CE and the NPC Standing Committee so agree) to decide whether the 4th-term CE and all members of the 5th-term LegCo should be elected by universal suffrage.

[23] In internal communications within the British government, its Foreign and Commonwealth Office expressed the view that 'all the provisions of the Joint Declaration [were] reflected in the [second] draft Basic Law': see Chen and Ng (n 15) fn 120 and the accompanying text.

inconsistent with the Basic Law or legal procedures. However, under Article 17 of the second draft, the exercise of the veto power is limited to circumstances in which the Hong Kong law is considered to be inconsistent with Basic Law provisions relating to matters within the jurisdiction of the central authorities or the relationship between the central authorities and the HKSAR.

Thirdly, as regards the scope of the jurisdiction of the HKSAR courts, Article 18 of the first draft had provided that Hong Kong courts should have no jurisdiction over cases concerning matters of defence and foreign affairs, or concerning 'executive acts' of the Central People's Government. Under Article 19 of the second draft, the exclusion of the courts' jurisdiction is limited to cases concerning 'acts of state'. This was considered an improvement, as the concept of 'act of state' already existed under the English common law and was well understood by judges and lawyers in Hong Kong.

Fourthly, as regards the enactment of legislation in the HKSAR to safeguard national security, Article 22 of the first draft had provided that the HKSAR should prohibit by law any act that harms national unity or subverts the Central People's Government. The wording of the prohibited acts was changed in Article 23 of the second draft to treason, splitting up the country (secession), sedition and theft of state secrets.

Less than two months after the publication of the second draft of the Basic Law, the student movement sparked off by the public grief over the passing of Hu Yaobang – former liberal-minded Chinese Communist Party General Secretary – began to engulf Beijing, culminating in the infamous 'June 4th incident' at Tiananmen Square. Hong Kong saw the largest demonstrations in its history, with hundreds of thousands of people marching in support of the student movement and against the crackdown. The actions taken by the Chinese authorities to quell the movement precipitated an unprecedented crisis of confidence in Hong Kong's future.

For a while, all activities of the BLCC were suspended. Szeto Wah and Martin Lee – two members of the BLDC, who had led the Hong Kong protests and formed the Hong Kong Alliance in Support of Patriotic Democratic Movements in China, were expelled from the BLDC. Two other members – Louis Cha and Bishop Kwong Kong-kit Peter – resigned from it on their own accord.

On the whole, the demand within the Hong Kong community for more rapid democratisation in the city gained strength. Even some leading members of the BPG now joined forces with the 'moderates' and a few 'democrats' to propose a new political model known as the

'4–4–2 model'.[24] Compared to the BPG's previous proposals, this new 4–4–2 model incorporated more directly elected elements and allowed for a faster pace of democratisation. At the same time, unofficial members of the Executive and Legislative Councils jointly promoted a model with even more democratic components. The British government proposed further revisions to the draft Basic Law on a large number of issues, including a faster pace of democratisation in Hong Kong. Sino-British diplomacy behind the scenes finally achieved a 'compromise', which entailed an increased number of directly elected LegCo members in 1991 and an arrangement for a 'through train' transition of the last colonial LegCo elected in 1995 to constitute the first LegCo of the HKSAR in 1997.[25]

The ninth and last plenary session of the BLDC was held in Beijing in February 1990. Revisions to the second draft of the Basic Law were finalised and voted on. The final version of the draft was presented to the NPC on 28 March 1990 and was adopted on 4 April 1990. The process of the drafting of the Basic Law, which took four years and eight months, was finally concluded.

When one compares the final enacted version of the Basic Law with the second draft published in 1989, the most significant new provisions in the final version are those on the electoral arrangements for the Chief Executive and LegCo. On other matters, the differences between the second draft and the final version are considerably less than the earlier differences between the first and second drafts.

It is noteworthy that in the final version, the provisions regarding the qualifications for the Chief Executive, principal officials, Executive Council members and the majority of LegCo members were tightened to exclude those with a right of abode in foreign countries. In previous drafts, there were qualification rules regarding Chinese nationality and Hong Kong permanent residency, but there was no express rule prohibiting any overseas right of abode. As regards Article 23 of the Basic Law, the final version reinstated the concept of subversion in the first draft, adding it to the other prohibited acts stipulated in Article 23 of the second draft. Also added to Article 23 was a prohibition on foreign political bodies from engaging in political activities in the HKSAR, and

[24] '4–4–2' referred to the following composition of the first LegCo of the HKSAR: 40% of the seats being elected by direct election/universal suffrage; 40% elected by functional constituencies; and 20% elected by an election committee. See So (n 16) 155–82; Sing (n 20) 114–22.

[25] Chen and Ng (n 15) 66–67.

a prohibition on Hong Kong political bodies from establishing ties with foreign political bodies.

IV. DEVELOPMENTS IN COLONIAL HONG KONG IN THE 1990s

In 1991, 18 seats in LegCo were opened to direct election by universal suffrage for the first time. The 'pro-democracy' politicians, who had led the massive demonstrations in Hong Kong in support of the student movement in Beijing in 1989, won a landslide victory.[26]

Another major constitutional milestone reached at this time was the enactment of the Hong Kong Bill of Rights Ordinance (HKBORO) in 1991.[27] This legislative initiative was part of the Hong Kong government's efforts to assuage the crisis of confidence in Hong Kong precipitated by the 'June 4th incident' in 1989. The HKBORO incorporated into Hong Kong's domestic law the provisions of the International Covenant on Civil and Political Rights (ICCPR), which Britain had already applied to Hong Kong in 1976. Corresponding amendments were made to the Letters Patent, Hong Kong's colonial constitutional instrument.[28] Hong Kong courts acquired the power to review and strike down laws and administrative actions that the courts determined to be inconsistent with the human rights guarantees in the HKBORO. Since 1991, a body of case law has developed in which Hong Kong courts have exercised this power of constitutional review, and have applied the 'proportionality analysis' to determine whether a restriction on a relevant right is justified.[29]

In 1992, the newly arrived Governor Christopher Patten announced an ambitious plan for political reform in Hong Kong, which involved a radical broadening of the franchise for the functional constituencies (increasing the number of eligible voters in these constituencies from less than 100,000 to over two million).[30] The Chinese government condemned

[26] See Lau Siu-kai and Louie Kin-sheun (eds), *Hong Kong Tried Democracy: The 1991 Elections in Hong Kong* (Hong Kong Institute of Asia-Pacific Studies, Chinese University of Hong Kong, 1993).

[27] See J Chan and Y Ghai (eds), *The Hong Kong Bill of Rights: A Comparative Approach* (Butterworths Asia, 1993).

[28] These amendments sought to ensure that the laws of Hong Kong would be consistent with the human rights standards set out in the ICCPR. See A Byrnes and J Chan (eds), *Public Law and Human Rights: A Hong Kong Sourcebook* (Butterworths, 1993).

[29] See AHY Chen, 'The Interpretation of the Basic Law – Common Law and Mainland Chinese Perspectives' (2000) 30 *Hong Kong Law Journal* 380, 418–20. The judicial practice of constitutional review on the basis of HKBORO and the ICCPR has continued after the 1997 handover as discussed in chs 4 and 5 below.

[30] See So (n 16) ch 7.

the plan as being inconsistent with the Basic Law and contrary to the understanding reached by an exchange of letters in 1990 between the Chinese and British governments. Seventeen rounds of negotiation between the two governments took place in 1993, but no settlement was reached. Governor Patten then unilaterally put the reform Bill to LegCo,[31] which passed it by a narrow majority. The 1995 LegCo election was thus conducted in accordance with the new electoral scheme.[32] The Chinese government responded by 'establishing another stove' (ie establishing an alternative institutional arrangement for the 1997 handover) and rescinding its previous consent (given tacitly in 1990) for the LegCo elected in 1995 to continue as the first LegCo of the HKSAR in 1997. China established a Provisional Legislative Council of the HKSAR in 1997 to take charge of HKSAR legislative matters before the first LegCo could be elected in accordance with the Basic Law.

V. MAJOR CONSTITUTIONAL AND LEGAL DEVELOPMENTS IN THE HKSAR

At the stroke of midnight between 30 June and 1 July 1997, a handover ceremony took place in Hong Kong, with the lowering of the British flag and the hoisting of the PRC national flag and HKSAR regional flag. The HKSAR was formally established. From the perspective of Hans Kelsen's legal theory, there was a shift in the *Grundnorm* (basic norm) of the legal order at this constitutional moment when power was transferred. Hong Kong's legal order, which drew its authority from the British Crown and Parliament, now derives its validity from the Constitution of the PRC, particularly Article 31, in pursuance of which the Basic Law was enacted. The Basic Law stipulates how the different branches of the SAR government will be constituted, defines their powers, identifies the sources of law in the SAR, guarantees the human rights of its residents, stipulates the social and economic systems and policies to be practised in the SAR, and, most important of all, defines the scope of the SAR's autonomous powers and its relationship with the central authorities.

[31] See *Representative Government in Hong Kong* (Hong Kong Government, February 1994).

[32] See Kuan Hsin-chi et al (eds), *The 1995 Legislative Council Elections in Hong Kong* (Hong Kong Institute of Asia-Pacific Studies, Chinese University of Hong Kong, 1996).

Since 1997, the HKSAR has had a chequered history, marked by constitutional controversies and social movements often fuelled by rambunctious legal and constitutional debates. We chronicle below what we consider the most significant law-related events in Hong Kong's post-1997. They will be discussed in greater detail in the chapters that follow.

A. Aborted Attempt to Implement Article 23 of the Basic Law, 2002–03

Article 23 of the Basic Law (BL 23) requires the HKSAR to 'enact laws on its own to prohibit any act of treason, secession, sedition, subversion against the Central People's Government'. It also requires Hong Kong to pass laws to protect state secrets and prohibit foreign political organisations from conducting political activities in Hong Kong. These 'national security' concerns raised by BL 23 were considered politically sensitive. Ever since the Basic Law was enacted in 1990 and enforced in July 1997, there had been local anxieties over the implementation of BL 23.

The publication of the HKSAR government's consultation document on 'Proposals to Implement Article 23 of the Basic Law' on 24 September 2002 opened a three-month consultation exercise on a legislative proposal to introduce national security legislation for the first time in the HKSAR. On 28 January 2003, the government published the results of the consultation and announced nine sets of clarifications or modifications of the original legislative proposal.[33] This was followed by the publication of the National Security (Legislative Provisions) Bill on 13 February 2003 and its first reading in LegCo on 26 February 2003. During the Bills Committee's deliberations on the Bill, the government agreed to some amendments. However, critics said that these amendments were insufficient; they also argued that the government's timetable for passing the Bill over LegCo's week-long meeting beginning on 9 July did not provide sufficient time for deliberation.

On 1 July 2003, a public holiday marking the anniversary of Hong Kong's return to China, an estimated half a million people took to the streets to protest against the BL 23 legislative exercise and to express

[33] For discussion of these clarifications and modifications, see CJ Petersen, 'Hong Kong's Spring of Discontent: The Rise and Fall of the National Security Bill in 2003' in H Fu, C Petersen and S Young (eds), *National Security and Fundamental Freedoms: Hong Kong's Article 23 under Scrutiny* (Hong Kong University Press, 2005) 13, 38–42.

their grievances against Tung Chee-hwa – the first Chief Executive of the HKSAR – and his administration. These grievances related to the government's perceived ineffectiveness in handling the SARS epidemic earlier in the year, and its failure to bring Hong Kong out of the economic recession triggered by the Asian financial crisis in 1997.

The demonstration had the effect of tilting the balance in LegCo in favour of legislators who opposed the BL 23 Bill. The Liberal Party, a pro-government political party which had hitherto supported the Bill, now advocated its postponement and opposed the Tung administration's decision to proceed with its passage on 9 July. Without enough votes in the legislature to pass the Bill, the government decided to postpone it.[34] On 17 July 2003, Tung announced that the government would reopen public consultation on the Bill. However, in an about-turn on 5 September 2003, he announced that the Bill would be withdrawn. Since the demise of the BL 23 Bill in 2003, the implementation of BL 23 was shelved for almost two decades. As discussed below, the failure of the HKSAR to legislate on BL 23 eventually paved the way for the central authorities' intervention in 2020 to legislate directly on the protection of national security in the HKSAR.

B. Interpretations of the Basic Law by the National People's Congress Standing Committee, 1999–2016

Under Article 158 of the Basic Law, and as further discussed in chapters two and four below, the National People's Congress Standing Committee (NPCSC) possesses the power of interpretation of the Basic Law. In the first 25 years of the HKSAR's history, a total of five interpretations were issued. The first interpretation was promulgated in 1999 in response to the request by Chief Executive (CE) Tung Chee-hwa for an NPCSC interpretation of the 'right of abode' provisions in the Basic Law. This gave rise to the first major constitutional controversy in the HKSAR's history. The interpretation had the effect of overruling the interpretation of the relevant Basic Law provisions adopted by Hong Kong's Court of Final Appeal (CFA) in the *Ng Ka Ling* and *Chan Kam Nga* cases – two related cases both decided on 29 January 1999.[35] According to the estimate of

[34] A Chen, 'A Defining Moment in Hong Kong's History' *South China Morning Post* (4 July 2003); 'How the Liberals Stopped a Constitutional Crisis' *South China Morning Post* (8 July 2003).

[35] See chs 2 and 5 below.

the HKSAR government, the CFA's rulings, if allowed to stand, would have resulted in more than 1.67 million residents in mainland China gaining the right to settle in Hong Kong over the next 10 years.

After the 1999 Interpretation that overruled the two above-mentioned CFA cases, the NPCSC in 2004, acting on its own initiative this time, issued an interpretation of the Basic Law provisions relating to the procedures for electoral reform.[36] Subsequently, in 2005, upon the request of the Acting CE of the HKSAR, the NPCSC issued an interpretation to clarify the length of the term of office of a CE who has succeeded to the office upon his predecessor's resignation mid-term.[37] In 2011, the CFA in the *Congo* case[38] used for the first time the judicial reference procedure in Article 158(3) of the Basic Law to refer two Basic Law provisions relating to foreign affairs and 'acts of state' to the NPCSC for interpretation.[39] This case concerned whether the applicable law on state immunity in the HKSAR should be the same as that on the mainland.

In November 2016, the NPCSC, acting again on its own initiative, issued an interpretation of Article 104 of the Basic Law, which relates to the oath-taking requirements applicable to the Chief Executive, judges and members of the Legislative and Executive Councils. This interpretation was particularly controversial, as it was issued three days after the Court of First Instance of the High Court of Hong Kong (CFI) heard a case on the validity of two legislative oaths-of-office but before the court delivered judgment. In this case, the HKSAR government argued that two newly elected pro-Hong Kong independence LegCo members had been disqualified from office by operation of law because of their failure to comply with the oath-taking requirements stipulated in Article 104 of the Basic Law and other Hong Kong legislation.[40]

C. Pace of Democratisation, 2003–15

The Basic Law provides for the development of the political system of the HKSAR over the long term. It declares that the 'ultimate aim'[41] of

[36] A Chen, 'The Constitutional Controversy of Spring 2004' (2004) 34 *Hong Kong Law Journal* 215.

[37] A Chen, 'The NPCSC's Interpretation in Spring 2005' (2005) 35 *Hong Kong Law Journal* 255.

[38] (2011) 14 HKCFAR 95, 395.

[39] A Chen, 'The *Congo* Case' (2011) 41 *Hong Kong Law Journal* 369.

[40] See chs 2 and 5 below.

[41] Arts 45 and 68 of the Basic Law.

Hong Kong's political evolution is for the election of both the CE and all members of LegCo by universal suffrage. Such political evolution would depend on 'the actual situation in the [HKSAR]' and should be 'in accordance with the principle of gradual and orderly progress'. The Basic Law does not provide any timetable for the eventual realisation of universal suffrage. However, Annexes I and II to the Basic Law expressly provide that the methods for electing the CE and LegCo may change after 2007. They also expressly provide for the procedure for such constitutional change, which involves the support of a two-thirds majority in LegCo, the CE's consent and the approval of the NPCSC (when there is a change in the electoral method for the CE) or 'reporting for the record' to the NPCSC (when there is a change in the electoral method for LegCo).[42]

In the second half of 2003, after the failure of the Hong Kong government's attempt to enact a BL 23 law as discussed above, the 'pan-democrats', who led the movement against the Bill, launched a movement to speed up the pace of democratisation in the HKSAR.[43] In early 2004, Beijing decided to respond to the demands of the democracy movement. On 6 April 2004, the NPCSC issued its second interpretation of the Basic Law.[44] This interpretation elaborated upon Annexes I and II to the Basic Law by stipulating a procedure for initiating changes to the methods of electing the CE and the LegCo members. The procedure requires the CE to submit a report to the NPCSC on whether there is a need to introduce electoral reform, after which the NPCSC will decide the matter in accordance with Article 45 (as regards CE election) or 68 (as regards LegCo election) of the Basic Law, as applicable.

Since April 2004, three reports on electoral reforms have been submitted to the NPCSC by CEs in Hong Kong – in 2004, 2007 and 2014, respectively. In response to the 2007 report, the NPCSC decided that

> the election of the fifth CE of the HKSAR in the year 2017 may be implemented by the method of universal suffrage; that after the CE is selected by universal suffrage, the election of the LegCo of the HKSAR may be implemented by the method of electing all the members by universal suffrage.[45]

[42] See Annexes I and II to the Basic Law (as originally enacted in 1990 and before their amendment in 2021).

[43] See M Sing, 'Public Support for Democracy in Hong Kong' (2005) 12 *Democratization* 244; LT White III, *Democratization in Hong Kong – and China?* (Lynne Rienner, 2016).

[44] See n 36 above.

[45] See A Chen, 'A New Era in Hong Kong's Constitutional History' (2008) 38 *Hong Kong Law Journal* 1.

In 2013, some activists mooted the idea for an 'Occupy Central' campaign – a proposal to occupy parts of the Central District in Hong Kong – to put pressure on Beijing and the Hong Kong government to introduce a model for universal suffrage in 2017 that would be consistent with international standards of democratic elections.[46] On 15 July 2014, CE Leung Chun-ying initiated the procedure for electoral reform and submitted a report to the NPCSC. On 31 August 2014, the NPCSC rendered its decision on political reform in the HKSAR. It stated that the 'broadly representative nominating committee', which would nominate candidates for election of the CE by universal suffrage in accordance with Article 45 of the Basic Law, should be modelled after the existing Election Committee for the election of the CE.[47] Furthermore, the nominating committee shall nominate two or three candidates, each of whom must have the endorsement of more than half of all the members of the nominating committee. The NPCSC Decision was explained as follows:

> [T]he principle that the Chief Executive has to be a person who loves the country and loves Hong Kong must be upheld. This is a basic requirement of the policy of 'one country, two systems'. It ... is called for by the actual need to maintain long-term prosperity and stability of Hong Kong and uphold the sovereignty, security and development interests of the country. The method for selecting the Chief Executive by universal suffrage must provide corresponding institutional safeguards for this purpose.

The NPCSC's decision was met with strong protests from 'pro-democracy' forces in Hong Kong, which derided the electoral model as 'fake universal suffrage', because they believed that only pro-China political figures, and not any member of the 'pro-democracy' camp, would be able to gain majority support from the nominating committee and be shortlisted as CE candidates who can be voted on by the people via universal suffrage. Students and other democracy activists launched the 'Umbrella Movement' or 'Occupy Central Movement', which started in late September and continued until mid-December 2014.[48] The Bill to introduce universal suffrage for the election of the CE was eventually

[46] See generally AY Cheung, 'Road to Nowhere: Hong Kong's Democratization and China's Obligations under Public International Law' (2014) 40 *Brooklyn Journal of International Law* 465, 494–98; MC Davis, 'The Basic Law, Universal Suffrage and Rule of Law in Hong Kong' (2015) 38 *Hastings International and Comparative Law Review* 275, 289.

[47] Art 45 refers to 'the selection of the Chief Executive by universal suffrage upon nomination by a broadly representative nominating committee in accordance with democratic procedures'.

[48] See generally Y Cai, *The Occupy Movement in Hong Kong* (Routledge, 2017); N Ma and EW Cheng (eds), *The Umbrella Movement* (Amsterdam University Press, 2019).

rejected by LegCo on 18 June 2015. With the 'pan-democrats' in LegCo voting against the proposal, it failed to secure the requisite two-thirds majority for an amendment of Annex I to the Basic Law. This veto meant that the existing system of electing the CE by a 1200-member Election Committee would continue for the time being.[49]

D. Failed Attempt to Introduce an Extradition Bill, 2019[50]

On 9 June 2019, Hong Kong became the focus of international attention once again as hundreds of thousands of demonstrators marched to oppose the imminent enactment of a Bill – the Fugitive Offenders and Mutual Legal Assistance in Criminal Matters Legislation (Amendment) Bill 2019 (the Extradition Bill). The Extradition Bill would introduce a rendition arrangement between Hong Kong and other parts of China (including mainland China, Taiwan and Macau), as well as new extradition arrangements between the HKSAR and over 170 states with which the HKSAR had not entered into an extradition treaty. This Bill not only led to the largest protests in Hong Kong's history; it also brought about the most serious crisis of governance in the HKSAR and precipitated a fundamental change in Beijing's policy towards Hong Kong. In view of the historical importance of this episode as a watershed event, we will discuss it in considerable detail here.

The saga began with a murder committed by a Hongkonger in Taiwan. In March 2018, Chan Tong-kai, a 20-year-old Hong Kong permanent resident, went on holiday in Taiwan with his girlfriend, murdered her there and returned to Hong Kong alone. He was subsequently arrested in Hong Kong and prosecuted for money laundering.[51] At that time, the Taiwan authorities requested Chan's extradition to Taiwan. Under the existing law, Hong Kong courts had no jurisdiction to try a murder case where the murder had been committed outside Hong Kong.[52]

[49] See generally AHY Chen, 'The Law and Politics of the Struggle for Universal Suffrage in Hong Kong, 2013–15' (2016) 3 *Asian Journal of Law and Society* 189; C Chan, 'Legalizing Politics: An Evaluation of Hong Kong's Recent Attempt at Democratization' (2017) 16 *Election Law Journal* 296.

[50] This section draws on A Chen, 'A Perfect Storm' (2019) 49 *Hong Kong Law Journal* 419, which contains relevant source materials.

[51] The prosecution was based on the fact that he had used his girlfriend's credit card after she was murdered.

[52] Under Hong Kong's existing law, the courts have extraterritorial jurisdiction over a number of criminal offences, but they do not include murder: see *Archbold Hong Kong, 2019* (Sweet & Maxwell, 2018) ss 2-111–2-155F.

Hong Kong's law of extradition was contained in the Fugitive Offenders Ordinance (FOO), enacted in April 1997. This Ordinance authorises extradition between Hong Kong and foreign states with which the HKSAR has entered into an extradition treaty. Since 1997, the HKSAR had entered into extradition treaties with 20 countries;[53] more than 100 persons – largely foreign nationals – had been surrendered by Hong Kong pursuant to these treaties, with the USA being the destination of the largest number of surrenders.[54] However, it was expressly provided in the FOO that it was not applicable to 'any other part of the PRC' (ie mainland China, Taiwan and Macau). Apparently, at the time of the FOO's enactment, given the vast differences between Hong Kong's common-law-based legal system and the socialist legal system practised in mainland China, Hong Kong was not ready to enter into rendition arrangements with the mainland.

Given the exclusion of other parts of China, including Taiwan, from the application of the FOO, the Hong Kong government determined that there was no legal basis for Chan Tong-kai's extradition to Taiwan. CE Carrie Lam therefore decided to undertake a legislative exercise to introduce a mechanism of allowing ad hoc extradition arrangements on a case-by-case basis (in the absence of extradition treaties) with any foreign jurisdiction – including more than 170 states with which Hong Kong had not entered into any extradition treaty, as well as mainland China, Taiwan and Macau. The original version of the proposal was published on 13 February 2019 and was then discussed in LegCo's Panel on Security. After some consultation, the proposal was refined to take into account the business community's concerns over rendition to the mainland for business-related offences that may have been committed in the past. The Bill was gazetted on 29 March 2019 and then introduced in LegCo.

Hong Kong politicians and civil society became highly polarised after the introduction of the Bill, with the pro-China camp (also known as the 'pro-Establishment' camp) supporting the Bill and the pro-democracy camp (ie the 'pan-democrats') strongly opposed to it. Opposition against the Bill gained momentum gradually, with the first demonstration against it taking place on 31 March 2019, followed by another demonstration of a larger size on 28 April.

[53] See www.doj.gov.hk/eng/laws/table4ti.html. Some of these treaties were suspended or abrogated by relevant Western states after China's enactment of the National Security Law for the HKSAR in 2020 (discussed below).

[54] See generally G Cross, 'Fugitive Surrender: Rights and Responsibilities' *China Daily* (12 June 2019) www.chinadailyhk.com/articles/186/73/64/1560307116859.html.

Many politicians and members of the legal community[55] opposed the Bill on the ground that it would subject innocent people in Hong Kong to the risk of being extradited to the mainland. The legal system on the mainland was not trusted by many Hong Kong people, who had doubts about whether an accused could get a fair trial. Furthermore, if the rendition process was initiated in a particular case by the CE upon the request of Beijing, there were concerns that Hong Kong courts could do little to reject the request. The existing law on extradition (which is still in force today) only requires the requesting state to provide written evidence that would constitute a prima facie case against the accused, and the accused cannot adduce evidence or call witnesses to prove their innocence. The existing law did not permit extradition to mainland China and the Hong Kong public was mainly concerned about the proposed legislative removal of this safeguard. It may also be noted that some of those who opposed the Bill did not fully understand the scope of the Bill's application. Some were fearful that they could be extradited to mainland China even if the alleged crimes were committed in Hong Kong rather than in mainland China. Others worried that they might be framed and falsely accused to facilitate extradition to mainland China.

LegCo formed a Bills Committee to study the Bill and it met for the first time on 17 April 2019. However, the Committee failed to function due to filibustering by the pan-democrats at its first two meetings that led to its failure to elect the Committee's Chairman. The pro-Establishment legislators then convened further meetings of the Committee, the legal validity of which were contested by the pan-democrats. On 20 May 2019, the government decided to bypass the Bills Committee and to commence the final stage of the legislative process on 12 June. In an attempt to compensate for the lack of deliberations on the Bill in the Bills Committee, the LegCo Panel on Security was convened to discuss the Bill between 31 May and 5 June. A slightly revised package was announced by the government on 30 May 2019 to narrow down the offences covered by the proposed extradition arrangement and to enhance safeguards for the accused's rights.

The social movement against the Bill culminated in a march of hundreds of thousands of people on 9 June 2019 (with 1.03 million participants as estimated by the organisers and 240,000 as estimated by

[55] On 6 June 2019, more than a thousand lawyers joined a 'silent march' against the Bill; this was the fifth march of its kind since 1997: see '"Record 3,000" Hong Kong Lawyers in Silent March against Controversial Extradition Bill' *South China Morning Post* (6 June 2019).

the police). Notwithstanding that the demonstration on 9 June 2019 was the largest of its kind since the march against the BL 23 Bill in 2003, CE Carrie Lam decided to press ahead with the final stage of the legislative process, which was scheduled to begin with the LegCo debate over the Bill on 12 June.

On the morning of 12 June, Hong Kong's downtown area and streets surrounding the LegCo building were occupied by tens of thousands of demonstrators. In the afternoon, the protest escalated into what the Hong Kong police called a 'riot' (a label which opponents of the Bill contested), and the police responded by deploying tear gas, pepper balls, baton rounds, rubber bullets and bean bag rounds. In view of the developing crisis, the President of LegCo decided to shelve the series of meetings on the Bill that were originally scheduled for 12–20 June. Then, on 15 June, CE Carrie Lam announced that the legislative process on the Bill would be immediately suspended.[56]

Even after the Bill's suspension, an even larger protest occurred on 16 June (with close to two million participants as estimated by the organisers and 338,000 as estimated by the police) to demand a complete withdrawal of the Bill and to protest against the alleged use of excessive force by the police against demonstrators on 12 June. In response, CE Lam publicly apologised on 18 June for 'deficiencies in the work of the HKSAR government' on the legislative amendment exercise, which 'has led to controversies, disputes and anxieties in society'. However, as the CE did not accede to the 'principal demands' of the protestors (including the withdrawal of the Bill, the retraction of the label 'riot' to describe the 12 June protest, non-prosecution of protestors and the establishment of an independent commission of inquiry to investigate the incident), civil unrest continued in Hong Kong even after legislative proceedings on the Bill had been shelved, and the protests subsequently escalated into large-scale rioting.[57]

The incidents relating to the civil unrest are too numerous to recount here, but we will highlight a few. For example, crowds of protestors laid

[56] For the full text of the CE's statement, see www.info.gov.hk/gia/general/201906/15/P2019061500707.htm. The government subsequently explained that all work on the Bill had ceased, and stated that the Bill would lapse upon the expiration of the current term of the Legislative Council in summer 2020. However, opponents were not satisfied and insisted that the Bill must be 'withdrawn'.

[57] See generally Z Ibrahim and J Lam (eds), *Rebel City: Hong Kong's Year of Water and Fire* (World Scientific, 2020); S Lo, S Hung and J Loo, *The Dynamics of Peaceful and Violent Protests in Hong Kong: The Anti-Extradition Movement* (Palgrave Macmillan, 2021).

siege to the Police Headquarters in Wanchai on 21 and 26 June 2019. On 1 July 2019, protestors stormed the LegCo building and damaged its facilities to such an extent that the legislature was unable to meet for the next few months. On 21 July 2019, the building of the Liaison Office of the central government was besieged, and the national emblem on the building was defaced. There was a public outcry when suspected triad society members assaulted protestors and other commuters at the Yuen Long subway station that same evening, with suspected acquiescence by the police.

On 4 September 2019, the CE announced the formal withdrawal of the Extradition Bill.[58] However, this still fell short of what the protestors demanded. Three months on from the first community-wide protests, the movement had evolved into a larger campaign for universal suffrage in CE and LegCo elections, and for an independent investigation into the police's use of force against protestors. Between September and November 2019, the use of force on the part of both radical protestors and the police escalated, culminating in warlike clashes on the campuses of the Chinese University of Hong Kong and the Hong Kong Polytechnic University in November, with riots breaking out in many locations in Hong Kong, and attacks on MTR facilities and shops and companies considered pro-China.

Meanwhile, on 4 October 2019, the CE in Council (ie the Executive Council) invoked the Emergency Regulations Ordinance (ERO) to promulgate the Prohibition on Face Covering Regulation, which criminalised mask-wearing by protestors. Pan-democrat legislators immediately brought a court action to challenge the Regulation. On 18 November 2019, the CFI found parts of the Ordinance and Regulation unconstitutional.[59] This judgment provoked a rebuke from a spokesman of the Legislative Affairs Commission of the NPCSC, who stated that the NPCSC was the only body that could decide whether a Hong Kong law complied with the Basic Law[60] – a position at odds with the long-standing practice of constitutional review by Hong Kong courts post-handover – and that the ERO was not amongst those colonial laws deemed unconstitutional by an NPCSC decision in February 1997.

[58] The Bill was formally withdrawn from LegCo on 23 October 2019.

[59] *Kwok Wing-hang v Chief Executive in Council* [2019] HKCFI 2820, [2020] HKCA 192, [2020] HKCFA 42.

[60] See A Chen, 'Constitutional Controversies in the Aftermath of the Anti-Extradition Movement' (2020) 50 *Hong Kong Law Journal* 609.

The constitutional crisis was subsequently alleviated when the Court of Appeal reversed the CFI's ruling and upheld the constitutionality of the ERO. On appeal to the CFA, the CFA also affirmed the ERO's constitutionality.

On 24 November 2019, the 'pan-democrats' and anti-government activists in the anti-extradition movement won a landslide victory in the District Council elections.[61] That month, the USA also enacted the Hong Kong Human Rights and Democracy Act, which some pan-democrat politicians and anti-government activists in the anti-extradition movement had lobbied for.[62] In the ensuing months, smaller-scale violent demonstrations and larger-scale peaceful ones with slogans such as 'five principal demands, not one less' and 'liberate Hong Kong, revolution of our times' still occurred sporadically until the COVID-19 pandemic struck in spring 2020.

Anti-extradition activists were not content with the indefinite suspension and subsequent withdrawal of the Extradition Bill, and many continued rioting to express their discontent with the state of affairs under OCTS. In retrospect, this social movement, using both peaceful and violent actions to campaign for the protestors' visions of liberty, democracy, and governmental and police accountability in Hong Kong, ultimately backfired, and had the effect of triggering the central authorities to impose even tighter controls over the HKSAR. This is the subject of the next section.

E. Beijing's Interventions on National Security Law and Electoral Reform, 2020–21

The Hong Kong and international community was taken by surprise when the NPC's agenda released on 21 May 2020 – for the upcoming NPC meeting set to commence in Beijing on 22 May – included the following legislative item: a proposed 'decision on establishing and improving the

[61] With an unprecedentedly high voter turnout, the pan-democrats won 57% of the popular votes and 85% of the seats: see *Ming Pao* (26 November 2019, in Chinese); 'Hong Kong Elections: Pro-democracy Camp Wins 17 out of 18 Districts while City Leader Says She Will Reflect on the Result' *South China Morning Post* (25 November 2019). The predecessors of District Councils were the District Boards established in 1982, as discussed earlier in this chapter. In 2000, the latter were reconstituted as District Councils. See ch 3 below, text accompanying nn 1 and 2.

[62] The Act (S1838, Pub L116-76) was passed by both Houses of Congress in November 2019 and was signed into law by President Trump on 27 November 2019.

legal system and enforcement mechanisms for the HKSAR to safeguard national security'.[63]

In his speech on the Bill for the Decision, Wang Chen, one of the vice-chairmen of the NPCSC, explained that the arrangements proposed in the Bill were designed to plug a loophole in existing Hong Kong law that was revealed by the 2019 riots. He pointed out that the HKSAR had a constitutional duty under Article 23 of the Basic Law to legislate to protect national security, but this legislative task had remained unfulfilled 23 years after the handover. He added that Article 23 legislation had been demonised over the years by opposition politicians in Hong Kong, and in practice it was difficult in the present circumstances for the HKSAR government to introduce Article 23 legislation on its own. It was therefore legitimate for the central authorities to step in to make the proposed Decision. Wang also commented that the Decision was to be made in pursuance of the decision of the fourth plenum of the 19th Central Committee of the Chinese Communist Party in late October 2019, which, inter alia, expressly called for the 'establishment and improvement of the legal system and enforcement mechanisms for safeguarding national security in the SARs'.

In a press conference on the evening of 22 May, CE Carrie Lam admitted that 'Hong Kong society must recognise the reality that it would be difficult for the executive and legislative organs of the HKSAR to complete the task of legislating on national security within a period in the foreseeable future'. A press statement from a spokesman of the Hong Kong and Macau Affairs Office of the State Council on 22 May explained that the power to legislate on national security is part and parcel of the legislative power of the central authorities of the state. Although the central authorities have, through Article 23 of the Basic Law, authorised the HKSAR to exercise part of the legislative power on national security matters, this has not changed the fundamental principle that, by its very nature, national security legislation is the power and responsibility of the central authorities.

In his speech at the NPCSC, Wang disclosed that the central authorities had considered several policy options for dealing with the loophole in Hong Kong law regarding national security, and finally decided to adopt a 'two-step approach', ie an NPC Decision followed by a law made by the NPCSC on the protection of national security in the HKSAR. The proposed Decision would set out the basic policies and principles; it would also authorise the NPCSC to make a national security law for the

[63] The discussion below draws on the article cited at n 60 above.

HKSAR. The law would then be inserted into Annex III of the Basic Law and applied to the HKSAR by direct promulgation in accordance with Article 18 of the Basic Law.[64]

The proposed Decision would specify four subject matters that would be covered by the national security law to be enacted by the NPCSC: (i) secession; (ii) subversion against the state; (iii) terrorism; and (iv) collusion with foreign forces to endanger national security. These subject matters overlap, but do not coincide completely, with the subject matters covered by Article 23 of the Basic Law. According to the proposed Decision, even after the NPCSC law has been made, the HKSAR still has to fulfil its constitutional duty of legislating on other areas of national security, such as the subject matters of Article 23 that are not covered by the NPCSC law.[65] Presumably, the four subject matters to be covered by the NPCSC law were the most pressing ones that had to be dealt with immediately.

The proposed Decision was passed by the NPC on 28 May 2020.[66] Thereafter, a specially expedited procedure was adopted by the NPCSC to enact the new national security law for the HKSAR. Departing from its usual practice of having one session of meetings every two months, two sessions of the NPCSC were held in the second half of June 2020, at which the Hong Kong national security law was – together with several other mainland legislative items – put on the agenda. The Bill for the Hong Kong national security law was introduced in the NPCSC on the first day of the NPCSC session held on 18–20 June.

Although the PRC Law on Legislation usually requires the publication of a legislative Bill for public consultation, it also permits a departure from this practice if so authorised by the Council of Chairpersons of the NPCSC.[67] In the case of the HKSAR national security law, the Bill was not published before its eventual enactment, and there was only consultation with selected individuals and institutions in Hong Kong and the mainland. The speech explaining the Bill to the NPCSC was published by

[64] Art 18(2) provides that a national law may be applied to the HKSAR either 'by way of promulgation or legislation by the Region'.

[65] Art 23 covers seven subject matters, only two of which have been expressly covered by the national security law. Matters not covered in the national security law include treason, sedition, theft of state secrets, foreign political bodies operating in Hong Kong, and ties between local and foreign political bodies.

[66] See Decision of the NPC on Establishing and Improving the Legal System and Enforcement Mechanisms for the HKSAR to Safeguard National Security, HKSAR Government Gazette, LN 135 of 2020, p B2335 (unofficial English translation; there is no English translation with official status or legal force).

[67] See Art 37 of the PRC Law on Legislation.

the Xinhua News Agency on 20 June, which publicised the main features of the Bill.

The Bill was further considered by the NPCSC in its session of 28–30 June. On the morning of the last day of this session, the NPCSC enacted the Law of the PRC on Safeguarding National Security in the HKSAR (NSL). On the afternoon of the same day, the NPCSC (after consultation with the HKSAR government and the Hong Kong Basic Law Committee of the NPCSC in accordance with Article 18 of the Basic Law) decided to insert the NSL into Annex III of the Basic Law, and the NSL was gazetted in Hong Kong in the evening of 30 June.[68] The controversial and internationally spotlighted legislative exercise was thus completed, and the NSL came into force shortly before midnight between 30 June and 1 July 2020 – the twenty-third anniversary of the establishment of the HKSAR.

The NSL creates four categories of offences, relating to secession, subversion, terrorism and collusion with foreign forces to endanger national security. As is the case with the Basic Law, although the Hong Kong courts may interpret and apply the NSL when adjudicating cases, the NPCSC enjoys an overriding authority to promulgate interpretations of the NSL.[69] The NSL establishes extraterritorial jurisdiction by stipulating that the NSL applies to relevant offences committed by persons outside Hong Kong regardless of nationality.[70] The NSL also provides for the establishment by Beijing of a national security office (NSO) in Hong Kong.[71] Although the NSL empowers Hong Kong's law enforcement authorities and courts to investigate, prosecute and try cases arising from the NSL, it also gives the NSO powers of investigation and rendition to the mainland for prosecution before mainland Chinese courts in certain exceptional circumstances.[72] The exercise of such powers in particular cases is subject to approval by the central government. The HKSAR government has no jurisdiction over actions of the NSO.

The NSL was highly controversial and attracted international attention. The official view of the Chinese government was that the new

[68] See Promulgation of National Law 2000, HKSAR Government Gazette, LN 136 of 2020, p B2345 (in Chinese); GN(E) 72 of 2020 (unofficial English translation of the Law of the PRC on Safeguarding National Security in the HKSAR; there is no English translation with official status or legal force).

[69] NSL, Art 65.

[70] ibid Art 38.

[71] ibid ch 5.

[72] ibid Arts 55–57.

legislative scheme on Hong Kong's national security merely drew a red line to protect the 'One Country' component of OCTS, and would enable the OCTS policy to be more successfully practised in the future. On the other hand, critics of the law accused Beijing of abandoning the 'Two Systems' component of OCTS, leaving only 'One Country'. Some Western countries have adopted new policies towards Hong Kong in response to the enactment of the NSL, such as terminating existing extradition agreements with the HKSAR. The USA has imposed sanctions against China and Hong Kong, including their officials, on the ground that the NSL threatened civil liberties and infringed upon Hong Kong's autonomy. The UK accused China of breaching the Joint Declaration. Some states, particularly the UK, have made it easier for Hong Kong residents to migrate to their territories. The effects and impact of the NSL in the long run would depend crucially on how the authorities interpret and apply it. This and other details of the NSL will be considered in chapter two below.

The central authorities' legislative intervention in restructuring the law and politics of the HKSAR did not end with the enactment of the NSL. On 11 August 2020, the NPCSC adopted a decision to extend the term of office of LegCo in light of the postponement of the LegCo election originally scheduled for September 2020. (Invoking its power under the Emergency Regulations Ordinance, the Hong Kong government had decided on 31 July 2020 to postpone the LegCo election because of the COVID-19 pandemic.) On 11 November 2020, the NPCSC passed another decision on the qualifications of LegCo members and rules on disqualification. The decision had the immediate effect of disqualifying four LegCo members from continuing to serve during LegCo's extended term of office. These four legislators had previously been disqualified as candidates for the LegCo election originally scheduled for September 2020. In protest against this NPCSC decision, most of the legislators in the pan-democrat camp resigned en masse.[73]

In spring 2021, the NPC itself acted once again to adopt another major Decision on the HKSAR. This was the Decision on the Improvement of the Electoral System of the HKSAR enacted on 11 March 2021, followed by the amendment of Annexes I and II to the Basic Law by the NPCSC on 30 March 2021. The electoral system of the HKSAR was completely overhauled, as will be discussed in chapter four below.

[73] See ch 4 below.

In a booklet entitled *Improve Electoral System, Ensure Patriots Administering Hong Kong*,[74] the HKSAR government described its justifications for the electoral overhaul in the following terms:

> Most of the Hong Kong citizens love the Country and love Hong Kong. Nonetheless, Hong Kong has long been a hub of cultural exchange with the West and is a diverse society. Some citizens have limited understanding of the Country and the Mainland and may even harbour prejudices and biased views. Coupled with inadequate national education over a long period of time after Hong Kong's return to the motherland, local and external forces with ulterior motives often fanned anti-China sentiments and sabotaged relations between people in Hong Kong and those on the mainland. All these developments have engendered serious threats towards 'One Country, Two Systems'.
>
> The emergence of anti-China forces seeking to destabilise Hong Kong can be traced back to the 'anti-national education' incident in 2012, the illegal 'Occupy Central Movement' in 2014, 'Mong Kok riots' in 2016, the surfacing of the 'Hong Kong National Party' advocating 'independence' and 'self-determination' and the chaos occurred in the 2016 LegCo General Elections for the Sixth Term LegCo. By exploiting the electoral system to worm their way into the political structure of the HKSAR, these radical forces have attempted to make use of their status as public officers to shamelessly obstruct and paralyse the operation of the Government.
>
> The saga arising from the proposed legislative amendments to the Fugitive Offenders Ordinance in mid-2019 pushed such anti-China forces to the boiling point. Unscrupulous acts and activities of the rioters, such as desecrating the national emblem and the national flag which symbolise the dignity of the Country, openly colluding with foreign forces, and pleading western countries for sanctions on Hong Kong with utter disregard for the interest of Hong Kong people, have seriously undermined the constitutional order and public safety of the HKSAR. Exploiting loopholes in the electoral system, they won the majority of seats in the District Councils, and then organised illegal 'primaries' as well as the '35+' in an attempt to control the LegCo through elections and seize the jurisdiction of the HKSAR. These plots and activities constituted significant security risks to the political structure of the HKSAR, and endangered national sovereignty, security and development interests of the Country.
>
> Although the National Security Law promulgated in mid-2020 has successfully curbed violence and chaos as well as brought peace and stability back to the Hong Kong society, with a few elections scheduled for the coming year, a political storm is already at our doorstep.

[74] www.cmab.gov.hk/improvement/filemanager/content/pdf/en/resource-centre/booklet.pdf.

VI. CONCLUSION

In 1982, the pending expiration of the 99-year lease over Hong Kong's New Territories prompted the UK government to open negotiations with the PRC over Hong Kong's future. In response, the PRC decided to transplant the idea of 'One Country, Two Systems', which it developed to reunify Taiwan with the mainland, to the governance of Hong Kong after reclaiming it from the British. The terms of OCTS were first stipulated in the Sino-British Joint Declaration 1984, and then further elaborated and codified as China's domestic law in the Basic Law of the HKSAR enacted in 1990.

The transitional period between colonial rule and the establishment as a special administrative region of the PRC saw the beginnings of constitutional reform in Hong Kong, termed by the colonial government as the development of 'representative government' in Hong Kong. This generated considerable tension between the British and Chinese governments; both attempted to steer the future direction of development of Hong Kong's political system towards their preferred models. China was determined to ensure that the design of the HKSAR's political system to be established in 1997 would not be stymied by constitutional reforms introduced unilaterally by the British before 1997. A compromise was reached when the colonial government published its White Paper on the development of representative government in 1988, which postponed the introduction of direct election to the Legislative Council until the Basic Law was enacted by China's legislature in 1990. However, the subsequent constitutional reforms introduced unilaterally by Chris Patten, the last Governor of Hong Kong, were considered objectionable by the Chinese side, which led to the 'derailing' of the originally contemplated 'through train' arrangement for the Legislative Council in 1997.

The constitutional journey of the HKSAR after 1997 has not been plain sailing. The single most important source of conflict and instability was the opposing views on what OCTS meant to the 'pan-democrats' and other opposition politicians in Hong Kong on the one hand, and the Chinese government and its supporters – particularly the 'pro-establishment camp' in Hong Kong – on the other hand. The two camps had very different visions of how OCTS should operate in practice, particularly the balance to be struck between the 'One Country' and 'Two Systems' components of

OCTS. They also had different understandings of the autonomy of, and the degree of democratic rule permissible in, the HKSAR.

The short history of the HKSAR has been marked by social movements fuelled by this tension between 'One Country' and 'Two Systems'. For example, the strong and widespread opposition against the Article 23 Bill on national security was due to fears that the people of Hong Kong would lose their civil liberties if the Bill were passed. Subsequently, the pan-democrats, who had led the opposition against the Article 23 Bill, campaigned vigorously and persistently for the realisation of the universal suffrage enshrined in Articles 45 and 68 of the Basic Law. The democracy movement achieved some success when it secured a timetable – promulgated by the NPC Standing Committee in 2007 – for universal suffrage in the election of the Chief Executive in 2017, subject to the candidates being shortlisted by a nominating committee.

The conflict between the PRC's vision of democracy in Hong Kong and the pan-democrats' differing vision culminated in the Occupy Central movement of autumn 2014. After the failure of the movement, some opposition politicians were radicalised and began to promote ideas of Hong Kong's self-determination or independence.

The Extradition Bill of 2019, like the Article 23 Bill of 2003, was widely perceived as a grave threat to human rights in Hong Kong, and it catalysed the most serious public outbursts of discontent against the existing practice of OCTS. Ironically, the 2019 movement proved to be counter-productive, and it only prompted the central authorities to adopt unprecedented and severe measures to re-tilt the institutional balance between 'One Country' and 'Two Systems' in favour of the former.

FURTHER READING

Carroll, JM, *A Concise History of Hong Kong* (Rowman & Littlefield, 2007).

Ho, H, *City on the Edge: Hong Kong under Chinese Rule* (Cambridge University Press, 2022).

Lim, CL, *Treaty for a Lost City: The Sino-British Joint Declaration* (Cambridge University Press, 2022).

Miners, N, *The Government and Politics of Hong Kong*, 4th edn (Oxford University Press, 1986).

Ng, MHK and Wong, JD (eds), *Civil Unrest and Governance in Hong Kong: Historical and Cultural Perspectives* (Routledge, 2017).

Tsang, S (ed), *Government and Politics: A Documentary History of Hong Kong* (Hong Kong University Press, 1995).
Wacks, R (ed), *The Law in Hong Kong 1969–1989* (Oxford University Press, 1989).
Wacks, R (ed), *The Future of the Law in Hong Kong* (Oxford University Press, 1989).

2

The Autonomy of the HKSAR and the Powers of the Central Authorities

Autonomy – Devolution – Central–Local Relationship – Basic Law Interpretations – National People's Congress – National Security

In the previous chapter, we reviewed Hong Kong's constitutional history. In this chapter, we proceed to discuss the autonomy of the Hong Kong Special Administrative Region (HKSAR) under Chinese sovereignty. The concept of autonomy, which is well recognised globally, is the key concept underpinning the constitutional arrangement of 'One Country, Two Systems' (OCTS). This chapter first introduces the relevant provisions of the Chinese Constitution and the Basic Law of the HKSAR, which collectively constitute the constitutional and legal foundation of the HKSAR. It discusses the basic concepts developed by the Chinese authorities to explain the nature of autonomy conferred on the HKSAR. It then examines the respective powers of the HKSAR authorities and the central authorities under OCTS and the exercise of such powers, including the central authorities' imposition of the HKSAR National Security Law in 2020. Finally, the chapter concludes by analysing Hong Kong's autonomy from the perspective of comparative theories on multi-level governance and devolution.

I. THE CONCEPT OF AUTONOMY

Both the Joint Declaration and the Basic Law stipulate that Hong Kong as a Special Administrative Region (SAR) of the PRC shall enjoy a 'high degree of autonomy'.[1] Autonomy is a well-recognised concept under international and comparative law. Basically, autonomy refers to a constitutional arrangement that allows for separate allocations of governmental power to the national government and the local government. Although it may be said that each constituent unit (or member state) of a federation enjoys autonomy, the term 'autonomy' is more commonly used to describe the partial self-rule enjoyed by a territorial unit (of a nation state) when the national government of a unitary state confers on that unit some degree of autonomy or internal self-determination under a 'devolution' arrangement.[2] While the USA is representative of the federal model of autonomy, devolution is exemplified by Scotland, which enjoys autonomy within the UK.[3]

The fourth Constitution of the PRC, which was enacted in 1982, contains a provision that authorises the establishment of SARs within the PRC. This is provided in Article 31 of the Constitution. SARs may practise economic, social and other systems different from those practised in other parts of the PRC. Article 31 empowers the National People's Congress (NPC) to enact laws that constitute SARs. To date, the Basic Law of the HKSAR, enacted in 1990, together with the Basic Law of the Macau SAR, enacted in 1993, are the only two laws adopted by the NPC in pursuance of Article 31 of the Constitution.

There are two most fundamental principles embodied in the Hong Kong Basic Law: the principle of PRC sovereignty over Hong Kong and the principle that the HKSAR is authorised by the central authorities of the PRC to enjoy a high degree of autonomy. As Chinese constitutional law scholars and officials have emphasised, the PRC is a unitary state, and therefore all powers that the HKSAR exercises are delegated by the central authorities through the Basic Law.[4] The high degree of autonomy enjoyed by the HKSAR and specific powers conferred on the HKSAR are expressly delineated in the Basic Law. At the same time, the Basic Law also codifies the constitutional powers that the central authorities may exercise with regard to the HKSAR. Both types of powers will be

[1] Joint Declaration, para 3(2); Basic Law, Art 2.

[2] See s VII below.

[3] See the Scotland Act 1998 enacted by the UK Parliament.

[4] S Wang (ed), *Introduction to the Basic Law of the Hong Kong Special Administrative Region* (Law Press, 2000) 66–70, 177–79. See also J Cheng, 'Jurisprudential Basis for the New Constitutional Order of Hong Kong: Separation of Powers or Delegation of Powers' (2017) 5 *China Legal Science* 56; Information Office of the State Council White Paper, *The Practice of the 'One Country, Two Systems' Policy in the Hong Kong Special Administrative Region* (2014) www.china.org.cn/chinese/2014-06/19/content_32637202_2.htm.

discussed in this chapter. In addition to regulating the constitutional relationship between the HKSAR and the central authorities, the Basic Law also stipulates the political system of the HKSAR, the rights and duties of its residents, and policies relating to economic and social affairs in the HKSAR. Some of these aspects will be considered in subsequent chapters.

II. THE PRC CONSTITUTION AND THE BASIC LAW

Although the Basic Law was enacted in 1990, it only came into effect in Hong Kong upon the establishment of the HKSAR on 1 July 1997. The shift in *Grundnorm* (basic norm) may be used to explain the legal significance of the 1997 handover. As Hans Kelsen has argued,[5] the validity of all legal norms within the legal order of a modern state can be ultimately traced back to a basic norm that confers validity on the constitution of the state concerned.

Applying Kelsen's theory, there was a shift in the basic norm of Hong Kong's legal order upon the PRC's resumption of sovereignty on 1 July 1997. Before the handover, the basic norm of the colonial legal order in Hong Kong was the same as that of the legal order in the UK. Upon the establishment of the HKSAR, the *Grundnorm* that confers validity on the PRC Constitution became the basic norm of Hong Kong's legal order. The Basic Law of the HKSAR is valid because it was enacted in accordance with the PRC Constitution. As mentioned above, Article 31 of the Constitution provides specifically for the establishment of SARs and the enactment of basic laws governing the SARs.

From this perspective, Chinese scholars and officials are correct in pointing out that the constitutional foundation of the HKSAR is jointly constituted by the PRC Constitution and the Basic Law.[6] This principle was expressly emphasised in the NPC Decision on electoral reform in the HKSAR dated 11 March 2021.[7] Most Chinese scholars also hold the view that, generally speaking, the PRC Constitution as a whole is applicable to the HKSAR, although whether a particular provision in the PRC

[5] H Kelsen, *Pure Theory of Law* (trans Max Knight, University of California Press, 1970).

[6] President Xi Jinping emphasised this in his speeches in Hong Kong on 1 July 2017 and 1 July 2022 at the 20th and 25th anniversary celebrations of the establishment of the HKSAR respectively: www.chinadaily.com.cn/china/hk20threturn/2017-07/01/content_29959860.htm; http://en.qstheory.cn/2022-07/02/c_786009.htm.

[7] Discussed later in this chapter.

Constitution is applicable to or should be implemented in the HKSAR depends on the nature and content of that provision and whether the Basic Law expressly or implicitly excludes its application.[8]

III. THE CONTINUITY OF LAWS

Despite the PRC's resumption of sovereignty in 1997, there is a high degree of continuity in the legal system and the applicable laws in Hong Kong before and after the handover. This is secured partly by Articles 8 and 18 of the Basic Law and partly by the Decision of the National People's Congress Standing Committee (NPCSC) on 23 February 1997, read together with Article 160 of the Basic Law.[9] Article 160 provides for the adoption of the laws previously in force in Hong Kong except those declared by the NPCSC to be in contravention of the Basic Law.[10] In the 1990s, the Chinese government conducted a comprehensive review of the existing laws in Hong Kong for the purpose of deciding which laws should not survive the handover under Article 160. Eventually, the February 1997 Decision of the NPCSC listed those laws that would not remain in force after the handover.

IV. 'PLENARY POWER' AND 'PATRIOTS RULING HONG KONG'

As mentioned above, the fundamental principles underlying the Basic Law are the principle of Chinese sovereignty and the principle of a high degree of autonomy exercisable by the HKSAR. Apart from these principles, two additional concepts have also been promoted by the central authorities.

The first is the concept of the 'plenary power' (*quanmian guanzhi quan*, 全面管治權, alternatively translated as 'overall jurisdiction' or

[8] See Y Wang, *Lun xianfa zai tebie xingzhengqu de shiyong* [*On the Application of the Constitution in the Special Administrative Regions*] (Joint Publishing Macau, 2019); speech by T Cheng, Secretary for Justice of the HKSAR on 27 May 2022 at the HKSAR 25th Anniversary Legal Conference on Basic Law: Stability to Prosperity, https://webcast.info.gov.hk/revamp/eng/video/0000001654_mp4.html.

[9] The NPCSC Decision was on the 'treatment of the laws previously in force in Hong Kong in accordance with Article 160 of the Basic Law'. See also the Hong Kong Reunification Ordinance enacted by the Provisional Legislative Council of the HKSAR in 1997.

[10] On the continuity of the common law in Hong Kong, see also the *Ma Wai Kwan* case [1997] HKLRD 761.

'comprehensive jurisdiction') of the central authorities over Hong Kong. The phrase 'plenary power' made its first appearance in the White Paper entitled *The Practice of One Country, Two Systems in the HKSAR*, issued by the Information Office of the State Council in 2014.[11] Since then, Chinese officials have often underscored the 'organic unity' between the plenary power possessed by the central authorities and the high degree of autonomy exercisable by the HKSAR.[12]

The concept of 'plenary power' is used to highlight the fact that all the powers of the HKSAR, including the autonomy it enjoys, are delegated by the central authorities, and the HKSAR cannot exercise any power that has not been delegated to it. The 'plenary power' of the central authorities over Hong Kong is a corollary of the PRC's sovereignty over Hong Kong and the fact that the PRC is a unitary state. In exercise of their 'plenary power', the central authorities have delegated numerous powers to the HKSAR. The central authorities' 'plenary power' includes the powers that may be directly exercised by the central authorities over the HKSAR, as well as any other power that has not been delegated to the HKSAR and therefore remains vested in the central authorities.

Article 20 of the Basic Law provides that the HKSAR may enjoy other powers granted to it by the central authorities. 'Other powers' in this context would mean powers that have not been expressly conferred upon the HKSAR by the Basic Law. Thus, Article 20 implies that any 'residual' power not conferred upon the HKSAR vests in the central authorities. Even for powers delegated to the HKSAR, the central authorities' plenary power also includes the power to exercise supervision over the exercise of such delegated powers.[13]

The second concept promoted by the central authorities is that of 'patriots ruling Hong Kong' (alternatively translated as 'patriots administering Hong Kong'). This phrase can be traced back to speeches made by Deng Xiaoping in the 1980s, when the Basic Law was being drafted.[14] After the handover, the discourse on patriots ruling Hong Kong was actively promoted by the central authorities on several occasions. Those occasions include public discussions on electoral reform in early 2004, proposed reforms in 2013–14 of the electoral model for electing the Chief Executive (CE) by universal suffrage and the discussion on the

[11] See n 4 above.

[12] See, eg President Xi Jinping's speech, n 6 above.

[13] See, eg State Council Information Office White Paper, *Hong Kong Democratic Progress Under the Framework of One Country, Two Systems* (December 2021) s II(3), www.news.cn/english/2021-12/20/c_1310383032.htm.

[14] See *Deng Xiaoping on 'One Country, Two Systems'* (Joint Publishing, 2004).

electoral revamp in Hong Kong in 2021. Notably, the Decision of the NPCSC dated 31 August 2014 on the election of the CE by universal suffrage expressly specifies that the CE has to be a person who loves the country and loves Hong Kong. The Decision of the NPC on electoral reform in the HKSAR dated 11 March 2021 also expressly mentions that 'patriots' should comprise the 'main body' (*zhuti*) of 'Hong Kong people ruling Hong Kong'.[15]

The Basic Law itself does not refer to 'patriots', but it can be argued that Article 104, which requires the CE, principal officials, legislative and executive councillors, and judges to take an oath to uphold the Basic Law and swear allegiance to the HKSAR of the PRC, embodies this 'patriots' principle. The exact criteria for determining whether a person upholds the Basic Law and owes allegiance to the HKSAR have now been set out in the Public Offices (Candidacy and Taking Up Offices) (Miscellaneous Amendments) Ordinance 2021.[16]

V. THE POWERS OF THE HKSAR

Under the Basic Law, the HKSAR authorities (including the executive, legislative and judicial branches) exercise jurisdiction over a wide range of subject matters. From this perspective, the scope of the autonomous powers conferred on the HKSAR is broader than those exercisable by member states in federations or autonomous regions governed under most devolution schemes.[17] The matters mentioned below are illustrative, but by no means exhaustive, of the HKSAR's autonomy:

1. More than 95 per cent of the laws enacted by China's national legislature (the NPC and its Standing Committee) are not applicable to the SAR; the pre-existing common law system and legislation are largely preserved in Hong Kong. The only national laws that apply to Hong Kong are those listed in Annex III to the Basic Law, and there are currently 14 such laws, such as the Nationality Law, National Flag Law, National Emblem Law, Law on the Territorial Sea, Law on the Garrisoning of the Hong Kong SAR, Regulations

[15] See ch 4 below.
[16] This law was enacted as part of the electoral reform package of 2021. See ch 4 below.
[17] H Hannum, *Autonomy, Sovereignty and Self-Determination*, revised edn (University of Pennsylvania Press, 1996) 137–49.

on Diplomatic Privileges and Immunities, and HKSAR National Security Law.[18] The legislature of the SAR can legislate over almost all subject matters in or relating to Hong Kong.
2. Cases litigated before the Hong Kong courts are entirely resolved within the Hong Kong court system, with the Hong Kong Court of Final Appeal (CFA) serving as the highest appellate court, replacing the Judicial Committee of the Privy Council, Hong Kong's final appellate court during the colonial era. No appeal lies from a Hong Kong court to any court or institution in mainland China. But Article 158 of the Basic Law requires the CFA to refer relevant provisions of the Basic Law to the NPC Standing Committee (NPCSC) for interpretation in certain circumstances. However, interpretations made by the NPCSC cannot overturn a final court judgment previously rendered. In other words, litigants in a case that the court has previously decided would not be affected by a subsequent NPCSC interpretation.
3. Hong Kong residents do not have to pay any tax to the central government, and the tax that they pay to the SAR government will be used for the SAR exclusively – no part of it will be handed over to the central government.
4. The SAR can continue to have and issue its own currency, the Hong Kong dollar.
5. The SAR can control and regulate entry and exit of persons into and out of the SAR.
6. The SAR is a customs territory separate from other parts of China.
7. The SAR, using the name of 'Hong Kong, China', can enter into economic and cultural relations with other countries, sign international agreements in these domains and participate in some international organisations (such as the World Trade Organization) whose membership is not restricted to sovereign states.[19] The Basic

[18] See Art 18 of the Basic Law. Annex III has been amended five times since the Basic Law was enacted in 1990. On 1 July 1997, the NPC Standing Committee added to it five new laws enacted between 1990 and 1997: the Law on the Garrisoning of the HKSAR; the National Flag Law; the National Emblem Law; the Law on the Territorial Sea and the Contiguous Zone; and Regulations concerning Consular Privileges and Immunities. Since 1 July 1997, four more laws have been added: the Law on the Exclusive Economic Zone and the Continental Shelf was added to Annex III in December 1998; the Law on Judicial Immunity from Compulsory Measures Concerning the Property of Foreign Central Banks was added in October 2005; the National Anthem Law was added in November 2017; and the HKSAR National Security Law was added in June 2020.

[19] R Mushkat, 'Hong Kong's Exercise of External Autonomy' (2006) 55 *ICLQ* 945.

Law authorises the SAR government to handle certain 'external affairs' even though, generally speaking, 'foreign affairs' are within the power of the central government.[20]

VI. THE POWERS OF THE CENTRAL AUTHORITIES

Under the Basic Law, the major powers that the central authorities can exercise over the HKSAR include Article 15 (appointment of the Chief Executive and principal officials), 17 (invalidation of Hong Kong legislation), 18 (application of national laws to Hong Kong), 158 (interpretation of the Basic Law) and 159 (amendment of the Basic Law). Some of these powers have not been used in practice. For example, under Article 17, the NPCSC has the power to nullify SAR laws that exceed the scope of the SAR's autonomy. However, since the HKSAR was established in 1997, the central government has never exercised this power to nullify any SAR law. The NPC's power under Article 159 to amend the main text of the Basic Law has never been exercised, although Annexes I, II and III to the Basic Law have been amended.[21]

Under Article 158 of the Basic Law, the NPCSC may issue an interpretation of the Basic Law. The exercise of this power constitutes one of the most significant interactions and points of interface between the Hong Kong and mainland legal systems.[22] A total of five interpretations have been issued so far. These interpretations are summarised below; some of them will be discussed in greater detail in chapter five insofar as they interact with the judicial system of the HKSAR.

A. The First Interpretation

The first interpretation, promulgated in 1999, centred on Articles 22 and 24 of the Basic Law; it related to the right of abode in the HKSAR of children born on the mainland but to Hong Kong permanent residents. This interpretation was issued upon the request of the SAR government, which sought to overrule two decisions rendered by the CFA in

[20] See Art 13 and chs 5–7 of the Basic Law.

[21] For amendments to Annex III, see n 18 above. Annexes I and II to the Basic Law, which govern Hong Kong's electoral system, were amended in 2010 and in 2021. See ch 4 below.

[22] See ch 5 below.

the cases of *Ng Ka Ling*[23] and *Chan Kam Nga*.[24] In both cases, the CFA had conferred the constitutional right of abode in Hong Kong on a sizeable class of persons born on the mainland. The government estimated that, based on the CFA's interpretation of the relevant Basic Law provisions, 1.67 million mainland residents would be entitled to migrate to Hong Kong in the following 10 years. Whether the CFA's interpretation should remain was thus a matter of huge socio-economic importance. Responding to CE Tung Chee-hwa's request, the NPCSC issued its interpretation in June 1999, overruling the CFA's interpretation.

Under Article 158 of the Basic Law, the NPCSC's interpretation did not have the effect of reversing the CFA's judgments and orders concerning the litigants in the *Ng* and *Chan* cases; the interpretation only meant that Hong Kong courts in future cases must follow the NPCSC's interpretation instead of the CFA's interpretation of the relevant Basic Law provisions. In *Lau Kong Yung*,[25] the CFA addressed the effect of the NPCSC interpretation and recognised its binding force. It also acknowledged that the NPCSC's interpretative power is 'free-standing', in the sense that it may be exercised at any time, even in the absence of a judicial reference by the CFA under Article 158(3) of the Basic Law.

B. The Second Interpretation

After 1999, the NPCSC exercised the power of Basic Law interpretation on four other occasions. In 2004, the NPCSC promulgated an interpretation of the Basic Law provisions relating to the procedure on electoral reform. The procedure, nature, effect and impact of the 2004 Interpretation differ considerably from the 1999 Interpretation.

First, unlike the 1999 Interpretation, the 2004 Interpretation was not requested by the CE, but was issued by the NPCSC on its own initiative.

Secondly, unlike the 1999 Interpretation, the 2004 Interpretation does not deal with any ambiguity in the language of the Basic Law provisions that was addressed by a court in the course of litigation. Instead, it fleshes out – or purports to flesh out – the legislative policy underpinning the relevant provisions in Annexes I and II of the Basic Law. The Interpretation effectively supplements or adds to the provisions of the

[23] (1999) 2 HKCFAR 4.
[24] (1999) 2 HKCFAR 82.
[25] (1999) 2 HKCFAR 300.

Basic Law. Therefore, critics argue that the 2004 Interpretation is in substance an amendment of the provisions of Annexes I and II of the Basic Law rather than an interpretation that resolves an ambiguity in the Basic Law, as was the case with the 1999 Interpretation. However, it is noteworthy in this regard that the CFA has already held in *Chong Fung Yuen*[26] that under the mainland Chinese system of legislative interpretation by the NPCSC, an interpretation may have the effect of supplementing the text of a Basic Law provision.

Thirdly, the impact of the 2004 Interpretation may be considered more far-reaching than the 1999 Interpretation. In particular, the 2004 Interpretation has the effect of reshaping the procedural and substantive roles the HKSAR authorities and the central authorities play vis-à-vis any future electoral reform of the HKSAR's political system.

Before the 2004 Interpretation, the literal meaning of the relevant provisions of Annexes I and II of the Basic Law would suggest that the HKSAR authorities are allowed to initiate proposals for electoral reforms relating to the CE and the Legislative Council (LegCo). It would appear from these provisions that if such a proposal relating to the mode of election of the CE is endorsed by a two-thirds majority in LegCo and consented to by the CE, it will come into force upon approval by the NPCSC. And if the electoral reform relates to the LegCo, and is endorsed by a two-thirds majority in LegCo and consented to by the CE, it can come into force upon being reported to the NPCSC 'for the record'.

The 2004 Interpretation inserts two additional steps to the initial stage of this electoral reform process. First, the CE should make a report to the NPCSC on whether 'there is a need to amend' the existing mode of election of the CE or the LegCo. Secondly, the NPCSC, after considering the CE's report, will make a decision thereon.

It is noteworthy here that the phrase 'if there is a need to amend' the relevant electoral arrangement appears in the original provisions of Annexes I and II to the Basic Law. Hence, defenders of the 2004 Interpretation point out that there is a real ambiguity in the Basic Law regarding which party has the power to determine whether there is a need to amend the electoral arrangements, and the 2004 Interpretation thereby resolves this ambiguity by vesting this power in the NPCSC.[27]

[26] (2001) 4 HKCFAR 211.

[27] See A Chen, 'The Constitutional Controversy of Spring 2004' (2004) 34 *Hong Kong Law Journal* 215.

C. The Third Interpretation

In 2005, CE Tung Chee-hwa's resignation in the middle of his second term of office raised a constitutional issue concerning the length of his successor's term of office. Neither the Basic Law nor the Chief Executive Election Ordinance included any specific provision addressing such a scenario; Article 46 of the Basic Law simply stipulates a five-year term for the CE and provides that they may serve no more than two consecutive terms. In view of this uncertainty, the Acting Chief Executive followed the practice adopted by the CE in 1999 and referred this Basic Law issue to the central authorities for an authoritative determination. Thereafter, the NPCSC promulgated an interpretation of Article 53(2) of the Basic Law (which deals with vacancy in the office of the CE and an election being held to fill the vacancy), stipulating that if a vacancy in the office of the CE arises before the five-year term is completed, the new CE will serve the remainder of their predecessor's term of office.

D. The Fourth Interpretation

In 2011, the CFA, in the *Congo* case,[28] for the first time used the judicial reference procedure provided in Article 158(3) of the Basic Law, which requires the court to refer to the NPCSC for interpretation of relevant Basic Law provisions relating to affairs within the responsibility of the Central People's Government or the relationship between the central authorities and the HKSAR.[29] This *Congo* case centred on whether the law on foreign state immunity in the HKSAR was the same as that on the mainland. Before the handover, the 'restrictive' or 'qualified' version of the doctrine of state immunity in British law was applicable to colonial Hong Kong under both the common law and the UK State Immunity Act 1978, which was made applicable to Hong Kong by the State Immunity (Overseas Territories) Order 1979. According to this version of the doctrine, a state cannot assert immunity over commercial transactions it has entered into. This differs from the 'absolute' version of state immunity followed by the PRC, under which there is no 'commercial transactions' exception to this immunity.

In the *Congo* case, the defendants – including the Democratic Republic of the Congo – argued that they were immune from suit by virtue of

[28] (2011) 14 HKCFAR 95, 395.
[29] See A Chen, 'The *Congo* Case' (2011) 41 *Hong Kong Law Journal* 369.

the doctrine of state immunity, and that the 'absolute' version of the doctrine was applicable in the HKSAR. The plaintiff contended that the 'restrictive' version of the doctrine should be applied, as it was part of the common law that was applicable in the HKSAR. The Secretary for Justice, acting on behalf of the HKSAR government as 'intervener' in the proceedings, supported the defendants' view regarding state immunity. The Office of the Commissioner of the Ministry of Foreign Affairs in the HKSAR also issued letters expressing the view that the PRC adopts the 'absolute' version of state immunity, and this should apply to the HKSAR as it is part of the PRC.

The CFA decided, by a 3:2 majority (with the overseas non-permanent judge, Sir Anthony Mason, former Chief Justice of Australia, joining the majority), to make a judicial reference to the NPCSC under Article 158(3) of the Basic Law. In the majority's view, this case called for an authoritative interpretation by the NPCSC of Articles 13 and 19 of the Basic Law. In particular, Article 13(1) vests in the Central People's Government the responsibility for the 'foreign affairs relating to the HKSAR' and Article 19(3) excludes matters relating to 'acts of state such as defence and foreign affairs' from the HKSAR's jurisdiction. Therefore, whether the Hong Kong courts were bound to apply the law or policy of foreign state immunity determined by the central authorities, and whether such a determination would constitute an 'act of state' over which Hong Kong courts have no jurisdiction, would depend on the interpretation of these Basic Law provisions.

On 26 August 2011, the NPCSC promulgated an interpretation of Articles 13(1) and 19 of the Basic Law. The interpretation basically answered the two questions mentioned above in the affirmative. After the interpretation was issued, the CFA reconvened and gave judgment in favour of the defendants in this case.

E. The Fifth Interpretation

In November 2016, the NPCSC, acting on its own initiative, promulgated what is probably the most controversial interpretation of the Basic Law to date. The interpretation was issued in the midst of litigation in the case of *Chief Executive of the HKSAR v President of the Legislative Council and Leung Chung Hang Sixtus*.[30] The court proceedings

[30] *Chief Executive of the HKSAR v President of the Legislative Council and Leung Chung Hang Sixtus*, HCAL 185/2016 (Court of First Instance, 15 November 2016), [2017]

in this case were brought by the government for the purpose of disqualifying two 'pro-Hong Kong independence' Legislative Councillors from office after they had just been elected into office. Notably, both lawmakers had openly derided China at their swearing-in ceremony on 12 October 2016; they even referred to China as 'Sheen-na' – a derogatory term used by the Japanese to refer to the Chinese during the Second World War – and displayed banners advocating Hong Kong's independence.

Their oaths of office were naturally rejected by the President of the Legislative Council as invalid. But before the lawmakers were allowed to retake their oaths on a separate occasion, the government commenced judicial proceedings in the High Court, arguing that the two LegCo members had been disqualified by operation of law because they had failed to take their oaths in the prescribed manner as stipulated in Article 104 of the Basic Law and other Hong Kong legislation, particularly the Oaths and Declarations Ordinance (ODO). These oath-taking requirements are applicable to the Chief Executive, members of the Legislative and Executive Councils, and judges.

Three days after the High Court's Court of First Instance (CFI) concluded its hearing in this case, but before the court delivered judgment, the NPCSC – at a regular session convened to deal with various legislative matters on the mainland – promulgated its interpretation of Article 104 of the Basic Law. The Interpretation largely pre-empted the issues litigated in the *Leung* case and provides, inter alia, that 'If the oath taken is determined as invalid, no arrangement shall be made for retaking the oath'. Critics argued that this Interpretation is effectively an amendment of the Basic Law. Furthermore, while the Interpretation itself is silent on whether it applies retrospectively to events predating the promulgation, the courts proceeded to retrospectively apply it to the matters litigated in the *Leung Chung Hang* case. In essence, the CFI disqualified the two LegCo members mainly by applying the ODO, and the Court remarked that its decision would have been the same even if there had not been an NPCSC Interpretation on oath-taking. The CFI's decision was upheld by the Court of Appeal, which partly relied on the NPCSC Interpretation for its decision. The disqualified legislators' application for leave to appeal to the CFA was dismissed by the CFA. The CFA pointed out that existing case law has already established that an NPCSC Interpretation can supplement the text of the Basic Law and can also have retrospective effect insofar as the Interpretation is declarative of what the law is and has always been since the coming into effect of the Basic Law on 1 July 1997.

The two disqualified legislators were among six 'localist' activists who were elected into LegCo in 2016, collectively capturing 19 per cent of the popular votes.[31] Shortly after the first 'disqualification' case was resolved by the High Court, the government brought proceedings for the purpose of disqualifying four other legislators elected in 2016, on account that they too had failed to take their oaths properly. These cases were also resolved in favour of the government.[32]

In the by-elections held to fill the vacancies arising from the disqualification of these legislators, several 'localists' were barred from running for office.[33] The first case in which the disqualification of a LegCo election candidate was judicially challenged was *Chan Ho Tin v Lo Ying Ki Alan*.[34] Chan was one of the 'localists' barred from participating as a candidate in the 2016 LegCo election. The CFI upheld the decision of the returning officer to disqualify him. The judge ruled that the returning officer had the power under the relevant electoral law to determine whether the candidate's declaration that he upheld the Basic Law and owed allegiance to the HKSAR of the PRC – a declaration required of every candidate in a LegCo election – was sincerely and genuinely made, or whether this declaration did not correspond with the candidate's state of mind or belief (eg because the candidate actually believed that Hong Kong should become independent of the PRC) such that the declaration was invalid.

The NPCSC's 2016 Interpretation not only 'clarifies' the law on oath-taking by newly elected legislators; it also extends the application of Article 104 of the Basic Law to persons standing for elections. Thus, the Interpretation has the effect of strengthening the legal basis for disqualifying candidates in LegCo elections who are deemed not to have met the

1 HKLRD 460 (Court of Appeal), (2017) 20 HKCFAR 390 (leave to appeal refused by CFA). The two Legislative Councillors – Leung Chung Hang and Yau Wai Ching – were disqualified from office.

31 'Localists and Self-Determination Activists Capture 6 Seats, LegCo Divided into 3 Factions' and 'Localist Self-Determination Politicians Capture 400,000 Votes' *Ming Pao* (6 September 2016, in Chinese); CK Choy and JM Chan, 'Lifahui xuanju jieguo chubu pingxi' (立法會選舉結果初步評析; A Preliminary Analysis of the Outcome of the LegCo Election) *Ming Pao* (6 September 2016).

32 *Nathan Law Kwun Chung* [2017] 4 HKLRD 115 (CFI); *Leung Kwok Hung* [2019] HKCA 173 (CA). For an analysis, see H Zhu and AHY Chen, 'The Oath-Taking Cases and the NPCSC Interpretation of 2016' (2019) 49 *Hong Kong Law Journal* 381.

33 See, eg *Chow Ting v Teng Yu Yan* [2019] HKCFI 2135; *Au Nok Hin v Teng Yu Yan Anne* [2019] HKCFA 50 (candidates' disqualification successfully challenged on procedural grounds); *Lau Wing Hong v Chan Yuen Man* [2019] HKCFI 2287 (on the effect of such successful challenge on incumbent LegCo member).

34 [2018] HKCFI 345.

Article 104 constitutional requirement of upholding the Basic Law and owing allegiance to the HKSAR of the PRC.[35]

Subsequently, the 2016 Interpretation also constituted part of the legal basis for the enactment of the Public Offices (Candidacy and Taking Up Offices) (Miscellaneous Amendments) Ordinance in 2021, which, inter alia, sets out the criteria for determining whether someone upholds the Basic Law and owes allegiance to the HKSAR. Hence, the impact of the 2016 Interpretation on Hong Kong's electoral laws has been far-reaching.

F. The 'Decision-Making' Power of the NPCSC

In addition to interpretations, the NPCSC has also promulgated a number of 'decisions' with regard to the HKSAR. The constitutional and legal basis of these decisions vary, and some of the decisions are controversial in Hong Kong insofar as the Basic Law makes no mention of the applicability of these decisions as part of Hong Kong law, and their legal foundation rests solely with the PRC Constitution itself. However, as far as mainland Chinese law is concerned, legal instruments entitled 'decisions' made by the NPC and NPCSC have the same legal force as legal instruments entitled 'laws'.[36]

The NPCSC promulgated three decisions, in 2004, 2007 and 2014 respectively, on electoral reform in the HKSAR. These decisions were made in pursuance of the 2004 Interpretation of the Basic Law. As discussed above, this 2004 Interpretation requires the NPCSC to make a decision on electoral reform in the HKSAR after considering the CE's report on the matter.

Apart from these three decisions, the NPCSC also promulgated two decisions in 2006 and 2017 on the 'co-location' of mainland and HKSAR immigration and customs checkpoints at the Shenzhen Bay Port and at the West Kowloon Express Rail station respectively, and another two decisions in 2020 relating to the LegCo of the HKSAR.

[35] According to para 1 of the Interpretation, upholding the Basic Law and bearing allegiance to the HKSAR of the PRC 'are not only the legal content which must be included in the oath … but also the legal requirements and preconditions for standing for election'.

[36] For example, in practice, an amendment to an existing law is made by the NPCSC by passing a 'decision' rather than by passing a law providing for the amendment. The establishment of the HKSAR itself was effectuated by a Decision on the Establishment of the HKSAR enacted by the NPC on 4 April 1990, the same day as the date of enactment of the Basic Law of the HKSAR.

As far as these four decisions are concerned, only the legal basis for the 2006 Decision may be clearly found in the Basic Law. Article 20 of the Basic Law provides that the HKSAR 'may enjoy other powers granted to it' by the central authorities. The 2006 Decision of the NPCSC authorises the HKSAR to exercise power and jurisdiction over a port control area within the Shenzhen Bay Port. The Decision may therefore be regarded as having granted an additional power to the HKSAR as authorised under Article 20, even though Article 20 was not expressly mentioned in the NPCSC decision.[37]

The 2017 Decision of the NPCSC is also on the co-location of immigration checkpoints, but its nature and effect are quite different from the 2006 Decision. Unlike the 2006 Decision, the 2017 Decision does not grant any specific power to the HKSAR. Instead, it approved the 'Co-operation Arrangement' that had been entered into by the Guangdong and HKSAR authorities regarding the establishment of a port at the West Kowloon Express Rail Station, where the co-location of immigration facilities would be practised. The NPCSC Decision also confirmed that the Co-operation Arrangement was consistent with the PRC Constitution and the Basic Law, and the Decision required the HKSAR to legislate on the implementation of the Co-operation Arrangement.

The legal status of the 2017 Decision of the NPCSC was litigated in the case of *Leung Chung Hang v President of Legislative Council*.[38] In this case, the Guangzhou–Shenzhen–Hong Kong Express Rail Link (Colocation) Ordinance 2018, which allows mainland Chinese immigration and customs officers to be stationed in a port control area in the West Kowloon station and authorises the enforcement of mainland Chinese law therein, was challenged as being inconsistent with Article 18 of the Basic Law concerning the non-application of mainland laws in Hong Kong. The scheme was upheld by the CFI, which relied to some extent on the 2017 Decision of the NPCSC. The CFI's decision was upheld by the Court of Appeal. This case will be further discussed in chapter five below.

In 2020, the NPCSC promulgated two decisions on the HKSAR. Both relate mainly to the sixth-term Legislative Council (2016–20). The first Decision was made on 11 August 2020 after the HKSAR

[37] The NPCSC's grant of power provided the legal basis for the enactment by the HKSAR legislature of the Shenzhen Bay Port Hong Kong Port Area Ordinance 2007, which provides for the 'co-location' arrangement at the Shenzhen Bay Port.

[38] *Leung Chung Hang v President of Legislative Council* [2018] HKCFI 2657, [2021] HKCA 871.

government decided, in view of the COVID-19 pandemic, to postpone for one year the LegCo election originally scheduled for September 2020. The postponement was achieved by the government passing a regulation under the Emergency Regulations Ordinance.[39] However, the SAR government had no power to extend the term of office of the (sixth-term) LegCo, as the Basic Law limits the LegCo to a four-year term.[40] To prevent a legislative vacuum where there would be no legislature in place to make laws, the NPCSC made a Decision in August 2020 to authorise the sixth-term Legco to continue the discharge of its official functions for one more year.

However, no clear legal basis for this Decision can be found in the Basic Law itself. Arguably, Article 20 of the Basic Law is relevant here, because it authorises the central authorities, including the NPCSC, to grant a power to the HKSAR that is not provided for in the Basic Law itself. Nevertheless, the NPCSC Decision of August 2020 does not refer to Article 20.[41] The better view is that the decision was made in pursuance of the PRC Constitution itself. Article 31 of the PRC Constitution grants the NPC a general power to legislate on the systems to be practised in an SAR. As the NPC only meets once a year (in a session lasting for several weeks), there exists a practice or convention that the NPCSC may act on behalf of the NPC when the former is not in session. Furthermore, under Chinese constitutional law, the power to make 'decisions' on important matters is a general power exercisable by the NPC and its Standing Committee.

The NPCSC Decision of 11 August 2020 was soon followed by another Decision made on 11 November 2020. This Decision had the effect of disqualifying four members of the sixth-term LegCo from serving during its extended term, on the ground that they had already been disqualified by electoral returning officers from standing as candidates in the LegCo election previously scheduled for September 2020 before its postponement. In protest against the NPCSC Decision, 15 other LegCo members of the pro-democracy camp resigned en masse.[42]

[39] Emergency (Date of General Election) (Seventh Term of the Legislative Council) Regulation, gazetted on 31 July 2020.

[40] Basic Law, Art 69.

[41] The text of the NPCSC decision states that it was made in accordance with the 'relevant provisions of the PRC Constitution and the Basic Law of the HKSAR of the PRC'.

[42] J Lam et al, 'Hong Kong Opposition Lawmakers to Resign en Masse after Beijing Resolution Empowering Local Authorities to Bypass Courts and Unseat Politicians' *South China Morning Post* (11 November 2020) www.scmp.com/news/hong-kong/politics/article/3109330/top-beijing-body-makes-patriotism-mandatory-hong-kong.

Although this NPCSC Decision was expressed in general terms, setting out the circumstances in which a LegCo member may be disqualified,[43] the background to this Decision stemmed from the earlier Decision of the NPCSC to extend the term of office of the sixth-term LegCo. This earlier Decision gave rise to the legal question of whether members of the sixth-term LegCo could continue to serve during the extended term if they had already been disqualified by the returning officer when they were seeking to stand as candidates in the September 2020 election for the seventh-term LegCo.[44] Beijing came to the view that these LegCo members should not be allowed to serve during the extended term of the sixth-term LegCo, as they had already been determined to be ineligible as LegCo members. Hence the NPCSC Decision in November 2020. Like the NPCSC Decision of August 2020, the legal basis for the November 2020 Decision lies not in the Basic Law, but in the PRC Constitution itself.[45]

G. The 'Decision-Making' Power of the NPC

The NPC itself has, since the Basic Law came into effect in 1997, made two decisions relating to the HKSAR. They are the Decision on national security in the HKSAR (2020) and the Decision on electoral reform in the HKSAR (2021). These Decisions were made by the NPC in exercise of its power under the Constitution itself. They may be regarded as legislative acts of the NPC that supplement the Basic Law enacted by the NPC in 1990. In pursuance of and as authorised by these two Decisions, the NPCSC enacted the HKSAR National Security Law in June 2020, and amended Annexes I and II to the Basic Law in March 2021. The National Security Law has been mentioned in chapter one and will be further discussed later in this chapter. The amendments to Annexes I and II of the Basic Law will be discussed in chapter four on the political system of the HKSAR and the electoral revamp of 2021.

[43] See Art 1 of the NPCSC Decision. The circumstances include those instances in which a LegCo member will be deemed not to have upheld the Basic Law and owed allegiance to the HKSAR of the PRC (as required by the terms of the oath of office under Art 104 of the Basic Law) – eg where the LegCo member advocates or supports 'Hong Kong independence' or seeks foreign intervention into the affairs of the HKSAR.

[44] Four members of the 6th-term LegCo who intended to run for the September 2020 election had been disqualified by returning officers on the ground that their declarations (that they upheld the Basic Law and owed allegiance to the HKSAR of the PRC) were invalid.

[45] The preamble of the text of the Decision refers, inter alia, to Arts 52, 54 and 67(1) of the PRC Constitution.

H. Application of National Laws to the HKSAR

Apart from making interpretations of the Basic Law and decisions with regard to the HKSAR, the NPCSC has the power, under Article 18 of the Basic Law, to apply to the HKSAR national laws relating to defence, foreign affairs and other matters outside the limits of the autonomy of the HKSAR. Such national laws – listed in Annex III to the Basic Law – are added by the NPCSC from time to time. As mentioned above, 14 national laws are currently listed in Annex III, including the Law on Safeguarding National Security in the HKSAR (NSL) enacted by the NPCSC on 30 June 2020.

The context leading to the enactment of the NSL has been discussed in chapter one above. As mentioned there, the NSL has created four types of offences, relating to secession, subversion, terrorism and collusion with foreign forces to endanger national security. Critics have argued that the NSL is too draconian and is inconsistent with the international covenants on rights protection enshrined in the Basic Law.[46] There are, for example, criticisms of the putative vague language in some of the NSL offence-creating provisions, the list of 'designated judges' appointed by the Chief Executive (from among existing judges and in consultation with the Chief Justice) to hear national security cases,[47] exceptions made to jury trials,[48] limitations on bail,[49] broad powers granted to the police by the NSL and by its Implementing Rules,[50]

[46] See, eg J-P Cabestan and L Daziano, *Hong Kong: The Second Handover* (Fondation pour L'Innovation Politique, 2020); public letter dated 1 September 2020 to the Chinese government from several UN Special Rapporteurs and human rights experts on the PRC Law on Safeguarding National Security in the HKSAR, reference: OL CHN 17/2020, https://spcommreports.ohchr.org/TMResultsBase/DownLoadPublicCommunicationFile?gId=25487; China's reply: https://spcommreports.ohchr.org/TMResultsBase/DownLoadFile?gId=35721; Human Rights Committee, 'Concluding Observations on the Fourth Periodic Report of Hong Kong, China' (CCPR/C/CHN-HKG/CO/4, 27 July 2022) https://tbinternet.ohchr.org/Treaties/CCPR/Shared%20Documents/HKG/CCPR_C_CHN-HKG_CO_4_49295_E.pdf; HKSAR government's replies: www.cmab.gov.hk/doc/en/documents/policy_responsibilities/response_to_loi-iccpr-en.pdf.

[47] NSL, Art 44. See also the 'Statement by Chief Justice of Court of Final Appeal' on the implementation of Art 44: www.info.gov.hk/gia/general/202007/02/P2020070200414.htm (2 July 2020).

[48] NSL, Art 46; *Tong Ying Kit v Secretary for Justice* [2021] HKCFI 1397, [2021] HKCA 912.

[49] NSL, Art 42(2); *HKSAR v Lai Chee Ying* [2021] HKCFA 3.

[50] NSL, Art 43; Implementing Rules for Art 43 of the NSL, HKSAR Government Gazette, LN 139 of 2020, p B2397; Operating Principles and Guidelines for Application of Authorization to Conduct Interception and Covert Surveillance, HKSAR Government Gazette, GN(E) 74 of 2020.

the disqualification of persons convicted of offences under the NSL from holding public office possibly for life,[51] the broad extraterritorial reach of the NSL[52] and the exclusion from judicial review of decisions made by the National Security Committee of the HKSAR government.[53] The CFA has also ruled that the NSL itself is effectively immune from any constitutional challenge lodged on the ground that the NSL is incompatible with the Basic Law.[54]

A major criticism of the NSL is that it authorises the central authorities to establish the National Security Office (NSO) in Hong Kong.[55] The NSO is now one of four state organs in the HKSAR that are directly accountable to the central authorities in Beijing – the other three being the Liaison Office of the Central People's Government in the HKSAR, the Office of the Commissioner of the Ministry of Foreign Affairs in the HKSAR and the Hong Kong Garrison of the People's Liberation Army. Although the NSL empowers Hong Kong's law enforcement authorities and courts to investigate, prosecute and try cases arising from the NSL, it also confers on the NSO powers of investigation, arrest, detention and transfer of suspects to the mainland for prosecution and trial in three scenarios, specifically when the case is complex due to the involvement of foreign countries, the HKSAR government is unable to effectively enforce the law, or a major and imminent threat to national security has occurred.[56]

Any reliance on the NSO and mainland state apparatus for the enforcement of the NSL in these three types of cases is believed to be intended only for very special or exceptional circumstances. Nevertheless, this arrangement may be considered an inroad into the integrity of the HKSAR's legal system, insofar as it exposes people in Hong Kong to the risk of being transferred to mainland China for prosecution and trial. It is not easy to reconcile this arrangement with the Basic Law, which confers on the HKSAR courts 'jurisdiction over all cases in the Region', subject to restrictions on the courts' jurisdiction that existed before the handover.[57] It thus raises jurisprudential questions on whether the NSL may introduce institutional arrangements inconsistent with the Basic

[51] NSL, Art 35.
[52] NSL, Arts 37–38.
[53] NSL, Art 14.
[54] *Lai Chee Ying* (n 49).
[55] NSL, Arts 48–54.
[56] NSL, Arts 55–61.
[57] Basic Law, Art 19; see also Arts 80 and 81.

Law, or questions on the precise nature of the relationship between the NSL and the Basic Law. These questions, however, may be merely academic, as the Court of Final Appeal has held that the NSL is consistent with the Basic Law.[58]

Although the offence-creating provisions of the NSL are separate from the other substantive criminal law offences in Hong Kong, this does not mean that the NSL will not significantly impact the operation of Hong Kong's existing laws vis-à-vis non-NSL offences. This is because the NSL has made it clear that it is not the only law relating to national security in the HKSAR, and some of its provisions are applicable to other national security-related laws in Hong Kong.[59]

Notably, there is no definition of 'national security' in the NSL. However, the CFA in the *Lai Chee Ying* case[60]

> construe[d] 'acts endangering national security' in the context of Article 42(2) of the NSL – the provision on bail requirements – as referring to acts of that nature capable of constituting an offence under the NSL *or the laws of the HKSAR safeguarding national security*. (emphasis added)[61]

The CFA judgment provides examples of national security offences outside the NSL: 'the offences of treason, incitement to disaffection or sedition under Parts I and II of the Crimes Ordinance'.[62] This means that the statutory provisions on these offences also form part of HKSAR laws relating to national security. Subsequently, it was held specifically that the sedition offence constituted by sections 9 and 10 of the Crimes Ordinance is an offence against national security.[63]

The question of whether a particular law or legal provision concerns national security is significant because there are several NSL articles which apply to legal proceedings of cases concerning offences endangering national security. A prosecution pursuant to a legal provision relating to national security, irrespective of whether the provision is codified in the NSL or in another law, would trigger the operation of the NSL articles concerning trial by 'designated judges',[64] bail,[65] the possible

[58] *Lai Chee Ying* (n 49).
[59] NSL, Arts 3, 6(2), 7 and 8.
[60] See n 49 above.
[61] ibid CFA judgment, para 53(c)(ii).
[62] ibid CFA judgment, fn 40.
[63] *HKSAR v Ng Hau Yi Sidney* [2021] HKCFA 42 (on the applicability of Art 42(2) (the 'bail provision') of the NSL to the sedition offence under the Crimes Ordinance.
[64] *HKSAR v Lai Man-ling* [2022] HKDC 355.
[65] *Ng Hau Yi* (n 63).

dispensation of jury trials and the possibility of closed hearings. Where there is doubt over whether a case concerns national security, Article 47 of the NSL authorises the court to obtain a certificate from the CE to certify whether that relevant act concerns national security.

The passage of the NSL was highly controversial and attracted international attention. Some countries imposed sanctions on Hong Kong and the PRC, including their officials, on the ground that the NSL threatens civil liberties and infringes upon Hong Kong's autonomy. The UK responded by making it easier for Hong Kong residents holding British Nationals (Overseas) passports to migrate to Britain. The full effect of the implementation of the NSL remains to be seen as, at the time of writing, the enforcement of the NSL was still at the early stages.

As of 1 July 2022 – the second anniversary of the enactment of the NSL, 201 persons had been arrested for the alleged commission of offences against national security (including 44 suspected of sedition under the Crimes Ordinance), of whom 126 had been charged (including the 47 co-defendants in the 'primary election' case mentioned below and 26 defendants prosecuted for sedition). In addition, five companies, including the company that published the *Apple Daily*, which was well known for its anti-Chinese Communist Party stance, were also prosecuted for national security offences. Of those prosecuted, 12 persons had been convicted by the courts as of 1 July 2022, 81 persons were in custody pending trial and 33 persons were out on bail.[66]

The prosecution of 47 defendants in the 'primary election' case was probably the most politically significant case brought under the NSL, as many of the defendants were leading members of the political 'opposition' in Hong Kong.[67] In July 2019, they had organised or ran in an unofficial 'primary election' to select pro-democracy candidates for the September 2020 election. As part of their electoral platform, they stated that they would veto the government's budget proposal and all

[66] Data reported in *Ming Pao* (4 July 2022, in Chinese).

[67] Case numbers WKCC813/21, HCCC 69/2022; N Wong, 'Opposition Hit with Subversion Charges' *South China Morning Post* (1 March 2021); C Lau and B Wong, 'Hundreds Gather at Court as Bail Hearing Commences' *South China Morning Post* (2 March 2021). As of the beginning of June 2022, 17 of the defendants had been granted bail pending trial and 30 were in custody. For some of the bail judgments, see www.judiciary.hk, Case Nos HCCP 110/21, 111–120/21, 126/21, 134–137/21, 141/21, 294/21, 417/21. The trial of the case in the High Court before a three-judge bench began on 6 February 2023 but had not concluded at the time of writing. Sixteen of the 24 defendants pleaded not guilty and the others pleaded guilty. The trial was expected to take 90 days. See C Lau and B Wong, 'Biggest Trial of Opposition Figures Begins' *South China Morning Post* (7 February 2023).

government Bills in LegCo (so as to force the CE to dissolve LegCo and eventually resign) if the government did not accede to the 'five principal demands' of the anti-extradition movement of 2019.[68] In early 2021, they were arrested and charged with conspiracy to commit subversion under Article 22(3) of the NSL.[69]

As of 1 July 2022, the courts had concluded four NSL trials, all of which the defendants were convicted for (inter alia) incitement of secession, and they were sentenced to prison terms ranging between three years and seven months and 9 years.[70] Since the enactment of the NSL, the SAR government has also revived the use of the 'dormant' sedition offence under sections 9 and 10 of the Crimes Ordinance – which had not been used since the 1970s – to prosecute persons for inciting hatred against the government, the police or the judiciary, thus raising concerns about the shrinking space for free speech in Hong Kong.[71]

Since the enactment of the NSL in 2020, outspoken news media such as *Apple Daily*, *Stand News* and *Citizen News* have closed down, and leading civil society groups in the 'pro-democracy' camp such as the Hong Kong Professional Teachers' Union, the Hong Kong Confederation of Trade Unions, the Civil Human Rights Front and the Hong Kong Alliance in Support of Patriotic Democratic Movements of China have all chosen to disband.

Another controversy over the NSL related to whether a foreign-qualified barrister is eligible to serve as counsel in cases concerning national security. The background to this dispute, which led to the NPCSC's first ever

[68] See ch 1 above.

[69] For the official position of the HKSAR government, see its press releases: 'HKSAR Government Will Not Tolerate any Offense of Subversion' (6 January 2021) www.info.gov.hk/gia/general/202101/06/P2021010600675.htm; 'S for S Speaks on Police Arrest of People on Suspicion of Subversion' (6 January 2021) www.info.gov.hk/gia/general/202101/06/P2021010600580.htm. The persons arrested were suspected of attempting to implement the '10-step plan for mutual destruction' (攬炒 lanchao) proposed by former legal academic Benny Tai in an article published in *Apple Daily* on 28 April 2020: 'Zhen lanchao shibu, zheshi Xianggang xiuming' [真攬炒十步，這是香港宿命, Ten Steps for the True Mutual Destruction, This Is the Fate of Hong Kong] *Apple Daily* (28 April 2020).

[70] *HKSAR v Tong Ying Kit* [2021] HKCFI 2200, [2021] HKCFI 2239; *HKSAR v Ma Chun Man* [2021] HKDC 1325, [2021] HKDC 1406, [2022] HKCA 1151; *HKSAR v Chung Hon Lam* [2021] HKDC 1484; *HKSAR v Lui Sai Yu* [2022] HKDC 384.

[71] See the figures in the text accompanying n 66 above. Widely reported convictions for sedition include *HKSAR v Tam Tak Chi* [2022] HKDC 208, [2022] HKDC 343; *HKSAR v Lai Man-ling* [2022] HKDC 981, [2022] HKDC 1004. For the judicial implementation of the NSL, see M Jackson, 'Two Years On: Reviewing the Implementation of the National Security Law in the HKSAR' (2022) 52 *Hong Kong Law Journal* 875.

interpretation of the NSL under Article 65 of the NSL, is summarised as follows.

Under section 27(4) of the Legal Practitioners Ordinance, the court may admit a barrister whose qualification is acquired outside Hong Kong to practise in a particular case before the HKSAR court. This provision has been used by both the government and litigants in the HKSAR from time to time to engage British-qualified barristers in cases where the legal issues were considered to be particularly important and complex, and where there was a shortage of local legal expertise in the litigated matters.

In the *Lai Chee-ying* case, Lai, the owner of the influential *Apple Daily* newspaper, was prosecuted for various national security offences. The defence applied to the court for the admission of Timothy Owen KC, a senior English barrister who had previously been admitted to practise in several cases before the HKSAR courts. Despite the opposition of the government and the Hong Kong Bar Association to the application, the CFI granted Owen's admission. The government's appeal to the Court of Appeal was dismissed, and the CFA also refused to grant further leave to appeal.[72]

On the evening of 28 November 2022 – the day on which the CFA rendered its decision – CE John Lee, in response to the central government's request for a report on the implementation of the NSL, submitted such a report, requesting the NPCSC to exercise its power of interpretation under the NSL to address the issue of whether overseas lawyers 'not qualified to practise generally in Hong Kong' should be allowed to 'participate by any means in the handling of work in cases concerning' national security offences. Notably, under Article 65, the power of interpreting the NSL is vested in the NPCSC. In response, the NPCSC promulgated its first ever Interpretation of the NSL on 30 December 2022.[73]

The Interpretation does not directly answer the question posed by the CE. Instead, the Interpretation elaborates on Articles 14 and 47 of the NSL. It states that the question raised by the CE should have been dealt with in accordance with Article 47, which provides, inter alia, that the court should obtain a certificate from the CE on whether an act involves national security when this question arises in the adjudication of a case.

[72] *Re Timothy Wynn Owen KC* [2022] HKCFI 3233, [2022] HKCA 1689, [2022] HKCA 1751, [2022] HKCFA 23.

[73] HK Government press release, 'Statement by Chief Executive on Submitting Report to CPG on National Security Law and Recommendation to Request Interpretation of National Security Law from NPCSC' (28 November 2022) www.info.gov.hk/gia/general/202211/28/P2022112800736.htm.

In the NPCSC's opinion, the eligibility of overseas qualified lawyers' participation in national security cases was one such question. The Interpretation further provides that in the absence of a certificate issued by the CE on this matter, the issue should be determined and decided upon by the HKSAR National Security Committee (NSC) pursuant to Article 14.

After the Interpretation was issued, the NSC convened on 11 January 2023 and supported an amendment of the Legal Practitioners Ordinance to limit the participation of overseas qualified lawyers in national security cases.[74] However, it remains unclear under what other circumstances the CE's certificate issued under Article 47 would be required, what issues such a certificate may cover and the exact scope of the NSC's powers under Article 14.

At the time of writing, some of the most important national security cases have not been resolved by the courts. We do not have a full picture of the NSL's impact, or of how the NSL and related laws will be enforced by the authorities and interpreted by the courts. A more optimistic scenario would be that the NSL largely serves a deterrent function, that relatively few prosecutions are brought and only for clear violations of the NSL, and that the NSO does not rely on its powers under Article 55. On the other hand, if prosecutions are brought frequently, and these include high-profile cases where it is debatable as a matter of law and evidence whether the defendants are guilty, judges who seek to apply liberal values enshrined in the Basic Law and in the International Covenant on Civil and Political Rights[75] may be placed in an unenviable position. There will also be increased risks of conflict between the courts' interpretation of the NSL and the expectations of the central authorities, which may result in interpretations being issued by the NPCSC or even interventions by the NSO to transfer NSL proceedings to the mainland.

VII. CONCLUSION: AN ANALYSIS OF 'ONE COUNTRY, TWO SYSTEMS'

Both the text of the PRC Constitution and the writings of Chinese constitutional law scholars are unequivocal about the PRC being a unitary state. Indeed, the very idea of federalism has been flatly rejected as being

[74] HK Government press release, 'Committee for Safeguarding National Security of HKSAR actively Performs Duties and Functions to Safeguard National Security in Accordance with the Interpretation and Explanations of the National Security Law' (11 January 2023) www.info.gov.hk/gia/general/202301/11/P2023011100609.htm.

[75] See NSL, Art 4.

inconsistent with the theory and practice of the Chinese Constitution. The introduction of the 'One Country, Two Systems' policy has not changed this official doctrine that the PRC is a unitary state. The Basic Law has made it clear that the powers of the HKSAR government are delegated to it by the National People's Congress. Chinese scholars writing on the Basic Law unanimously emphasise that such delegation of power (*shouquan* 授權) is not a division of powers (*fenquan* 分權),[76] and that there is no element of federalism codified in the constitutional arrangement of OCTS.

According to the theoretical framework developed by Nicholas Aroney in a paper co-authored with one of the authors of the present volume,[77] the principal models of multi-level governance within a state include federalism and devolution. In the case of devolution, a unitary state establishes a constitutional arrangement whereby one or more of its regional units is granted broad executive and legislative powers of self-government. The typical case of devolution involves a process of 'disaggregation'. This stands in contrast to 'aggregation' in the case of federalism, where several pre-existing political communities or states join together to form a federation and establish a new federal system of government. On the other hand, devolution involves disaggregation insofar as the unitary state decides to create and empower new local political sub-units at the regional level. The existence and powers of such local autonomous institutions may or may not be expressly provided for in the national constitution. If they are so provided for and are thus constitutionally entrenched, the system of devolution may be said to be 'federated', even though it does not amount to a full federation or federalism.

From the perspective of the PRC state and its constitutional law, the establishment and operation of the HKSAR fits well into the model of devolution within a unitary state. Insofar as the institutional arrangements for Hong Kong's autonomy are not specified in the PRC Constitution itself but are provided for in a Basic Law enacted by the NPC, the case of Hong Kong falls within the category of 'non-federated' devolution under Aroney's framework.

[76] See n 4 above.

[77] N Aroney and AHY Chen, 'Multi-level Governance and Constitutions of "Plurality-in-Unity": "One Country, Two Systems" in the Hong Kong Special Administrative Region (1997–2019)', University of Hong Kong Faculty of Law Research Paper No 2022/07, http://ssrn.com/abstract=4025796.

The political institutions of the HKSAR, which became operational on 1 July 1997 – the establishment date of the HKSAR – were newly created institutions that did not have prior legal existence. But what is interesting and remarkable about the case of Hong Kong is that these constitutional issues may be viewed through another lens, which to some extent differs from the Chinese mainland perspective. This different perspective is held by those people in Hong Kong who identify Hong Kong as a political community separate and distinct from the political community of other PRC citizens on the mainland. The complexity of this identity amongst many Hongkongers can be attributed to the fact that under pre-1997 Hong Kong law, ethnically Chinese persons born in Hong Kong were legally British Dependent Territories Citizens or British Nationals (Overseas).[78] After 1997, under the law of the HKSAR, these people all became Chinese nationals with the right of abode in the HKSAR.

For ease of discussion, we will refer to the perspective of such Hong Kong people as the 'Hong Kong perspective'. From the Hong Kong perspective, the establishment of the HKSAR is not just about creating, by means of devolution, new political institutions of self-government or autonomy – a process of disaggregation from the PRC's perspective. From the Hong Kong perspective, the establishment of the HKSAR is also an act of aggregation, in which the pre-existing political community of Hong Kong and its institutions became connected to those of the PRC. For many Hongkongers, therefore, the terms 'reunification' or 'unification' – rather than devolution – may more accurately convey the significance of the handover in 1997. Whereas the mainland Chinese perspective sees the Basic Law as an instrument of devolution and disaggregation, the Hong Kong perspective views the Joint Declaration and the Basic Law as the bulwark that protects the rights and partially self-governing institutions of the pre-existing political community of Hong Kong as it undergoes unification and aggregation/integration with the PRC. The difference or even conflict between the Chinese perspective and the Hong Kong perspective as outlined above has far-reaching implications for the practical operation of OCTS, which has not been plain sailing.

Apart from aggregation and disaggregation, two other concepts used in Aroney's theoretical framework pertain to the 'preservative' and

[78] See generally AHY Chen, 'The Development of Immigration Law and Policy: The Hong Kong Experience' (1988) *McGill Law Journal* 631.

'transformative' aspects of a new constitutional arrangement for multi-level state governance. It has been pointed out that such constitutional multi-level arrangements are 'always preservative and transformative in this sense: they preserve aspects of an existing constitutional state of affairs while simultaneously transforming it into a new state of affairs that is federal in character.'[79] For example, in the formation of a federal system, existing political communities are preserved as member states of the new federation, while the transformative aspect of the new constitutional order involves the creation of a new federal system of government. In the case of devolution, an existing unitary state is preserved, while transformation is achieved insofar as the unitary state devolves new powers to a regional government.

In the case of the creation of the HKSAR, we can observe both preservative and transformative features in play. From the Chinese perspective, there is a process of devolution that preserves the unitary state, while at the same time transforming it by establishing a new SAR within it. And from the Hong Kong perspective, what is preserved is the existing system of Hong Kong as one of the 'two systems' in the OCTS arrangement, while the transformative element involves the Hong Kong system becoming a component of the 'one country' constituted by the PRC. What is interesting and remarkable in the case of Hong Kong is that what is perceived to be preservative from the Hong Kong perspective is deemed transformative from the Chinese perspective. The converse is equally true.

The basic design of the HKSAR's executive, legislative and judicial institutions, which will be elaborated on in chapters three and four, also have both preservative and transformative aspects. The constitutional roles of the Chief Executive, Legislative Council and judiciary of the HKSAR are essentially the same as those of the colonial Governor, Legislative Council and judiciary, respectively. However, instead of the Governor being appointed by the British government, the CE is now elected by an Election Committee (designed to be representative of different sectors of Hong Kong society) and then appointed by the Chinese government as CE. LegCo continues to be what it was in the 1990s – a body partly elected by universal suffrage; the Basic Law also provides that the number of LegCo members directly elected by universal suffrage will gradually increase during the first 10 years of the HKSAR, though such moves toward democratisation have now been reversed by the electoral overhaul of 2021. Nevertheless, the Basic Law intended

[79] Aroney and Chen (n 77 above) 8.

that LegCo would become wholly elected by universal suffrage at some indeterminate time in the future, as would the CE. Whether this will pan out in reality is unclear.

As the courts did in colonial Hong Kong, the HKSAR courts continue to interpret and apply the law of Hong Kong, including its constitutional instrument (now the Basic Law instead of the Letters Patent issued by the British Crown), and they do so independently. At the apex of the Hong Kong judicial system is the Court of Final Appeal, which replaced the Privy Council as Hong Kong's final appellate court. As discussed above, and will be elaborated on in chapter five, the HKSAR courts' judicial power is now subject to interpretive interventions by the NPCSC on the Basic Law.

There has also been preservation of and continuity in the autonomous powers of LegCo after 1997. It continues to exercise general legislative powers over a broad range of matters that it had exercised in the past, subject to several significant powers reserved for the central authorities. These reserved powers for the central authorities include the powers to apply national laws to Hong Kong on matters outside the HKSAR's autonomy, to invalidate Hong Kong laws, to issue overriding interpretations of the Basic Law and to amend the Basic Law, as we have discussed above.

Another important element of Aroney's theoretical framework is the concept of 'effective constituent authority', alternatively termed 'effective constitutive authority'. This may be usefully employed to analyse the constitution-making process of the Basic Law. Aroney points out that each constitution is 'premised on a unique configuration of effective constitutive authority'.[80] The effective constitutive authority that is empowered to craft a constitution has a decisive effect on the constitution because that authority can shape the features of the constitution-making process and influence the political environment within which the strategic negotiations over those features occur.

An effective constitutive authority may be either unitary or plural in nature. In a typical case of devolution or decentralisation within a unitary state, the effective constitutive authority is unitary, and it is this unitary authority that is responsible for establishing regional institutions and conferring autonomous powers of self-government upon them. This may be contrasted with the formation of a federal state, in which the effective constitutive authority is pluralistic in nature as it involves the

[80] ibid 3.

peoples of separate states agreeing to become constituent member states of a single federation. Aroney also mentions another possible scenario where a 'third power' plays a significant role in the formation of the constitutional arrangement for multi-level state governance. This takes the form of a third party supervising or controlling the constitution-making process, as exemplified by the British imperial government in the case of Australia and Canada.[81]

In light of our discussion above, it is evident that the OCTS constitutional model is not a simple case of devolution where the effective constitutive authority is unitary in nature. Although the Basic Law of the HKSAR was enacted in 1990 by the National People's Congress pursuant to the PRC Constitution, the terms on which jurisdiction over Hong Kong was transferred from the UK to the PRC were negotiated between the British and Chinese governments and codified in the Sino-British Joint Declaration. The Joint Declaration, particularly Annex I thereto, set out the institutional arrangements for Hong Kong's post-1997 governance in considerable detail. Approximately half of the provisions in the Basic Law were largely reproduced from the Joint Declaration.[82] The British government also provided input behind the scenes through diplomatic channels during the drafting of the Basic Law.[83] It may therefore be said that Britain in practice participated in and shared with the PRC the exercise of effective constitutive authority over the design of the HKSAR's constitutional order. Also, as discussed in chapter one, although the people of Hong Kong were not represented in the negotiation process, public opinion in Hong Kong and the views of the business and political elites of colonial Hong Kong were canvassed widely during consultative processes as the Basic Law was drafted.

Vis-à-vis the 'high degree of autonomy' granted to Hong Kong under the Joint Declaration and the Basic Law, it is noteworthy that the HKSAR government (including its executive, legislative and judicial branches) exercises considerable powers over a wide range of subject matters in which the HKSAR has jurisdiction. As mentioned above, it may be said that the autonomy exercised by the HKSAR is more extensive than the powers granted to member states of many federations. Of course, in assessing the degree of autonomy exercised by the people of Hong Kong,

[81] ibid 6.

[82] Based on the authors' article-by-article comparison of the text of the Basic Law with that of the Joint Declaration.

[83] AHY Chen and M Ng, 'The Making of the Constitutional Order of the Hong Kong SAR' in KYL Tan and M Ng (eds), *Constitutional Foundings in Northeast Asia* (Hart Publishing, 2022) ch 3.

the range of subject matters that fall within the autonomous powers of the HKSAR government is not the only key criterion. Another important criterion is whether the constitutional arrangement for the selection of the political leaders and lawmakers of the HKSAR is sufficiently and effectively representative of the will and interests of the people of Hong Kong. Thus, the electoral models of the CE and LegCo will be paramount. This will be considered in the next chapter.

Finally, according to Aroney's framework on multi-level state governance, one important subject relates to 'the capacity to amend the fundamental features of the system'.[84] In the case of the HKSAR, the Basic Law may be amended by the NPC, though the Basic Law provides that no amendment can 'contravene the established basic policies' of the PRC towards Hong Kong as enshrined in the Joint Declaration. However, this is essentially a policy declaration rather than a justiciable constitutional provision enforceable by a HKSAR court, whose power to interpret the Basic Law is in any event subject to the overriding authority of the NPC Standing Committee to promulgate interpretations of the Basic Law.

The manner by which the Basic Law is amendable can be contrasted with the devolved regions within the UK and Spain.[85] In the devolution arrangement for Scotland, there exists a constitutional convention, known as the Sewel Convention, that the UK Parliament will not normally exercise its right to legislate with regard to devolved matters without the consent of the Scottish Parliament, although this convention is not judicially enforceable.[86] In Spain, the powers of self-government in the autonomous communities such as Catalonia are delegated from the unitary Spanish state, but are guaranteed under the Spanish constitution.[87]

With regard to Hong Kong, one can argue that the enactment of the NSL, as discussed in this chapter, and the extensive amendments to the electoral system codified in Annexes I and II to the Basic Law, as discussed in the next chapter, are substantial amendments of the

[84] Aroney and Chen (n 77) 5.

[85] ibid 36.

[86] See the famous Brexit case *R (on the application of Miller and another) v Secretary of State for Exiting the European Union* [2017] UKSC 5.

[87] See, eg N Krisch, 'The Spanish Constitutional Crisis: Law, Legitimacy and Popular Sovereignty in Question' (*VerfBlog*, 7 October 2017) https://verfassungsblog.de/the-spanish-constitutional-crisis-law-legitimacy-and-popular-sovereignty-in-question/; M Helmich, 'Spain, Catalonia, and the Supposed Authority of the Judiciary' (2020) 2 *Jus Cogens* 259, https://link.springer.com/article/10.1007/s42439-020-00026-x.

original constitutional order established by the Basic Law. They were also unilateral actions taken by the central authorities without prior public consultation in the HKSAR. The draftsmen of the Basic Law originally intended that it was for the HKSAR to legislate 'on its own' laws protecting China's national security interests in Hong Kong.[88] The enactment of the HKSAR National Security Law by the NPCSC in 2020 would probably not be within the contemplation of the original draftsmen. As we will also examine in chapter four, the electoral revamp of 2021, introduced by the decisions of the NPC and NPCSC in 2021, was a fundamental overhaul of the HKSAR's pre-existing political system established by the Basic Law. But China has equally defended the NSL and the electoral overhaul as necessary responses to the national security risks inherent within the OCTS model, which surfaced during the 2019 street protests against the extradition Bill. In retrospect, that months-long social movement became the watershed event that transformed the constitutional order of Hong Kong.

FURTHER READING

Chan, C and de Londras, F (eds), *China's National Security: Endangering Hong Kong's Rule of Law?* (Hart Publishing, 2020).

Chan, JMM, Fu, HL and Ghai, Y (eds), *Hong Kong's Constitutional Debate: Conflict over Interpretation* (Hong Kong University Press, 2000).

Fu, H, Harris, L and Young, SNM (eds), *Interpreting Hong Kong's Basic Law: The Struggle for Coherence* (Palgrave Macmillan, 2007).

Fu, H and Hor, M (eds), *The National Security Law: of Hong Kong: Restoration and Transformation* (Hong Kong University Press, 2022).

[88] Basic Law, Art 23.

3

The Political System: The Executive and the Legislature

Chief Executive – Executive–Legislative Relations – Legislature – Legislative–Judicial Relations – Emergency Powers

In the previous chapter, we discussed the relationship between the Hong Kong Special Administrative Region (HKSAR) and the central authorities. We now turn to the internal political system of the HKSAR, which comprises the executive, the legislature and the judiciary. The judiciary will be the subject of chapter five; the executive and the legislature will be discussed in chapters three and four. Chapter three examines the structural and institutional features of the executive and the legislature, particularly their powers, functions and interrelationship. Chapter four then considers the electoral system for the Chief Executive and the Legislative Council, the electoral politics and the dynamics of constitutional change over the years.

I. HONG KONG'S POLITICAL SYSTEM: FROM COLONY TO SAR

The political institutions established by the Basic Law were largely modelled on the pre-existing colonial system. These offices and institutions comprise the Chief Executive (CE) (equivalent to the former Governor), principal officials (appointed by the central government upon the CE's nomination), the Executive Council (a top advisory body, of a similar nature to its colonial predecessor, with members appointed by the CE), the 'Executive Authorities' (including the civil service), the Legislative Council (LegCo – the legislature of the HKSAR, with powers and functions similar to its colonial predecessor, such as law-making, approval of annual budgets and other items of public expenditure, questioning the work of the government) and the courts. The Basic Law provides that the HKSAR is a 'local administrative region' of the PRC which 'come[s] directly under the Central People's Government [CPG]' (Article 12). The CE is accountable to both the CPG and the HKSAR in accordance with the provisions of the Basic Law (Article 43).

Shortly after the handover, the colonial system, with its 'three-tier' system of councils (LegCo; Urban and Regional Councils; District Boards), was revamped and became a 'two-tier' one. Specifically, in 2000, the government introduced a new framework for the administration of municipal affairs such that the Urban Council and the Regional Council were abolished.[1] Some of their existing functions were transferred to LegCo and some to the Executive Authorities. At the same time, the existing District Boards were reformed and reconstituted as District Councils, of which there are 18. These advisory district bodies comprise elected members and some appointed members, but appointed seats were all phased out in 2015.[2]

We begin the study of the HKSAR's political system with an examination of the relevant provisions of the Basic Law and their operation in practice. Chapter four of the Basic Law is entitled 'Political Structure'. It consists of six sections: (i) the CE; (ii) the Executive Authorities (also known as the 'Government of the HKSAR', as defined in Article 59); (iii) the legislature; (iv) the judiciary; (v) district organisations; and (vi) public servants.

II. THE CHIEF EXECUTIVE

The CE occupies a pre-eminent position in the constitutional system of the HKSAR. This office is characterised by the 'dual headship' and 'dual accountability' roles it performs. The CE is the head of the HKSAR and 'shall represent the Region' (Article 43). At the same time, the CE is also the 'head' of the 'Executive Authorities' of the HKSAR (Articles 59–60). As mentioned above, the CE is accountable to both the CPG (which exercises the power of appointment of the CE) and the HKSAR. The accountability of the CE to the CPG is also formally manifested in the CE's periodic visits – at least once a year – to Beijing, where they meet

[1] See the Provision of Municipal Services (Reorganization) Ordinance. For the Urban Council and District Boards, see ch 1 above. The Regional Council, which was established in 1986, was the counterpart in the New Territories of the Urban Council; it had jurisdiction over the New Territories similar to the Urban Council's jurisdiction in the urban areas.

[2] See the amendment enacted in 2013 to the District Councils Ordinance.

with the Premier of the CPG (ie the State Council) and the President of the PRC (who, by convention, is also the General Secretary of the Chinese Communist Party) to report on their duties (*shuzhi*, 述職).

The Basic Law prescribes the eligibility criteria for the CE.[3] They must be a Chinese citizen of not less than 40 years of age. They must be a permanent resident of the HKSAR, with no right of abode in any foreign country, and must have ordinarily resided in Hong Kong for a continuous period of not less than 20 years. The CE is appointed by the CPG on the basis of an election by the Election Committee, which we discuss below. Notably, the Sino-British Joint Declaration did not require the CE to be elected. It provided that the CE 'will be appointed by the [CPG] on the basis of the results of elections or consultations to be held locally'.[4] This provision has been reproduced in Article 45(1) of the Basic Law. However, Articles 45(2) and 45(3) provide more specifically that the CE shall be selected by election rather than by consultation.

The principles governing the CE election and the composition of the Election Committee are specified in Annex I to the Basic Law and further elaborated upon in the Chief Executive Election Ordinance. According to this ordinance, the CE cannot be a member of any political party.[5] The removal of the CE by the CPG is not expressly provided for in the Basic Law, but is addressed in section 4(c) of the Chief Executive Election Ordinance.

The Basic Law stipulates that the CE's term of office is five years, and they may not serve more than two consecutive terms.[6] In practice, none of the CEs of the HKSAR have served two full consecutive terms. The first CE, Tung Chee-hwa, resigned in the middle of his second term. Upon his resignation in 2005, a constitutional issue arose as to whether his successor would serve a full five-year term or only the remainder of Tung's second term. As discussed in chapters one and two, the issue was resolved by the National People's Congress Standing Committee's (NPCSC's) second interpretation of the Basic Law, which opted for the successor serving the remainder of the predecessor's unfinished term. Donald Tsang Yam-kuen was elected and appointed CE in 2005 to succeed Tung. Upon the completion of his term in 2007, Tsang was re-elected and reappointed for a five-year term. He was succeeded in 2012 by Leung Chun-ying, who served one term and was succeeded by Carrie

[3] Basic Law, Art 44.
[4] Sino-British Joint Declaration, para 3(4).
[5] Chief Executive Election Ordinance, s 31.
[6] Basic Law, Art 46.

Lam Cheng Yuet-ngor in 2017. Lam served one term and was succeeded by John Lee Ka-chiu, the sixth-term CE, on 1 July 2022.

The powers and functions of the CE are provided for in Article 48 of the Basic Law, which has 13 sub-sections. As the CE is the head of the government, Article 48 should be read together with Article 62. Article 62 is divided into six sub-sections, and it governs the powers and functions of the Executive Authorities (or 'government') of the HKSAR.

Some of the most significant powers of the CE relate to the appointment of key personnel in the HKSAR. The 'principal officials' of the HKSAR government are nominated by the CE and appointed by the CPG.[7] The CE may also recommend to the CPG the removal of any principal official. The CE has powers of appointment and removal of many holders of public office. The Public Service Commission, whose members are appointed directly by the CE, has the statutory function of advising the CE regarding the filling of vacancies in the public service.[8] As discussed in chapter five of this volume, judges in Hong Kong are also appointed by the CE, on the basis of recommendations of the Judicial Officers Recommendation Commission, which is chaired by the Chief Justice and whose members include the Secretary for Justice and others appointed by the CE.

Most legislative Bills in the HKSAR are introduced to the legislature by the government. As we will discuss below, the right of individual LegCo members to introduce private members' Bills is very limited. After a Bill has been passed by LegCo, it can only become law after the CE signs it.

A. Executive Orders

The Basic Law expressly provides that the CE may issue 'executive orders';[9] the scope of this power has been clarified by case law. In the *Association of Expatriate Civil Servants* case,[10] the Court of First Instance ruled that, under the Basic Law, the CE may promulgate executive orders for the regulation of the civil service, just as in colonial Hong Kong, the Governor – acting on behalf of the Crown and by virtue of the Letters Patent – may make regulations on the appointment and dismissal of, and disciplinary matters relating to, civil servants.

[7] ibid Arts 15 and 48(5).
[8] Public Service Commission Ordinance, s 6.
[9] Basic Law, Art 48(4).
[10] [1998] 1 HKLRD 615.

On the other hand, in the *Leung Kwok Hung* case,[11] the Law Enforcement (Covert Surveillance Procedure) Order made by the CE in 2005, which authorised law enforcement officials to engage in covert surveillance of criminal suspects, was held unconstitutional and invalid. The Court of Appeal ruled that the making of this order was beyond the power of the CE to make executive orders under the Basic Law. The court held that while an executive order may be valid as a set of administrative directions binding on civil servants, the CE's power to make executive orders cannot be used to impose restrictions on rights protected by the Basic Law, such as the right to privacy of communications in the present case. Such restrictions may only be imposed by a law made by the legislature, or by subsidiary legislation made by a person or body authorised by an enabling ordinance passed by the legislature for this purpose.

As in other common law systems, the legislature in Hong Kong may enact a law to authorise the making of subsidiary legislation by a relevant official, executive organ or designated office holder. Subsidiary legislation is recognised expressly by the Basic Law as one of the sources of law in Hong Kong.[12] Like other common law systems, HKSAR courts can review subsidiary legislation on the basis that it is ultra vires the enabling parent legislation, known as an 'ordinance' in Hong Kong.[13] The person or body making a piece of subsidiary legislation cannot go beyond the limits of power conferred on and delegated to the person or body by the enabling ordinance. Furthermore, subsidiary legislation, when made, must be tabled before and vetted by LegCo in accordance with either the 'negative vetting' or 'positive vetting' procedure specified in sections 34 and 35 of the Interpretation and General Clauses Ordinance respectively.[14]

B. Emergency Powers

One of the ordinances passed by the Hong Kong legislature in colonial times was the Emergency Regulations Ordinance (ERO), which authorised the making of subsidiary legislation by the Governor in Council

[11] [2006] HKEC 239, HCAL 107/2005, [2006] HKEC 816, CACV 73/2006.

[12] Basic Law, Arts 8, 56 and 62(5).

[13] See EC Ip, *Law and Justice in Hong Kong*, 3rd edn (Sweet & Maxwell, 2019) chs 3 and 5.

[14] s 35 applies where the enabling ordinance provides that the subsidiary legislation is subject to LegCo's approval. In other cases, LegCo may by resolution amend or repeal the subsidiary legislation when it is laid on the table of LegCo under s 34.

in times of 'emergency' or 'public danger'. The ERO is a pre-1997 law that survived the handover in 1997.[15] In response to the riots following the 2019 anti-extradition movement, the CE in Council (ie the Executive Council) in October 2019 invoked the ERO and enacted the Prohibition on Face Covering Regulation (PFCR). The PFCR was challenged in court, on the ground, inter alia, that its enabling legislation – the ERO – was inconsistent with the Basic Law and therefore unconstitutional.[16] The applicants for judicial review (who included all LegCo members belonging to the 'opposition' or 'pro-democracy' camp) argued that the Basic Law vests law-making power exclusively in LegCo, but the ERO purported to confer on the executive a plenary legislative power in times of 'emergency' or 'public danger', which was unlimited in scope and could be used to amend or repeal any pre-existing law and to create new legal rules.

Although the Court of First Instance invalidated the ERO insofar as it purported to confer general law-making power on the executive on occasions of 'public danger',[17] the constitutionality of the ERO was upheld on appeal both before the Court of Appeal and the Court of Final Appeal (CFA).[18] The CFA ruled that the power conferred on the CE in Council by the ERO on occasions of emergency or public danger was not unrestrained and uncontrolled. The courts can use traditional administrative law principles to control the exercise of this power to make regulations. Furthermore, any such emergency regulations are subject to 'negative vetting' by LegCo. Any restrictions on constitutional rights imposed by those regulations made under the ERO must also be 'prescribed by law' (ie clear, precise, publicly accessible) and proportionate.[19] Finally, if there is a dispute whether there genuinely exists an occasion of emergency or public danger that justifies the emergency power being invoked, the court will determine whether the decision of the CE in Council is bona fide and not *Wednesbury* unreasonable.

Although the PFCR was upheld in its entirety, its practical significance was blunted by the global onslaught of the COVID-19 pandemic in that mask-wearing had become mandatory in Hong Kong since spring 2020 (until 28 February 2023). In late July 2020, the CE in Council invoked

[15] For the use of the ERO in colonial times, see, eg M Ng, S Zhang and M Wong, '"Who but the Governor in Executive Council Is the Judge?" – Historical Use of the Emergency Regulations Ordinance' (2020) 50 *Hong Kong Law Journal* 425.

[16] See ch 1 above, fn 59 and the accompanying text.

[17] *Kwok Wing-hang v Chief Executive in Council* [2019] HKCFI 2820.

[18] [2020] HKCA 192, [2020] HKCFA 42.

[19] See ch 6 below.

the ERO for a second time. This time, the emergency power was used, citing the circumstances of the pandemic, to postpone the LegCo election originally scheduled for September 2020.[20]

However, as the Basic Law expressly limits LegCo to a four-year term, neither the legislature nor the executive of the HKSAR had the power to extend its existing term of office beyond September 2020. This extension was achieved instead by the NPCSC when it promulgated a decision on 11 August 2020, as discussed in chapter two.

C. Dual Accountability

The dual accountability of the Chief Executive – pursuant to Article 43 of the Basic Law – to both the central government and the HKSAR is probably the most important and distinctive feature of the HKSAR's political system. Insofar as the central authorities' interests in and views on Hong Kong's development converge with those of the general public in Hong Kong, there should be no conflict in the discharge of the dual roles. On the other hand, when there is a divergence in the interests of the central authorities in the HKSAR and the interests of Hong Kong as perceived by the majority of Hong Kong's population, the CE would be placed in an unenviable position. In these circumstances, it is not easy for the CE to win or retain the trust and confidence of both the central authorities and the people of Hong Kong concurrently.

As mentioned above, the CE reports to the central authorities on their work at least once a year. Under Article 48(8) of the Basic Law, the central government may issue 'directives' to the CE 'in respect of the relevant matters provided for' in the Basic Law. So far, no such directives have been formally and publicly issued.

However, there were at least two occasions when it was publicised that the central government had requested the CE to provide a report on a specified matter. As we will discuss in chapter four, after the pro-independence Hong Kong National Party was banned by the HKSAR government, the central government in February 2019 issued an 'official letter' to the CE expressing support for the decision and requiring the CE to submit a report on the matter. The report of the CE to the central government in November 2022, in which he requested the NPCSC to interpret the National Security Law (NSL), as discussed in chapter two,

[20] Emergency (Date of General Election) (Seventh Term of the Legislative Council) Regulation, gazetted on 31 July 2020.

had been preceded by a letter from the central government requiring the CE to report on the recent implementation of the NSL.

There were several other acts of the central authorities that were prompted by the CE's reports to the central government on the matters concerned. These include the NPCSC's first interpretation of the Basic Law, which concerned the right of abode, and the NPCSC's third Basic Law interpretation, which centred on the term of office of the CE. The NPCSC's decision in August 2020 (discussed in chapter two) to extend the term of office of the sixth-term LegCo was also prompted by the CE's report on the postponement of the LegCo election, which had originally been scheduled for September 2020, due to the local COVID-19 situation.

Apart from their close working relationship with the central government, the CE also liaises and works with officials of provincial authorities, particularly the provincial government of Guangdong and the municipal government of Shenzhen, to promote cooperation between Hong Kong and its neighbouring cities and regions. In 2017, the central government announced a strategy for the development of the Guangdong–Hong Kong–Macau Greater Bay Area (GBA), which was subsequently concretised in an Outline Development Plan published in February 2019.[21] A high-level Leading Group on the Development of the GBA was established under the State Council in 2019. It was chaired by Vice-Premier Han Zheng; its members include several senior Chinese officials, the CE of the HKSAR (who was Carrie Lam at the time) and the CE of the Macau SAR (Ho Iat Seng).

With regard to the CE's accountability to the HKSAR, one such formal manifestation is the delivery of an annual policy address at the Legislative Council, pursuant to Article 73(4) of the Basic Law. Furthermore, a convention has been established under which the CE would attend a 'CE's Questions and Answers Session' at LegCo four times a year. In addition, CE Carrie Lam introduced the practice of attending LegCo meetings monthly for shorter periods to respond to

[21] See the Chief Executive's 2020 Policy Address, para 64, www.policyaddress.gov.hk/2020/eng/pdf/PA2020.pdf. One of the central authorities' strategies regarding Hong Kong has been to incorporate Hong Kong into China's national development framework: see PTY Cheung, 'Changing Relations between Hong Kong and the Mainland since 2014' in Lam, P Liu and W Wong (eds), *Contemporary Hong Kong Government and Politics*, 3rd edn (HKU Press, forthcoming) ch 15. We are grateful to the author for making available the manuscript for this chapter.

members' questions.[22] CE John Lee introduced the practice of monthly 'antechamber exchanges' – informal meetings taking place in the antechamber of the LegCo building, attended by the CE and/or principal officials and all LegCo members. These sessions provide opportunities for informal exchange of views between LegCo members and leading members of government.[23]

III. THE EXECUTIVE COUNCIL

The CE in Council mentioned above refers to the CE acting in tandem with the Executive Council (ExCo). ExCo was a key governing institution in colonial Hong Kong, and the Basic Law provides for its continued existence. It is an organ for assisting the CE in policy-making.[24] ExCo members are appointed by the CE (unlike principal officials, who are appointed by the CPG). As in colonial times, ExCo members include some senior government officials, as well as some non-government members (known as unofficial members in colonial times), who may be LegCo members or other public figures.[25]

In practice, several LegCo members who are leaders of major 'pro-government' political parties have been among the non-government members appointed to the ExCo of the HKSAR. This practice was adopted after the HKSAR was established in 1997 and has continued since then. The Basic Law provides that ExCo meetings are chaired by the CE, who shall consult ExCo before making 'important policy decisions', introducing bills to LegCo and making subsidiary legislation.[26] There is a confidentiality rule governing internal ExCo deliberations. There is also a constitutional convention that ExCo members will bear collective responsibility for the decisions made by the CE in Council, which means that an ExCo member should not publicly disavow a decision made by the CE in Council.

[22] See the LegCo's Annual Reports, www.legco.gov.hk/en/about-legco/annual-reports-of-legislative-council.html.

[23] 'Hong Kong Lawmakers Are Not "Film or Pop Stars" Who Need Media Attention and Popularity, Legco President Says' *South China Morning Post* (16 December 2022).

[24] Basic Law, Art 54.

[25] The Executive Council appointed by Chief Executive John Lee, which took office on 1 July 2022, included 21 principal officials and 16 'non-official' members. Of the non-official members, seven were LegCo members.

[26] Art 56.

IV. PRINCIPAL OFFICIALS, BUREAUX AND DEPARTMENTS

The apex of the HKSAR government comprises the CE and the principal officials (appointed by the CPG upon the CE's nomination) who head the policy bureaux of the government. Beneath each policy bureau is one or more government departments, headed by their respective directors; the directors are responsible for the execution of policies adopted by the bureaux. Bureaux and departments are staffed by the civil service of the HKSAR.

The most senior principal officials are the Chief Secretary, the Financial Secretary and the Secretary for Justice (equivalent to the Attorney-General in colonial times). In the sixth-term HKSAR government, which took office on 1 July 2022, the other principal officials, also appointed by the CPG upon the CE's recommendation, are the Deputy Chief Secretary, the Deputy Financial Secretary, the Deputy Secretary for Justice, 15 Secretaries who head the 15 policy bureaux,[27] the Commissioner of Police, the Commissioner of the Independent Commission Against Corruption (ICAC), the Commissioner of Customs and Excise, the Director of Immigration and the Director of Audit.[28]

Each of the 15 Secretaries heads a policy bureau of the government. For example, the Secretary for Security is the head of the Security Bureau. Government departments or units under the jurisdiction of the Security Bureau include the Hong Kong Police, the Immigration Department, the Customs and Excise Department, the Correctional Services Department and the Fire Services Department. The current structure of the government is a result of a reorganisation of the government structure proposed by CE Carrie Lam on 12 January 2022, such that the number of policy bureaux (and the corresponding Secretaries) was increased from 13 to 15, and three new positions – Deputy Chief Secretary, Deputy Financial Secretary and Deputy Secretary for Justice – were created.[29]

In the colonial era (including the time the Basic Law was drafted in the late 1980s) and in the early years after the 1997 handover, the most senior officials of the Hong Kong government were employed as civil servants and had risen through the ranks of the civil service. Like other

[27] See the Organisation Chart of the HKSAR government, www.gov.hk/en/about/govdirectory/govchart/index.htm.

[28] See Basic Law, Art 48(5).

[29] C Chau, 'Hong Kong's Lam Unveils Plan for New Gov't Bureaux in First "Patriots-Only" Legislative Meeting' (*Hong Kong Free Press*, 12 January 2022) https://hongkongfp.com/2022/01/12/hong-kongs-lam-unveils-plans-for-new-govt-bureaux-in-first-patriots-only-legislative-meeting/.

civil servants who staffed the bureaucracy of the Hong Kong government, these senior officials were employed on permanent-tenured terms until their retirement. After Tung Chee-hwa began his second term of office as CE in 2002, he introduced a reform known as the 'Principal Officials Accountability System' (POAS).[30] Under this reform, the principal officials appointed by the central government – upon nomination by the CE – would no longer be employed on the terms applicable to civil servants (except for the Secretary for the Civil Service who would remain a civil servant). Instead, they would be appointed on fixed-term contracts that do not extend beyond the term of office of the CE who recommends them for appointment.

The person appointed as a principal official may or may not be a civil servant before their appointment, although in practice the civil service has been the major source from which principal officials were inducted after the POAS came into operation.[31] The principal official is accountable to the CE for their performance with regard to their policy portfolio, and the CE may recommend to the central government the removal of any principal official at any time. After the introduction of the POAS, there have been occasional resignations of principal officials due to scandals or perceived inadequate performance.[32]

Under this reformed system, the principal officials have been described as 'political appointees' or 'politically appointed officials', as opposed to civil servants. When the POAS was first introduced in 2002, the principal officials were the only 'political appointees' in the government. In 2007, CE Donald Tsang expanded the system of political appointees by creating two new classes of senior officials who would also be political appointees: the 'Under Secretary' of each policy bureau and the 'Political Assistant' to each of the Secretaries of the policy bureau. After this reform, the most senior civil servant in each policy bureau would be the Permanent Secretary of the bureau, who exercises supervision over the work of all civil servants who staff that bureau.

[30] See J Chan and CL Lim (eds), *Law of the Hong Kong Constitution*, 3rd edn (Sweet & Maxwell, 2021) ch 10.

[31] See EWY Lee and RLK Yeung, 'The "Principal Officials Accountability System: Its Underdevelopment as a System of Ministerial Government' (2017) 39 *Asia Pacific Journal of Public Administration* 120.

[32] The latest example to date was the resignation of Caspar Tsui Ying-wai, Secretary for Home Affairs, at the end of January 2022 after attending a banquet during the pandemic and behaving 'in an inappropriate manner': see his statement at www.info.gov.hk/gia/general/202201/31/P2022013100346.htm?fontSize=1.

The responsibilities and performance of politically appointed officials are currently governed by the 'Code for Officials under the Political Appointment System' promulgated by the Chief Executive's Office.[33] The original version of this document, which was subsequently revised from time to time, was known as the 'Code for Principal Officials under the Accountability System', and it was first promulgated in 2002.[34]

The current Code is a 22-page document divided into seven chapters. It provides that

> [p]rincipal officials are responsible for their respective portfolios ... and lead the executive departments within their respective portfolios. Principal officials are responsible for formulating, explaining and defending government policies as well as canvassing support from the public and the Legislative Council. They are accountable to the Chief Executive for the success or failure of their policies.

Vis-à-vis their 'responsibility in relation to civil servants', it provides that 'Politically appointed officials shall at all times actively uphold and promote a permanent, honest, meritocratic, professional and politically neutral civil service'.

Apart from the 'politically appointed officials' mentioned above, all the officials who staff the bureaux and departments of the HKSAR government are civil servants. Civil servants are governed by the provisions on 'public servants' in chapter 4, section 6 of the Basic Law and the following legal instruments: the Public Service (Administration) Order, promulgated by the CE; the Public Service (Disciplinary) Regulation made under this Order; and the Civil Service Regulations. The Regulations are supplemented by circulars and circular memoranda issued by the Civil Service Bureau. This bureau, led by the Secretary for the Civil Service, has the responsibility and authority to manage the civil service.[35]

Civil servants are also subject to a Civil Service Code, promulgated by the Civil Service Bureau in 2009. This is a 13-page document divided into seven sections: introduction; core values; standards of conduct; authority for the management of the civil service; role and responsibilities of civil servants in relation to politically appointed officials; relationship between civil servants and politically appointed officials; and communication, complaint and redress mechanism.

[33] www.cmab.gov.hk/en/issues/PAO_Code_1.7.2022.pdf.
[34] Lee and Yeung (n 31).
[35] See generally www.csb.gov.hk.

According to the Code:

> Civil servants support politically appointed officials in formulating policies. They are responsible for executing policies, carrying out executive tasks, managing and delivering services to the public, and undertaking law enforcement and regulatory functions, in accordance with the decisions of the Government of the day and directions of principal officials.

However, the Code also provides that 'politically appointed officials are generally not involved in issues relating to civil servants' careers, such as appointment, promotion and discipline'.

The Code provides for six 'core values' of the civil service: commitment to the rule of law; honesty and integrity; objectivity and impartiality; political neutrality; accountability for decisions and actions; and dedication, professionalism and diligence. 'Political neutrality' is defined to mean that 'Civil servants shall serve the Chief Executive and the Government of the day with total loyalty and to the best of their ability, no matter what their own political beliefs are'. Although this requirement appears unproblematic, the use of the term 'political neutrality' has become controversial in the aftermath of the anti-extradition movement of 2019. It was discovered that some civil servants had joined the 2019 street protests and supported the demands of this social movement, as they apparently believed that political neutrality meant they could legitimately distance themselves from the political stance of the government. At the time of writing, the Civil Service Code is in the process of being revised, and it is believed that the term 'political neutrality' might be dropped in the revised version. It is also noteworthy that since 2021, all civil servants have been required either to swear an oath or to sign a declaration to uphold the Basic Law and owe allegiance to the HKSAR of the PRC, a requirement that is comparable to the oath-taking requirement imposed by Article 104 of the Basic Law on the HKSAR's key personnel.[36]

V. ACCESS TO INFORMATION

As mentioned above, deliberations in the Executive Council are confidential. So are most internal deliberations within the government. This does not, however, mean that there is no public access to information

[36] See Civil Service Bureau, 'Oath-Taking/Declaration Requirement for Civil Servants', www.csb.gov.hk/english/admin/oathserving/2769.html. See also the Basic Law, Art 99.

about the operation of the HKSAR government. Even before the 1997 handover, the Hong Kong government had made efforts to improve the transparency of its operations and to allow public access to government information. A Code on Access to Information was promulgated in 1995 and has continued in force after the handover.

The Code

> provides a formal framework for access to information held by government departments. It defines the scope of information that will be provided, sets out how the information will be made available either routinely or in response to request, lays down procedures governing its release, as well as procedures for review or complaint.[37]

In particular, the Code 'authorises and requires civil servants … to provide information unless there are specific reasons for not doing so. These reasons are set out in Part 2 [of the Code].'[38]

The Code is a policy document; there is no legislation conferring a right to freedom of or access to information. It is noteworthy that the Law Reform Commission is currently considering proposals to codify such a right after the Commission's Access to Information Sub-committee published a consultation paper on the subject in December 2018.

As discussed in a later section of this chapter, one of the functions of the Ombudsman in the HKSAR is to receive and investigate complaints regarding government departments' compliance with the Code on Access to Information, and to make recommendations upon completion of its investigations.

VI. THE LEGISLATIVE COUNCIL

We now turn to the legislature of the HKSAR. The legislature is primarily regulated under chapter 4, section 3 of the Basic Law. Section 3 is entitled 'The Legislature', and begins with Article 66, which stipulates that LegCo is the legislature of the HKSAR. Members of LegCo must be permanent residents of the HKSAR who are Chinese citizens with no right of abode in any foreign country, but Article 67 allows up to 20 per cent of LegCo members to be HKSAR permanent residents who are either foreign nationals or have the right of abode in foreign

[37] http://www.access.gov.hk.

[38] www.csb.gov.hk/english/otherinfo/access/372.html.

countries.[39] 'Public servants' are disqualified from serving as LegCo members; for this purpose, 'public servants' include not only civil servants, but also principal officials under the above-mentioned Principal Officials Accountability System.[40]

LegCo is constituted by different types of elections, as we discuss below in chapter four. The right to vote is a fundamental right conferred on permanent residents of the HKSAR under the Basic Law, and it is not limited to Chinese citizens.[41] LegCo has a four-year term of office, with the exception of the first LegCo of the HKSAR, which had only a two-year term. LegCo meetings are chaired by its President, who is elected by members of LegCo;[42] their powers and functions are expressly provided for in the Basic Law. The operation of LegCo is governed by its Rules of Procedure, which are made solely by LegCo.[43] The quorum of LegCo meetings shall not be less than half of all its members.[44]

A. The Legislature and the Executive

At the time the Basic Law was enacted, Ji Pengfei, chairman of the Basic Law Drafting Committee, unequivocally stated that the executive and the legislature of the HKSAR should both coordinate with and check each other mutually.[45] The Joint Declaration also provided that the 'Executive Authorities shall … be accountable to the legislature'.[46] The precise nature of this accountability or responsibility is provided for in Article 64 of the Basic Law, which is located in chapter 4, section 2 ('The Executive Authorities') of the Basic Law. Article 64 first

[39] The Legislative Council Ordinance, s 37 requires candidates for LegCo elections to be Chinese citizens except for elections in the 12 'functional constituencies' specified in s 37(3).

[40] See Arts 79(4) and 101 of the Basic Law. In 2022, four LegCo members elected by the Election Committee on 19 December 2021 joined the new administration of the 6th-term HKSAR government led by Chief Executive John Lee, and they took office in July 2022. Their LegCo seats were thus vacated, and a by-election was held to fill the vacancies on 18 December 2022.

[41] Art 26 of the Basic Law.

[42] The following three persons have served as LegCo Presidents: Rita Fan (1997–2008), Jasper Tsang (2008–16) and Andrew Leung (2016–).

[43] Basic Law, Art 75.

[44] ibid. See also *Kwok Cheuk-kin v President of Legislative Council* [2021] HKCA 169.

[45] 'Explanations on "The Basic Law of the Hong Kong Special Administrative Region of the PRC (Draft)" and Its Related Documents' in *The Basic Law of the Hong Kong Special Administrative Region of the People's Republic of China and Related Documents* (Joint Publishing, 2007) 193, 202.

[46] Sino-British Joint Declaration, Annex 1, s 1.

reproduces the relevant provision in the Joint Declaration, and then goes on to provide that the government (ie the Executive Authorities) shall implement laws passed by LegCo, shall present regular policy addresses to LegCo, shall answer questions raised by LegCo members and shall obtain approval from LegCo for taxation and public expenditure.

Unlike the British Parliament in the UK, LegCo has no power to pass a vote of no confidence against the government to compel resignation. However, the Basic Law expressly provides that LegCo may impeach the CE on the ground of 'serious breach of law or dereliction of duty'.[47] This impeachment procedure can be initiated by LegCo and requires the establishment of an independent investigation committee chaired by the Chief Justice of the CFA.

After CY Leung was elected and appointed CE in 2012, opposition politicians in LegCo attempted to initiate this impeachment procedure against Leung but failed.[48] A motion proposed by opposition politicians to establish an investigation committee was voted down by LegCo in January 2013. Litigation was also brought to challenge the validity of his election, but again without success.[49] The allegations against Leung related mainly to his failure during the election campaign to disclose the existence of 'unauthorised structures' built inside his home. Towards the end of Leung's term of office, opposition politicians attempted to impeach him again, on the ground that he had interfered with the work of the LegCo select committee set up to investigate his acceptance of a large sum of money paid to him by UGL, an Australian engineering firm, under an agreement signed in 2011 in connection with UGL's takeover of DTZ Holdings, a real estate services firm of which Leung was a director.[50]

The Basic Law provides a mechanism to resolve conflicts between the executive and the legislature. The relevant provisions are found in Articles 49, 50 and 52 of the Basic Law. If the annual budget or any other 'important bill' introduced by the government is rejected by LegCo, the CE would have the discretion to dissolve LegCo, in which case a new

[47] Basic Law, Art 73(9).

[48] See E Chan, 'The Legislative Council of Hong Kong' in PJ Yap and R Abeyratne (eds), *Routledge Handbook of Asian Parliaments* (Routledge, 2023) 158, 171.

[49] Court proceedings were brought by HCY Albert (a defeated candidate in the CE election) and LK Hung: HCAL 83/2012, HCAL 84/2012, HKAL 85/2012, FAMV 21/2012, FACV 24/2012. For discussion, see H Litton, 'Election Fever' *The Standard* (23 December 2020) www.thestandard.com.hk/breaking-news/s/4/161834/(Viewpoint)-Henry-Litton:-Election-fever.

[50] See Chan (n 48) 171.

LegCo election shall be held. After the new election, if the budget or 'important bill' is once again rejected by LegCo, the CE must resign.[51] The CE may exercise the power to dissolve LegCo only once during each term of that CE's office.[52]

The argument that these Basic Law provisions authorise LegCo to substantively check the CE is potentially undermined by the case mentioned in chapter two, where 47 opposition politicians were prosecuted for conspiracy to engage in subversion under the NSL. According to Article 22 of the NSL, persons who organise, plan, commit or participate in certain prohibited acts by force, threat of force or 'other unlawful means' with a view to subverting state power are guilty of the offence of 'subversion'. Such prohibited acts include acts that seriously interfere with, disrupt or undermine the performance of duties and functions in accordance with the law by the 'body of power' of the HKSAR.

In the above-mentioned case, 47 opposition politicians organised or participated in an unofficial 'primary election' to select candidates for the LegCo election scheduled for September 2020. According to their electoral platform, their ostensible aim, if elected, was to compel the government to accept the 'five principal demands' of the anti-extradition movement of 2019 by threatening to veto the budget proposal and all other government Bills. These opposition politicians ostensibly believed that such a manoeuvre was within the powers of LegCo members under the above-mentioned provisions of the Basic Law.

However, the prosecution seemed to proceed on the premise that the indiscriminate act of voting down the budget and all other government Bills– without due consideration of their merits – would be an abuse of power akin to misconduct in public office. Therefore, the prosecution believed that such acts would constitute the 'unlawful means' (under Article 22 of the NSL) that interfere with, disrupt or undermine the performance of duties and functions by the HKSAR government. At the time of writing, the trial of the case (HCCC 69/2022), which began in the High Court on 6 February 2023, has not concluded.

B. 'Separate Counting' Mechanism and Private Members' Bills

In comparison with other legislatures in the world, two of the more distinctive features of the LegCo of the HKSAR relate to the use of

[51] Basic Law, Art 52.
[52] ibid Art 50.

the 'separate counting' (or 'split voting') mechanism and limitations on the right of individual LegCo members (as distinguished from the government) to introduce private members' Bills. The separate voting mechanism is provided in Annex II to the Basic Law. It applies not only to private members' Bills introduced by one or more LegCo members (as distinguished from Bills introduced by the government), but also to amendments of government Bills proposed by LegCo members and to motions proposed by LegCo members.

Such private members' Bills, amendments to government Bills and motions proposed by LegCo members may only be passed by LegCo if they get majority support in each of two groups of LegCo members present. Before the amendment of Annex II in 2021, the two groups were LegCo members elected from functional constituencies and members elected from geographical constituencies respectively. After the amendment of 2021, which will be discussed later in chapter four, the two groups are (i) members elected by the Election Committee and (ii) members elected from functional constituencies and geographical constituencies. On the other hand, Bills, amendments to Bills and motions proposed by the government can be passed by LegCo with a simple majority vote of all members present. The separate voting mechanism was apparently designed to facilitate the operation of an 'executive-led government', and to require a higher degree of consensus in LegCo for proposals initiated by individual members to pass. From this perspective, the HKSAR legislature may be regarded as a 'quasi-bicameral' legislature.

It is not only more difficult for Bills and motions proposed by individual LegCo members to get passed when compared with government proposals, there are also restrictions on the types of Bills and motions individual LegCo members can propose. These restrictions are codified in Article 74 of the Basic Law. Bills that relate to public expenditure, the political structure or the operation of the government may not be introduced by LegCo members at all. Bills that do not fall within the above rule but relate to 'government policies' can only be introduced by LegCo members with the written consent of the CE. Under the LegCo Rules of Procedure,[53] it is for the President of LegCo to determine whether a Bill relates to government policies. In practice, if a Bill is determined to be related to a government policy, it will not be easy to persuade the CE to give consent to its introduction.

[53] LegCo Rules of Procedure, rule 51(4).

Alongside Article 74, the LegCo Rules of Procedure also impose restrictions on motions and amendments to Bills proposed by LegCo members. In particular, a motion or amendment that, in the opinion of the LegCo President, has a charging effect on public revenue (in the sense that its implementation would require public expenditure) cannot be proposed without the consent of the CE.[54] This restriction was unsuccessfully challenged in the *Leung Kwok Hung* case.[55] The court held that it is within the power of LegCo under the Basic Law to enact the impugned provision as one of its Rules of Procedure, and the impugned provision does not contravene Article 74 or any other provision of the Basic Law. One of the factors the court took into account was that this restriction in the LegCo Rules of Procedure was not new. It already existed in the Standing Orders of the colonial Legislative Council, upon which the Rules of Procedure of the LegCo of the HKSAR were largely modelled when they were first adopted.

C. Powers and Functions

The powers and functions of LegCo are specified in considerable detail in Article 73 of the Basic Law. Like other legislatures, the major powers of LegCo include law-making, approval of budgets and public expenditure, monitoring and scrutinising the work of the government, and expressing views on and thus shaping public policy. As mentioned above, LegCo's powers also extend to the vetting of subordinate legislation.

In practice, the power to enact primary legislation known as ordinances and the power to approve taxation and public expenditure are the most significant powers exercised by LegCo. A Bill introduced by the government in the legislature will only become law after three readings and the affirmative vote of a majority of LegCo members present. Major Bills are carefully scrutinised in Bills Committees set up by LegCo specifically to study them.[56] LegCo members belonging to different political parties and groups may join together to lobby for amendments to a Bill. It is during this process that political bargaining and give-and-take occur, and the government may make concessions in response to the views and demands of legislators. Similarly, political negotiation also takes place

[54] ibid rules 31(1) and 57(6).

[55] *Leung Kwok Hung v President of Legislative Council* [2007] 1 HKLRD 387.

[56] See generally the information provided by the LegCo website, eg www.legco.gov.hk/general/english/bills/Bill_1620.htm; www.legco.gov.hk/en/legco-business/useful-information/legco-procedures/handbook-for-chairmen-of-bills-committees.html.

when the government applies to LegCo for public funding of any major project or exercise that the government proposes to engage in.[57]

In the first three annual sessions of LegCo, in 2016–19 (before its proceedings were disrupted by the intense opposition to the extradition Bill and the storming of the LegCo building in 2019), LegCo passed a total of 56 government Bills, 33 of which were amended in the course of LegCo proceedings.[58] The overwhelming majority of amendments were proposed by the government itself after taking into account the views of LegCo members. As pro-government legislators had a majority in LegCo and the 'separate counting' mechanism was applicable to amendments proposed by individual LegCo members, only two Bills were passed that included amendments proposed by LegCo members.[59]

Because of the restrictions on private members' Bills under Article 74 of the Basic Law and the separate counting mechanism, very few such Bills have been enacted by LegCo. In 2016–19, only four were passed.[60] Hence, it has been observed that LegCo has not been effective in initiating legislation that challenges government policy.[61] On the other hand, LegCo has been more effective in exercising its power of financial control. There have been numerous occasions on which proposed policies or projects associated with government requests for funding were modified or rejected by LegCo's Finance Committee.[62]

During the fifth-term LegCo (2012–16), and especially in the first four years of the sixth-term LegCo (2016–21), the fractious relationship between opposition lawmakers and the government resulted in increased filibustering and disruptive behaviour in LegCo, which significantly hampered the operation of the government. What happened was described by an experienced legislator as a 'vicious spiral racing to the bottom of chaos and dysfunction'.[63] The power of the President of LegCo to terminate a legislative filibuster was tested in the *Leung Kwok Hung* case.[64] The CFA affirmed the power of the President under the

[57] See, eg 'Finance Committee Procedure', www.legco.gov.hk/en/legco-business/useful-information/legco-procedures/finance-committee-procedure.html.

[58] See the LegCo's Annual Reports, www.legco.gov.hk/en/about-legco/annual-reports-of-legislative-council.html. In 2020–21, LegCo passed a total of 46 bills; the high number was due to the backlog resulting from the disruptions in 2019–20.

[59] PLT Lui, 'The Legislature' in Lam et al (n 21) ch 3. We are grateful to the author for making available the manuscript for this chapter.

[60] ibid.

[61] ibid.

[62] ibid.

[63] M Ng, 'The Legislature' in Chan and Lim (n 30) 285, 315. Actually there were at least three types of filibuster: see Chan (n 48) 167–68.

[64] *Leung Kwok Hung v President of the Legislative Council (No 1)* (2014) 17 HKCFAR 689.

Basic Law and LegCo Rules of Procedure to preside over LegCo meetings and to terminate a legislative debate. The Court made it clear that it will exercise jurisdiction only to determine the existence of such a power; it will not 'consider whether or not the power was properly exercised'.[65] To allow the legislature to function efficiently, the court would not lightly displace the principle of non-intervention in the internal proceedings and operations of LegCo.[66]

After the disqualification of several opposition lawmakers in late 2016 and 2017, the LegCo Rules of Procedure were amended several times to address the issue of filibuster and other problems that had plagued LegCo's operation for years. These amendments were only successfully pushed through because, by that time, opposition legislators – as a result of some of them having been disqualified – had lost their majority amongst the lawmakers elected from the geographical constituencies. Notably, motions for the amendment of the LegCo Rules of Procedure are not proposed, and cannot be proposed, by the government, but can only be proposed by LegCo members themselves. Such motions are therefore subject to the separate voting mechanism mentioned above. Before 2017, opposition politicians had consistently outnumbered pro-government legislators among the group of legislators elected from the geographical constituencies, although pro-government legislators had consistently formed the majority amongst the group of lawmakers elected by the functional constituencies. Hitherto, opposition politicians had enjoyed a de facto veto power on proposed amendments to the Rules of Procedure until the Rules were changed in 2017.

One of the amendments to the Rules of Procedure made in 2017 was to reduce the quorum requirement at the 'committee stage' of the legislative proceedings on a Bill from one half of LegCo members to 20.[67] This amendment was challenged as unconstitutional in the case of *Kwok Cheuk Kin*.[68] The challenge was dismissed by the court mainly on the ground that the quorum requirement imposed by Article 75 of the Basic Law applies only to the plenary meetings of LegCo and not to the committee stage for Bills, even though in practice the legislators participating in that stage typically include all LegCo members.

With regard to LegCo's function of monitoring and scrutinising the administration, this is mainly discharged by members raising questions

[65] ibid para 46.

[66] ibid paras 30–31. The doctrine of judicial non-intervention in LegCo proceedings has been established in the HKSAR since *Cheng Kar Shun v Li Fung-ying* [2009] 4 HKC 204.

[67] Rule 17(1A).

[68] *Kwok Cheuk-kin* (n 44).

on the government's work and, if necessary, conducting inquiries on matters of public concern. In the first three annual sessions of LegCo, between 2016 and 2019, there were 114, 150 and 114 oral questions asked in LegCo respectively, and there were 448, 499 and 422 questions seeking written replies by officials. In the 2020–21 legislative session, the number of questions posed for each of the two types were 191 and 595 respectively.[69]

The most significant power that LegCo has vis-à-vis the scrutiny and checking of the administration pertains to its power of investigation under the Legislative Council (Powers and Privileges) Ordinance (P&PO). This ordinance, enacted by the colonial LegCo in 1985, empowers LegCo to act like a court in compelling the attendance of witnesses and the production of documents in the course of a LegCo investigation into any matter. In the *Cheng Kar Shun* case,[70] the power of a LegCo committee to compel the attendance of witnesses was challenged on the ground that Article 73(10) of the Basic Law only authorises LegCo acting in its plenary session to summon witnesses to give evidence, and that this power may not be exercised by a committee of LegCo. The court held that in order to facilitate the effective exercise of the legislature's power of investigation, Article 73(10) of the Basic Law should be interpreted flexibly and purposively so as to enable a LegCo committee, established by LegCo for the purpose of investigation, to exercise the power concerned.

In recent years, select committees with the powers to compel the attendance of witnesses and the production of documents have rarely been established by LegCo, as opposition politicians' proposals to set them up have almost invariably been voted down. For example, in the 2018–19 session, three motions proposing to appoint select committees with powers of inquiry under the P&PO to investigate matters relating to the poor quality of the construction work of the Mass Transit Railway's Shatin-Central link were rejected when voted on. On the other hand, in 2016, LegCo did establish a select committee – with no powers of inquiry under the P&PO – to investigate the agreement between UGL and CY Leung and the former's payment to the latter, as mentioned above.[71]

Another function of LegCo is to express views on government policies and to exert influence on them. Articles 73(4) and 73(6) of the Basic Law provide for LegCo's power to debate the policy addresses of

[69] See the LegCo's Annual Reports (n 22).
[70] n 66 above.
[71] See the LegCo's Annual Reports (n 22).

the CE and to 'debate any issue concerning public interests'. In every annual session of LegCo, there are two major debates – one on the CE's annual policy address and the other on the Financial Secretary's budget proposal in the Appropriation Bill and Estimates of Expenditure. There are also many debates on motions proposed by members that are categorised as 'motions without legislative effect'. This means that even if the motions are passed by LegCo, they are not legally binding on the government. However, motion debates do provide an opportunity for LegCo members to express their views and public opinion on matters of public policy. For example, in the 2016–17 legislative session, 30 motions without legislative effect were debated, 20 of which were passed. In the 2020–21 session, 35 such motions were debated, with 30 of them passed.[72]

Another forum for LegCo members to express views on policies, particularly at the earlier stages of policy formulation, is the meetings of the panels of LegCo. Eighteen panels have been established by LegCo, each responsible for a particular domain of government affairs. They monitor and examine the work of the respective policy bureau, and they meet periodically with the senior officials concerned.

Finally, it is noteworthy that Article 73(8) of the Basic Law tasks LegCo 'to receive and handle complaints from Hong Kong residents'. Like other functions of LegCo discussed above, this function can be traced back to colonial times. Under this 'redress system', LegCo members take turns to be on 'ward duty' every week to receive and handle complaints and representations from persons and bodies who have been aggrieved by government actions or would like to make representations on governmental matters. In the legislative session of 2020–21, more than 2000 cases were handled by LegCo members under this redress system.[73]

VII. INDEPENDENT AGENCIES

As discussed above, one of the major functions of the Legislative Council is to monitor and scrutinise the executive government's conduct. Apart from the legislature, several independent office-holders and agencies have been established to check the operations of government departments and officials, to receive and investigate complaints, and to promote the protection of citizens' rights. Some of the most important institutions will be briefly discussed in this section.

[72] ibid.
[73] ibid.

First of all, there are three independent agencies within the executive which do not report to any of the principal officials, government bureaux and departments, but are accountable only to the CE. They are the Audit Commission, the Independent Commission Against Corruption (ICAC) and the Office of the Ombudsman.

The Audit Commission is headed by the Director of Audit, an office-holder provided for in Article 48(5) of the Basic Law. The powers and duties of the Director of Audit were first stipulated in the Audit Ordinance enacted in 1971.[74] The Director of Audit is the auditor of the government's accounts. Every year, the Director prepares a report on the government accounts and those of relevant statutory bodies ('regularity audit'), and two other reports on the results of 'value for money audits'. The reports typically contain occasional criticisms of the conduct of government departments and officials. The Public Accounts Committee of LegCo considers these reports in the exercise of LegCo's powers of financial control.

The ICAC, headed by a Commissioner Against Corruption, is provided for in Article 48(5) of the Basic Law. It is a reputable institution globally known for its effectiveness in combating corruption, which was rampant in colonial Hong Kong before the ICAC was established in 1974. With a staff of approximately 1500, the ICAC is responsible for enforcing Hong Kong's anti-corruption laws, which include the Prevention of Bribery Ordinance, the Elections (Corrupt and Illegal Conduct) Ordinance and the ICAC Ordinance.

The most senior government officials investigated and prosecuted by the ICAC include Donald Yam-kuen Tsang (CE, 2005–12) and Raphael Si-yan Hui (Chief Secretary – the second most senior official of the HKSAR – from 2005 to 2007). Tsang was convicted in 2017 by a jury in the High Court for misconduct in public office and was sentenced to 20 months' imprisonment. As CE, Tsang had presided over Executive Council meetings in which a company's applications for sound broadcasting licences were considered and approved. The company in question was controlled by Billy Wong, and at the time, Tsang was also negotiating a lease with Wong over a residential property Wong owned in Shenzhen, which Tsang planned to move into upon retirement. However, Tsang failed to declare or disclose these circumstances to the Executive Council. On appeal to the Court of Appeal, the sentence was reduced to 12 months. On further appeal, the conviction was quashed by the CFA

[74] www.aud.gov.hk/eng/aboutus/about_history.htm.

in 2019 – after Tsang had already served his prison sentence – on the ground that the trial judge's directions to the jury were inadequate.[75]

Rafael Hui had been Chief Secretary under the Tsang administration in 2005–07. In 2014, he was convicted of five offences, including conspiracy to commit misconduct in public offence and conspiracy to offer an advantage to a public servant, and he was sentenced to imprisonment for seven years and six months. His appeals to the higher courts were dismissed. The facts of the case were that, prior to and in anticipation of his taking office as Chief Secretary, Hui had accepted payments totalling HK$8.5 million from one of Hong Kong's major real estate developers in exchange for a favourable predisposition to the developer's interests while Hui was in office.[76]

With regard to the Office of the Ombudsman, its history dated back to 1989, when the Commissioner for Administrative Complaints Ordinance was enacted by the colonial legislature. In 1996, the Commissioner was renamed the Ombudsman, whose powers and functions are now governed by the Ombudsman Ordinance. The Office of the Ombudsman receives and investigates complaints by aggrieved persons regarding alleged maladministration (as defined in the Ordinance) by government departments or specified public bodies. It also deals with complaints about non-compliance with the Code on Access to Information mentioned above. It has the power to initiate direct investigations itself, and may also provide mediation services. After an investigation, the Ombudsman will prepare a report and make recommendations therein. Although the recommendations are not legally enforceable, in practice most of the Ombudsman's recommendations have been complied with.[77]

It should be noted, however, that a major limitation vis-à-vis the Ombudsman's jurisdiction is that it does not entertain complaints against the police, except for those regarding any non-compliance with the Code on Access to Information. Complaints relating to the police are instead dealt with by the Independent Police Complaints Council. However, this institution does not have any powers of investigation; it only oversees the investigation of complaints against the police conducted by the Complaints Against Police Office of the Hong Kong Police Force itself.[78]

[75] *HKSAR v Tsang Yam Kuen* HCCC 484/2015, [2018] HKCA 425, [2019] HKCFA 24.
[76] *HKSAR v Hui Rafael* HCCC 98/2013, CACC 444/2014, FACC 12/2016.
[77] See generally www.ombudsman.hk/.
[78] www.ipcc.gov.hk/en/what_we_do/two_tier_police.html.

Apart from the above agencies, two other independent agencies deserve to be mentioned here, as they also receive and handle complaints by aggrieved persons, conduct investigations and mediations, take some law enforcement actions, draft codes of practice and engage in public education to promote human rights in the community. They are the Equal Opportunities Commission (EOC) and the Office of the Privacy Commissioner for Personal Data; they were both established in 1996 and have continued to play increasingly active roles since the handover. The EOC oversees the implementation of Hong Kong's anti-discrimination laws, which include the Sex Discrimination Ordinance, Disability Discrimination Ordinance, Family Status Discrimination Ordinance and Race Discrimination Ordinance. The Privacy Commissioner is responsible for the enforcement of the Personal Data (Privacy) Ordinance.

VIII. CONCLUSION

In her Policy Address on 25 November 2020,[79] CE Carrie Lam described the principal features of the government system of the HKSAR as follows:

> The Chief Executive (CE) is responsible to both the HKSAR and the Central People's Government (CPG). Under the constitutional function of 'dual responsibility', the CE is required to comprehensively, accurately and firmly implement the 'One Country, Two Systems' principle and uphold the Basic Law (BL). Under the BL, the CE is vested with the dual role as head of the Executive Authorities of the HKSAR … and that of the HKSAR representing the whole Region. One can see the extensive powers conferred upon the CE by referring to Chapter IV of the BL. In addition to leading the Executive Authorities, the CE has specific roles and functions to play in respect of the exercise of powers and functions by the legislature and the judiciary of Hong Kong. This demonstrates the HKSAR's adherence to the executive-led structure under the core leadership of the CE, who is directly accountable to the CPG. Under this framework, the powers of the Executive Authorities, the legislature and the judiciary are 'individually positioned' with a division of work. There is no conflict between an executive-led system and an independent Judiciary, since one of the CE's duties is to uphold judicial independence which is protected under the BL.

The concept of 'executive-led' government emphasised by Lam in the above passage and its relationship with the doctrine of 'separation of powers' will be further discussed in chapters four and five below.

[79] www.policyaddress.gov.hk/2020/eng/pdf/PA2020.pdf.

The central authorities have resisted the 'separation of powers' discourse as they consider it more relevant to the political system of independent Western states, while the HKSAR is no more than a local administrative region of the PRC. Notably, the doctrine of 'separation of powers' also does not exist in the constitutional law of the PRC. Furthermore, to suggest that the executive, legislature and judiciary in the HKSAR are on an equal footing would contradict the central authorities' view that constitutionally the CE occupies a pre-eminent position in the HKSAR's political system by virtue of the CE's relationship with the central government.[80]

Putting aside this unique relationship between the CE and the central authorities, and if we just examine the internal operations of Hong Kong's political system, it may be said that Hong Kong's system is more similar to a presidential system than a parliamentary one. This is because the CE and LegCo are elected separately and, unlike in a parliamentary system, the CE is not the leader of a political party or coalition of parties that occupies the majority of seats in the legislature.

Hong Kong has never been ruled by popularly elected politicians. Three of the five CEs who have held office so far were civil servants of the British colonial government, while CH Tung and CY Leung were inducted from the business and professional sector respectively and had no political party background. The overwhelming majority of principal officials who have served in the HKSAR government had a civil service background. Although the introduction of the POAS has been described as the 'single most important institutional reform since the colonial era',[81] its actual impact on the operation and performance of the executive and its accountability to the public has been limited, as most of the appointed principal officials were originally civil servants. Therefore, the political system of the HKSAR essentially comprises bureaucrats in charge of the executive, seeking to work with a legislature consisting of elected politicians.

Although Hong Kong's political system is more akin to a presidential system than to a parliamentary system, it is very different from the American-style presidential system. As discussed above, the power of members of the legislature to initiate Bills in the HKSAR is severely limited by Article 74 of the Basic Law. The 'separate counting' mechanism as discussed above also makes it difficult for a mere majority of

[80] For further discussion of 'executive-led' government in the HKSAR, see chs 4 and 5 below.

[81] Lee and Yeung (n 31) 131.

the members of the legislature to get motions passed, unless they also command a majority in each of the two groups of lawmakers.

If the legislature has only a minor role in initiating and enacting public policies, one may rightly ask whether it is effective in monitoring and scrutinising the administration. It has been pointed out that the extent to which LegCo is assertive and aggressive in exercising its powers and functions depends crucially on its membership composition.[82] An experienced legislator in the HKSAR has identified four factors that condition LegCo's effectiveness: 'the active cooperation of the Government, the unity of purpose among members, the support of the public, and finally, the resourcefulness of the individual members'.[83] Unfortunately, as the study of the electoral politics of the HKSAR in the next chapter will reveal, these favourable conditions necessary for LegCo's effectiveness have been lacking in recent years. As a result, 'the Government's ability to achieve good governance which required the partnership of the legislature was also impaired'.[84] And after the electoral overhaul of 2021 and the establishment of a 'patriots-only' legislature, some may equally wonder how effective the revamped legislature will be in checking the operations of the government, especially on issues concerning civil liberties.

FURTHER READING

Ghai, Y, *Hong Kong's New Constitutional Order: The Resumption of Chinese Sovereignty and the Basic Law*, 2nd edn (Hong Kong University Press. 1999).

Lam, W, Lui, PLT and Wong, W (eds), *Contemporary Hong Kong Government and Politics*, 2nd edn (Hong Kong University Press, 2012).

Lau, S, *The Practice of 'One Country, Two Systems' Policy in Hong Kong* (Commercial Press, 2017).

[82] Lui (n 59).
[83] Ng (n 63) 312.
[84] ibid.

4

The Political System: Electoral Politics and Constitutional Changes

Constitutional Reform – Electoral System – Elections – Political Parties

As discussed in the last chapter, the extent to which the legislature can meaningfully check and balance the executive's exercise of powers depends crucially on the membership composition of the legislature. The last chapter has also referred to the fact that the members of the Hong Kong Special Administrative Region (HKSAR) legislature – prior to the electoral overhaul of 2021 – were divided into the 'pro-government' camp and the political 'opposition'. In this chapter, we will study the HKSAR's relatively unique electoral system at its founding, and the peculiar pattern of political polarisation it engendered. The chapter also discusses the phenomenon of a 'ruling coalition' in the HKSAR, which exists even though there has not been a dominant political party whose leaders are appointed or elected to the executive or the legislature. The chapter then reviews the complex and turbulent dynamics of constitutional reform in the HKSAR, which eventually culminated in the electoral overhaul of 2021 and the introduction of 'patriots ruling Hong Kong' as an overriding principle of constitutional design.

I. THE ELECTORAL SYSTEM

With respect to the selection of the Chief Executive (CE), a National People's Congress (NPC) Decision adopted at the same time as the enactment of the Basic Law in 1990 provided that the first CE would be chosen by a Selection Committee of 400 members. Annex I to the Basic Law stipulated that the second and third CEs would be elected by an Election Committee (EC) of 800 members. After the election, the Central People's Government (CPG) would appoint the elected candidate as CE.

Annex I to the Basic Law (as originally enacted in 1990) specified the four sectors of society from which EC members were to be elected, with an equal number of members drawn from each sector. The sectors were: (i) business (comprising mainly corporate voters in various commercial, financial and industrial fields); (ii) members of professional bodies; (iii) labour, religious and other social sectors; and (iv) the political sector (including legislators, Hong Kong deputies to the NPC and Hong Kong members of the Chinese People's Political Consultative Conference (CPPCC)). Therefore, in the 800-member EC, there were 200 members from each of the four sectors. Annex I to the Basic Law was amended in 2010, whereby the size of the EC was increased to 1200 members, comprising 300 members from each of the four sectors.[1] A more extensive amendment to Annex I was introduced in 2021, as discussed below.

Regarding the composition of the Legislative Council (LegCo), Annex II to the Basic Law (as originally enacted in 1990) provided for three separate types of elections for three respective groups of lawmakers: (i) direct election by universal suffrage in geographical constituencies (GC); (ii) election by functional constituencies (FCs); and (iii) election by the EC (mentioned above). Annex II (as originally enacted in 1990) provided for the progressive reduction of LegCo members elected by the EC from 10 (in the first-term LegCo) to six (in the second-term LegCo), and the EC election of LegCo members would be phased out in the third-term LegCo. The first-term LegCo comprised 20 GC members elected by universal suffrage, 30 members elected by FCs and 10 elected by the EC. As provided in Annex II, the number of GC members elected by universal suffrage increased to 24 in the second-term LegCo, then to 30 in the third-term LegCo, while the number elected by FCs remained unchanged during the corresponding period.

In accordance with Annex II as amended in 2010, the total number of LegCo members was increased from 60 to 70 for the fourth-term LegCo commencing in 2012, half of whom were elected by universal suffrage and the other half by FCs, which included five District Councillors elected by 'quasi'-universal suffrage in the 'super-District Councils' FC.[2]

[1] The political reform of 2010 is discussed below.

[2] See AHY Chen, 'An Unexpected Breakthrough in Hong Kong's Constitutional Reform' (2010) 40 *Hong Kong Law Journal* 259; N Ma, 'Negotiating Democracy and "High Autonomy"': The 2010 Political Reform' in R Yep (ed), *Negotiating Autonomy in Greater China: Hong Kong and its Sovereign before and after 1997* (Nordic Institute of Asian Studies Press, 2013) 242.

Simply put, all registered voters who previously did not have the right to vote in any pre-existing FC could now vote for candidates contesting for these five new FC seats, but eligible candidates had to be District Councillors nominated by fellow elected District Councillors.

In view of the social unrest, following from the Occupy Central movement of 2014 and culminating in the anti-extradition movement of 2019, the central authorities introduced a two-pronged approach to bring the 'One Country, Two Systems' (OCTS) model back onto what Beijing perceived to be the correct path. The first measure was the National Security Law, discussed in chapter two. The second measure was an overhaul of Hong Kong's electoral system introduced by the NPC Decision on Improving the Electoral System of the HKSAR (dated 11 March 2021), in pursuance of which the National People's Congress Standing Committee (NPCSC) amended Annexes I and II to the Basic Law. The amendments fundamentally changed the existing electoral system,[3] and will be discussed in a later section of this chapter.

The use of FCs (and the EC) to constitute part of the membership of LegCo has been one of the most controversial features of the HKSAR's political system. The number of persons entitled to vote for members of the EC and for the FC seats in LegCo (except the five 'super-District Councils' FC seats created in 2010 but abolished in 2021) has constituted less than 10 per cent of the general electorate in Hong Kong.[4] In contrast, more than four million registered voters are entitled to vote for the GC seats.[5] Furthermore, the number of electors in each FC varies greatly, even though most FCs have one seat each in LegCo. This means that the weight of the voting power of each individual in different FCs varies and is unequal. FCs enable business interests to be given disproportionate representation in LegCo.[6]

[3] See Annex I to the Basic Law (as amended in 2021); Improving Electoral System (Consolidated Amendments) Ordinance 2021.

[4] This refers to the situation before 2021. After the electoral reform of 2021 discussed below, the number of persons entitled to vote for members of the EC was drastically reduced. Before the 2021 reform, there were over 200,000 registered voters in the EC and the FCs (other than voters for the 'Super District Councils' seats). After the reform, the number of registered voters in the FCs still exceeded 200,000, but that of the EC was reduced to less than 8000. See the sources in n 5 below.

[5] 'Elector Registers to Be Published' (27 October 2021), www.news.gov.hk/eng/2021/10/20211027/20211027_144615_408.html; Registration and Electoral Office, 'Voter Registration Statistics', https://data.gov.hk/tc-data/dataset/hk-reo-reopsi01-voter-registration-statistics.

[6] Of the 28 FCs that exist in 2022, 18 represent business interests in various sectors of the economy.

Moreover, corporate voting, which applies to many FCs, has given rise to 'inequalities and anomalies'.[7] When corporate voting applies, it is the corporate bodies in the FCs that vote, not the individuals from that constituency. FCs also vote for members of the EC. Therefore, the EC and FC elections have been criticised as 'small circle' elections, from which the vast majority of the Hong Kong population are excluded.

The constitutionality of FCs had been unsuccessfully challenged in colonial Hong Kong on the ground that it infringed the right of equal suffrage.[8] After the handover, corporate voting in FCs was challenged on the ground that the Basic Law only conferred voting rights on HKSAR permanent residents, but that challenge too was unsuccessful.[9]

II. POLITICAL POLARISATION IN HONG KONG

Since direct elections to the legislature were introduced in colonial Hong Kong in the early 1990s, a distinctive type of political polarisation developed that shaped the politics of the HKSAR until the electoral revamp of 2021. This was the division of Hong Kong's political forces between pro-China forces (also known after 1997 as 'pro-Establishment' or 'pro-government' forces, or 'patriots') and 'pro-democracy' or 'non-Establishment' forces (comprising the 'pan-democrats' and other 'opposition' politicians such as 'localists').[10] The pro-China camp supports the policies of the PRC government towards Hong Kong, including its conservative or gradualist approach to Hong Kong's democratisation. This camp also supports, or at least does not question, Chinese Communist Party rule in mainland China, and generally refrains from criticising the country's human rights record. On the other hand, the pro-democracy camp advocates Western-style liberal democracy for Hong Kong, particularly universal suffrage for the election of the CE and all LegCo members, and the protection of civil liberties and human rights in accordance with international standards. They are also critical of the authoritarian one-party rule in China and its human rights record.

[7] S Young and A Law, 'Privileged to Vote: Inequalities and Anomalies of the FC System' in C Loh and Civic Exchange (eds), *Functional Constituencies: A Unique Feature of the Hong Kong Legislative Council* (Hong Kong University Press, 2006) ch 3.

[8] *Lee Miu Ling v Attorney-General* (1995) 5 HKPLR 23.

[9] *Chan Yu Nam v Secretary for Justice* (2012) 3 HKC 38.

[10] See, eg N Ma, 'The Rise of "Anti-China" Sentiments in Hong Kong and the 2012 Legislative Council Elections' (2015) 15 *China Review* 39; J Jang, 'Competing Political Visions in the Legislative Council of Hong Kong' (2016) 21 *Journal of Chinese Political Science* 89.

Since the pro-democracy camp emerged in the 1980s, it had consistently enjoyed significant support from civil society and the electorate in Hong Kong. It is noteworthy that for a quarter of a century since direct election by universal suffrage to a portion of LegCo seats was introduced in 1991, the pro-democracy politicians and parties – but not any single political party – consistently won 55–60 per cent of the popular votes for those LegCo seats elected by universal suffrage.[11] Beijing was naturally concerned that if completely free and unrestricted elections by universal suffrage were introduced in Hong Kong, and the CE and all LegCo seats were elected by universal suffrage, the office of the CE and a majority of LegCo seats might be captured by members of the pro-democracy camp.

The pro-democracy camp's understanding of Hong Kong's autonomy as stipulated in the Sino-British Joint Declaration of 1984 and the Basic Law is based on the idea that such autonomy can only be fully realised if Hong Kong's political system allows for the CE and all legislators to be elected by universal suffrage. This is different from Beijing's understanding of the HKSAR's autonomy under OCTS. Although Beijing is committed to 'Hong Kong people ruling Hong Kong' (instead of mainland officials doing so), in its view, the Hong Kong people who hold key governmental positions in Hong Kong must be 'patriots', which in practice means people whom Beijing considers acceptable and trustworthy for this purpose.[12] Hence Beijing has emphasised that under the Basic Law it has reserved the power to appoint the CE (after an election held in Hong Kong) and other principal officials of the SAR. Mainland scholars and officials have always stressed that the power of appointment of the CE, who is accountable both to the central government and the HKSAR,[13] is a substantive power and is by no means merely formal or ceremonial.[14] They have also stressed that Hong Kong's system

[11] N Ma, *Political Development in Hong Kong* (Hong Kong University Press, 2007) 154, 223; Ma, 'The Rise of "Anti-China" Sentiments' (n 10) 58, 62.

[12] Thus Wang Guangya, Director of the Hong Kong and Macau Affairs Office of the State Council, pointed out a few months before the CE election in March 2017 that the CE should meet four criteria: loving the nation and loving Hong Kong; being trusted by the central government; being capable of governing Hong Kong; and enjoying the support of Hong Kong people: 'Beijing Not Ready to Show Its Hand on Hong Kong Chief Executive Preference, Top Official Hints' *South China Morning Post* (31 December 2016); 'Crucial for Next Hong Kong Leader to Have Central Government's Trust, According to Beijing Official' *South China Morning Post* (17 February 2017).

[13] Basic Law, Art 43.

[14] See, eg S Wang (ed), *Introduction to the Basic Law of the Hong Kong Special Administrative Region* (Law Press, 2000) 364–65; R Yep, '"One Country, Two Systems" and Special Administrative Regions: The Case of Hong Kong' in JH Chung and TC Lam (eds), *China's Local Administration* (Routledge, 2010) 86, 98.

of government is an 'executive-led' system and must not become a 'legislative-led' one.[15] This emphasis on 'executive-led government' may be explained on the basis that it is the executive (including the CE and the principal officials) – and not LegCo – that is appointed by Beijing and enjoys the confidence and trust of Beijing, and it is primarily the executive that discharges the governing powers and authority directly conferred by the central authorities.

III. THE 'RULING COALITION' IN THE HKSAR

Since the establishment of the HKSAR, the success of the 'executive-led' government in Hong Kong has depended on a loose coalition of pro-China political parties and independent legislators who occupied a majority of seats in LegCo.[16] But there has never been any ruling party in the HKSAR. No single political party has ever occupied a majority of, or any number close to half of, the seats in LegCo. As mentioned above, the CE is elected independently of LegCo by the EC, which has never been dominated by political parties, although the majority of them are considered 'pro-China' or are at least not members of the 'pro-democracy' camp. Members of the pro-China camp in LegCo have been generally supportive of the CE and the administration, although such support is not guaranteed in respect of every policy, Bill or item of financial expenditure, because these elected legislators also have to answer to their own constituencies.

In practice, the central authorities in Beijing and their Liaison Office in Hong Kong have played a significant role – informal rather constitutionally prescribed – in promoting, supporting and coordinating among this camp of pro-China politicians in Hong Kong. This has been the strategy of the 'patriotic United Front', a long-standing practice in the history of the Chinese Communist Party (CCP) that involves the cooperation, cultivation and establishment of a political alliance with friends and supporters of the CCP for the purpose of achieving the CCP's objectives.[17]

[15] Wang (n 14) 346–49; PK Li, 'The Executive' in WM Lam, PLT Lui and W Wong (eds), *Contemporary Hong Kong Government and Politics*, 2nd edn (Hong Kong University Press, 2012) 27.

[16] See PLT Lui, 'The Legislature' in Lam et al (n 15) 45.

[17] See generally SSH Lo, SCF Hung and JHC Loo, *China's New United Front Work in Hong Kong: Penetrative Politics and Its Implications* (Palgrave Macmillan, 2019); EWY Lee, 'United Front, Clientelism, and Indirect Rule: Theorizing the Role of the "Liaison Office" in Hong Kong' (2020) 29 *Journal of Contemporary China* 763.

In most other devolved or federal systems of government around the world, the political systems at both the national level and the regional level are liberal-democratic in nature, with free elections, multi-party competition and elected assemblies. In such systems, political parties that operate at the national level may also participate in regional politics, even though some political parties may be active only at the regional devolved level and not at the national level. The distinguishing feature of the OCTS model in the case of the HKSAR is that an authoritarian party-state led by the CCP exists at the national level, but the CCP does not directly and publicly participate in the electoral system and public life of the HKSAR. Instead, in order to implement the policy of 'patriots ruling Hong Kong', the Chinese central authorities, through their Liaison Office in the HKSAR, coordinate among and support the 'pro-China' political forces in Hong Kong to ensure that they occupy a majority of LegCo and EC seats.[18]

This objective was achieved between 1997 and 2020 for the following reasons. First, most of the functional groups that elected members of the EC for the CE had a pro-China orientation, or at least they were not outnumbered by members of the pro-democracy camp. Secondly, approximately half of the FCs for LegCo election were in the business sector, which was generally pro-China in orientation. (Among the professions-based FCs, some constituents were pro-China and some were pro-democracy.)

Thirdly, prior to 2021, those LegCo lawmakers who were elected by universal suffrage were elected in multi-member geographical district constituencies with the use of proportional representation, rather than in single-member constituencies that rely on 'first past the post' voting. Under this pre-2021 system, pro-China politicians had consistently garnered the support of at least 40 per cent of the popular vote in the GCs. In practice, this ensured that the pro-China camp had a majority in LegCo comprising (i) a majority of the members elected by FCs and (ii) a sizeable minority of lawmakers elected by universal suffrage in GCs.

However, before the electoral revamp of 2021, there was no constitutional mechanism in place to ensure that support for the 'pro-China' camp would not decline, and support for the 'pro-democracy' camp would not increase, to such levels that the 'pro-China' camp would lose its majority in LegCo or even the EC.[19] By 2020, this scenario became a

[18] For further details, see Lee (n 17).

[19] For example, if the support for the 'pro-China' camp among voters voting by universal suffrage in the LegCo geographical constituencies falls from 40% to 35% or 30%, and/or the 'pro-China' camp loses a few seats constituted by the professions-based functional constituencies, it could lose its majority in LegCo.

real possibility, given the surge of support for the 'pro-democracy' camp that resulted from the anti-extradition movement of 2019.[20] This partly explains the central authorities' introduction of the electoral overhaul of 2021, which will be discussed in a later section of this chapter.

IV. THE DYNAMICS OF CONSTITUTIONAL REFORM

The electoral overhaul of 2021 was the latest in a series of constitutional reforms, either attempted or realised, in the history of the HKSAR. This electoral revamp should be understood in light of the long-standing political struggles between the 'pro-China' and 'pro-democracy' camps.

After the failure of the Hong Kong government's attempt in 2003 to enact a national security law to implement Article 23 of the Basic Law, the 'pan-democrats' launched a movement to demand a speedier pace of democratisation in the HKSAR. As previously discussed in chapter two, the NPCSC on 6 April 2004 issued an Interpretation of the Basic Law that requires the CE to submit a report to the NPCSC on whether there is a need to introduce electoral reform; and the CE may only proceed to initiate electoral reform if the NPCSC gives the 'green light'.

Chief Executive Donald Tsang attempted twice to initiate electoral reform. The first attempt, made in 2005, failed.[21] Under Annexes I and II to the Basic Law (as originally enacted in 1990), electoral reforms introduced by the CE had to be passed by a two-thirds majority in LegCo. Tsang's reform package was vetoed in 2005 by the 'pan-democrats' – who occupied more than one-third of the LegCo seats at the time – on the grounds that it was not democratic enough and that there was no timetable given for the introduction of universal suffrage. Two years later, such a timetable – for electing the CE by universal suffrage in 2017 – was subsequently promulgated by the NPCSC in 2007 in response to Tsang's report on electoral reform.[22]

[20] See ch 1 above, fn 61 regarding the unprecedented victory of the 'pro-democracy' camp in the District Council election on 24 November 2019. However, 49 District Councillors were subsequently disqualified when their oaths of office were determined to be invalid. Many other District Councillors resigned on their own accord. By October 2021, only 151 of the total number of 479 District Councillors remained in office. See *Ming Pao* (22 October 2021).

[21] See AHY Chen, 'The Fate of the Constitutional Reform Proposal of October 2005' (2005) 35 *Hong Kong Law Journal* 537.

[22] See A Chen, 'A New Era in Hong Kong's Constitutional History' (2008) 38 *Hong Kong Law Journal* 1.

Tsang's second attempt at electoral reform was made in 2010. The 'pan-democrats' had planned again to veto the reform proposal on the ground that it was not democratic enough. However, a last-minute concession by Tsang, which took the form of a radical revision to the original reform package, finally resulted in the reform being passed by the requisite two-thirds majority in LegCo, with some pan-democrats voting in support of the reform together with the pro-Establishment camp. The reform included the expansion of the size of the EC to 1200 members (still elected by the four social sectors that elected the existing EC), and the addition of 10 seats in LegCo – five lawmakers elected by universal suffrage in GCs, and another five elected by 'quasi-universal suffrage' in the new 'super-District Councils' FC.[23]

As discussed in chapter one, CE CY Leung in July 2014 initiated the procedure for another round of electoral reform by submitting a report to the NPCSC. On 31 August 2014, the NPCSC rendered its Decision on political reform in the HKSAR. Pro-democracy politicians condemned the Decision for being inconsistent with international standards of democratic elections and characterised it as 'fake universal suffrage'. Opponents of the Decision protested by participating in the Occupy Central movement. The electoral reform was vetoed by LegCo in June 2015, with all the pan-democrats voting against it.

Political developments since 2015, which came to a head in the anti-extradition movement of 2019, attest to the increasing tensions and conflicts between pro-democracy forces and the central authorities, and increasing polarisation within Hong Kong society itself, especially between the 'pro-Establishment' forces and the opposition. These developments will be reviewed briefly here.

After the failure of political reform in 2015, a new generation of political activists emerged[24] who distanced themselves from the traditional pan-democrats; the latter had attempted to realise democracy for Hong Kong within the constitutional framework of OCTS. The new generation of younger activists were inclined to believe that the authoritarian PRC regime would not allow a true democracy with genuine universal suffrage to take root in the HKSAR. Therefore, they went one step further and questioned whether Hong Kong should remain part of the PRC. Political activists who held such views were known as the

[23] See n 2 above.

[24] See generally SSH Lo, 'Ideologies and Factionalism in Beijing–Hong Kong Relations' (2018) 58 *Asian Survey* 392.

'localists'. Some of the 'localists' advocated self-determination or even independence for Hong Kong.[25]

In the LegCo election of September 2016, some 'localists' were barred from standing as candidates[26] on the ground that their political views were inconsistent with their signed declarations (as required by the electoral law) that they would uphold the Basic Law and owe allegiance to the HKSAR.[27] Despite this move, a total of six 'localists' were elected to LegCo in this election, collectively capturing 19 per cent of the popular vote.[28] As far as LegCo was concerned, the success of the 'localists' proved to be short-lived, as some of them were subsequently stripped of their LegCo seats by the courts on the ground of their failure to comply with the oath-taking requirement codified in the Basic Law and local legislation.[29] These 'disqualification' cases were highly controversial as the NPCSC intervened in the course of the judicial proceedings in the first 'disqualification' case by issuing an interpretation of Article 104 of the Basic Law (which concerns the oath-taking requirement).[30] In the by-elections held to fill the vacancies arising from the disqualification of these legislators, some 'localists' were once again barred from participation.[31]

[25] For the 'localist' turn in Hong Kong politics, see JYS Cheng (ed), *New Trends of Political Participation in Hong Kong* (City University of Hong Kong Press, 2014); I Ip, *Hong Kong's New Identity Politics* (Routledge, 2020).

[26] See Hong Kong newspapers of 2–3 August 2016, eg 'Protests Shut Down Electoral Commission Briefing as "Hong Kong Indigenous" Edward Leung Disqualified from Legco Elections' *South China Morning Post* (2 August 2016); 'Hong Kong's Returning Officers' Power to Dismiss Potential Legco Candidates Called into Question' *South China Morning Post* (2 August 2016).

[27] Chan Ho Tin, one of the disqualified candidates, subsequently brought an election petition to challenge the returning officer's decision, but was unsuccessful: see A Chen, 'A Defining Moment in Hong Kong's History' *South China Morning Post* (4 July 2003); 'How the Liberals Stopped a Constitutional Crisis' *South China Morning Post* (8 July 2003).

[28] See 'Localists and Self-Determination Activists Capture 6 Seats, LegCo Divided into 3 Factions' and 'Localist Self-Determination Politicians Capture 400,000 Votes' *Ming Pao* (6 September 2016, in Chinese); CK Choy and JM Chan, 'Lifahui xuanju jieguo chubu pingxi' (立法會選舉結果初步評析; A Preliminary Analysis of the Outcome of the LegCo Election) *Ming Pao* (6 September 2016).

[29] See *Chief Executive of the HKSAR v President of the Legislative Council and Leung Chung Hang Sixtus*, HCAL 185/2016 (Court of First Instance, 15 November 2016), [2017] 1 HKLRD 460 (Court of Appeal), (2017) 20 HKCFAR 390 (leave to appeal refused by CFA); *Nathan Law Kwun Chung* [2017] 4 HKLRD 115 (CFI); *Leung Kwok Hung* [2019] HKCA 173 (CA); H Zhu and AHY Chen, 'The Oath-Taking Cases and the NPCSC Interpretation of 2016' (2019) 49 *Hong Kong Law Journal* 381.

[30] See ch 2, fn 30 and accompanying text.

[31] See *Chow Ting v Teng Yu Yan* [2019] HKCFI 2135; *Au Nok Hin v Teng Yu Yan Anne* [2019] HKCFA 50; *Lau Wing Hong v Chan Yuen Man* [2019] HKCFI 2287.

The pro-independence Hong Kong National Party, founded by Chan Ho Tin Andy, one of the 'localists' barred from standing as a candidate in the 2016 LegCo election,[32] was banned by the Secretary for Security as an 'unlawful society' under the Societies Ordinance on 24 September 2018.[33] The National Party's appeal to the Chief Executive in Council was dismissed on 19 February 2019.[34] On 26 February 2019, the Central People's Government issued an 'official letter' (*gonghan*, 公函) to the CE expressing support for the decision to ban the National Party, affirming that it was the constitutional duty of the HKSAR to 'safeguard national security in accordance with law', and requiring the CE to submit a report on the matter.[35]

The escalating tensions between opposition politicians in Hong Kong and the central authorities reached a climax in 2019 during the social movement against the proposed extradition law, which saw mass protests, riots and months of civil unrest that were unprecedented in the history of the HKSAR. This saga has been narrated in chapter one. It is also noteworthy that the pro-democracy camp's demand for universal suffrage in the CE and LegCo elections was resurrected during this anti-extradition movement, and it featured as one of the 'five principal demands' of the protestors.

The anti-extradition movement exposed the dissatisfaction that many people in Hong Kong, particularly young people, had over the policy of OCTS as practised in recent years. They did not trust either the HKSAR government or the central government, identified themselves as Hongkongers rather than Chinese citizens, and some even considered the PRC and mainland Chinese people to be an alien 'Other'. The movement underscored the contradictions between the 'Two Systems' in OCTS: the clash between the aspirations for liberty and democracy on the part of many Hong Kong people and the limits to the realisation of such aspirations imposed by the logic of 'One Country'.

[32] See n 27 above.

[33] See Hong Kong newspapers of 25 September 2018.

[34] 'Hong Kong National Party Ban Upheld by Panel Which Says It Doesn't Trust Group Not "to Resort to Violence" in Independence Bid' *South China Morning Post* (22 February 2019).

[35] 'Beijing Backs City Government's Ban on Hong Kong National Party, Says Leader Carrie Lam' *South China Morning Post* (26 February 2019). For the full Chinese text of the 'official letter', see www.gov.cn/zhengce/content/2019-02/26/content_5368672.htm. The Chief Executive's report was submitted on 16 April 2019: see 'Carrie Lam Submits Report on National Party' *Ming Pao* (19 April 2019, in Chinese). For the full Chinese text of the report, see http://gia.info.gov.hk/general/201904/18/P2019041800415_308614_1_155557219 9159.pdf.

In retrospect, the anti-extradition movement, which had resorted to both peaceful and violent means to pursue protestors' visions of liberty, governmental accountability and democracy in Hong Kong, ultimately backfired, and only had the effect of prompting the central authorities to tighten their control over Hong Kong by means of the HKSAR National Security Law (NSL) of 2020 and the electoral overhaul of 2021. The NSL has been discussed in chapters one and two above. In the next section of this chapter, we consider the electoral revamp.

V. THE ELECTORAL OVERHAUL OF 2021

The anti-extradition movement of 2019 convinced the central authorities that there was not only a lacuna in Hong Kong's legal system vis-à-vis national security, there were also defects in its electoral system that had to be addressed urgently. In particular, Beijing was convinced that there were inadequate institutional safeguards to ensure that the HKSAR would only be ruled by 'patriots' (instead of 'anti-China' political forces) and to secure the effective operation of an 'executive-led' system of government. Beijing therefore decided to adopt a two-pronged approach to reorient the OCTS policy and to restore what it perceived to be a derailed train back onto the right track. The approach comprised the enactment of the NSL and the overhaul of Hong Kong's electoral system. Chinese officials described this manoeuvre as analogous to two moves of the same martial arts exercise.[36]

On 11 March 2021, the NPC at its annual plenary session adopted a Decision on the 'improvement' of the electoral system of the HKSAR. The Decision set out the basic principles and the direction of the electoral reform, and authorised the NPCSC to amend Annexes I and II to the Basic Law for this purpose. On 30 March 2021, the NPCSC passed the amendments to the two Annexes. The electoral revamp was implemented by local legislation when LegCo enacted the Improving Electoral System (Consolidated Amendments) Ordinance on 27 May 2021.[37] The revamped electoral system was implemented for the first time in the election of the EC in September 2021, the election of the seventh-term

[36] 'Li Zhanshu: dachu falü zuhequan' *Ming Pao* (9 March 2021); 'Gangaoban: xunxujianjin fei cici kuo zhixuan' *Ming Pao* (13 March 2021, in Chinese).

[37] See the papers of the LegCo Subcommittee on Decision of the NPC on Improving the Electoral System of the HKSAR at www.legco.gov.hk/yr20-21/english/hc/sub_com/hs102/agenda/hs10220210401.htm.

LegCo in December 2021 and the election of the sixth-term CE in May 2022. The major features of the electoral overhaul may be summarised as follows.

First, we will consider the change in the composition of LegCo. According to Annex II to the Basic Law as amended in 2010, and prior to the 2021 overhaul, LegCo comprised 70 members. Half of them were elected by universal suffrage, that is, by proportional representation in the five GCs that Hong Kong was divided into. Thirty seats were constituted by 'traditional' FCs – 'traditional' in the sense that they already existed before the 2010 electoral reform. As mentioned above, five seats were created in 2010; they were known as the 'super-District Councils' seats. Voters in this new District Councils FC were those voters in the GCs (constituted by universal suffrage) who were ineligible to vote in the 'traditional' FCs. They may elect five members of the District Councils into LegCo. As of 2010, most members of the 18 District Councils were directly elected by universal suffrage. There was still a minority of appointed members; appointed members were abolished by the time of the 2016 District Council elections.

The electoral overhaul of 2021 increased the total number of LegCo seats to 90. Twenty seats are elected by universal suffrage in GCs. The whole of Hong Kong is divided into 10 GCs, with each constituency electing two LegCo members. Instead of relying on proportional representation, a modified first-past-the-post voting system is now adopted, with each voter allowed to vote for only one candidate, and the two candidates with the highest votes in each GC being duly elected. As for the remaining 70 seats, 30 are elected by the 'traditional' FCs and 40 are elected by a newly reconstituted EC.

A core element of the electoral revamp was the reconstitution and further empowerment of the EC. According to the original Annex I to the Basic Law, EC members were elected from four social sectors, as mentioned above. Each sector comprised a number of sub-sectors. Voters in the sub-sectors were largely the same as voters in the 'traditional' FCs that elected part of the LegCo seats. The number of these voters, which included both natural persons and corporate bodies, was slightly over 200,000 before the electoral overhaul of 2021.

According to the original Annexes I and II to the Basic Law, the EC would elect the CE. Furthermore, the EC also elected 10 members of the 60-member first-term LegCo and six members of the 60-member second-term LegCo. The original Annex II to the Basic Law provided that, commencing from the third-term LegCo, the EC would no longer elect any LegCo members.

The electoral revamp of 2021 not only revived but also expanded the functions of the EC in electing part of LegCo, while retaining the EC's function in electing the CE. Three features are particularly noteworthy. First, the EC now elects a substantial proportion of LegCo members – 40 out of 90. Secondly, EC members are now also given a new right to nominate candidates standing for LegCo elections. Under the revamped system, each LegCo candidate must be nominated by at least two EC members from each of the five sectors that constitute the new EC. This requirement applies not only to candidates running for the EC seats in LegCo (such candidates, incidentally, do not need to be EC members), but also to those who stand as LegCo candidates in any of the FC or GC elections.

Thirdly, under the revamped system, any person seeking to be a candidate in a LegCo election has to be screened by a new Candidate Eligibility Review Committee comprising top government officials and appointed non-government members. The law expressly provides that in making its decisions, this committee should consider the opinion of the national security department of the Hong Kong Police Force on whether the candidates satisfy the requirement that they would uphold the Basic Law and owe allegiance to the HKSAR.[38] The amended Annexes I and II expressly provide that no legal proceedings may be instituted in respect of the committee's decisions in this regard.

We now turn to the revamped composition of the EC. Instead of the pre-existing 1200-member EC comprising four sectors with 300 persons each, the new EC has 1500 members, comprising five sectors with 300 persons each. The five sectors include the original 'industrial, commercial and financial sectors' ('the first sector') and 'the professions' ('the second sector'). The third sector (originally labelled 'labour, social services, religious and other sectors') is reconstituted as 'grassroots, labour, religious and other sectors'. 'Grassroots' refers to designated grassroot social organisations in different parts of Hong Kong, associations of people from the same province in mainland China, etc. The fourth sector, originally known as 'the political sector', now comprises LegCo members and representatives of 'district organisations and other organisations'.

The original fourth sector had included, among others, 117 EC members elected by District Councillors; this was a feature of the reform introduced in 2010. The new fourth sector no longer has members elected

[38] The meaning of this requirement is stipulated in the Public Offices (Candidacy and Taking Up Offices) (Miscellaneous Amendments) Ordinance 2021.

by members of the District Councils. Instead, the district organisations entitled to elect EC members in the fourth sector are mainly district-level advisory bodies appointed by the government. They also include associations formed by Hong Kong people residing on the mainland.

The newly created fifth sector comprises all Hong Kong deputies to the NPC, Hong Kong members of the National Committee of the CPPCC and representatives of Hong Kong members of national (all-China) associations in various domains.

Another significant element of the revamp concerns the voter eligibility criteria in the first, second and third sectors of the EC. Departing from the pre-existing system, the sub-sectors within these three sectors no longer include individuals or natural persons as voters; they now only include office-holders or representatives of designated corporate bodies or organisations in the sub-sectors concerned.

A. 'Patriots Ruling Hong Kong'

The declared purpose of the electoral reform was to provide institutional safeguards for the realisation of the principle of 'patriots ruling Hong Kong', first enunciated by Deng Xiaoping in the late 1980s. Beijing hoped that this overhaul would put an end to the political instability and conflicts, constant filibuster in LegCo and frequent anti-China mobilisation of the public by opposition politicians and activists that had plagued post-1997 Hong Kong for years.

The overhaul reduced dramatically the space for political participation that the 'opposition' or 'non-Establishment' camp (such as the 'pan-democrats' and 'localists') previously had, and ensured that the overwhelming majority of the members of both the EC and LegCo are drawn from the 'pro-Establishment' camp. We may observe this from the results of the first elections of the EC and LegCo held after the revamp.[39] In the EC elected on 19 September 2021, only one member (out of its 1448 elected members) previously belonged to the 'opposition' or 'pan-democrats' camp. In the LegCo election held on 19 December 2021, there were a total of 153 candidates competing for 90 seats. Candidates were allowed to declare their political stance or affiliation in their electoral manifestoes. According to their own declarations,

[39] See Hong Kong newspapers (eg *Ming Pao*, *South China Morning Post*) of 20–21 September 2021 and 20–21 December 2021.

13 candidates belonged to the 'non-Establishment camp'. Only one of them, Mr Tik Chi-yuen, was elected into LegCo. Therefore, the seventh-term LegCo (2022–25) comprises only one 'non-Establishment' member, with the other 89 members widely perceived to be from the 'pro-Establishment' camp.

The political orientation of these 89 members was demonstrated when they all signed a joint statement in support of the police's law enforcement action against *Stand News*. Tik Chi-yuen was the only LegCo member who did not sign that statement.[40] *Stand News* was an influential online media published in Chinese that shared the political orientation of the pan-democrats. On 29 December 2021, the National Security Department of the Hong Kong Police Force arrested the leading members of *Stand News* and froze the company's assets for allegedly committing sedition. Sedition is criminalised under the Crimes Ordinance, but the CFA has affirmed that it also constitutes an offence against national security, even though it is not an offence prescribed under the NSL.[41]

B. The Policy Behind the Electoral Reform

China's view on the electoral overhaul was clearly articulated at the NPC session when the electoral revamp was passed. Mr Han Zheng, Vice-Premier in charge of Hong Kong affairs, commented publicly that the electoral reform was not a question of 'being democratic or not democratic', but was 'a struggle between subversion and anti-subversion'.[42] He implied that – and this point was expressly mentioned in some Chinese media – the purpose of the electoral revamp was to prevent 'anti-China' political forces in Hong Kong, with the support of hostile Western forces, from seizing power by electoral means.

For the Chinese authorities, the electoral revamp was necessary in light of the unprecedented and overwhelming electoral victory of opposition politicians in the District Council election held on 24 November 2019. This election took place in the heat of the anti-extradition movement,

[40] 'Stand News Pair Denied Bail as Lam Slams Critics' *South China Morning Post* (31 December 2021).

[41] *HKSAR v Ng Hau Yi Sidney* [2021] HKCFA 42.

[42] 'Han Zheng: *wanshan Xianggang xuanju zhidu shi baowei zhan*' *Hong Kong Economic Journal* (8 March 2021, in Chinese); 'Han Zheng: *gaizhi shi dianfu fandianfu wenti*' *Ming Pao* (8 March 2021, in Chinese).

which saw violent clashes between demonstrators and the police. The opposition, including 'pan-democrats' and 'localists', won 57 per cent of the popular vote and 85 per cent of the District Council seats, thereby occupying a majority in 17 out of 18 District Councils.[43] This election result was particularly shocking for the central authorities, as the pro-establishment camp had won a majority of District Council seats in past elections. Subsequently, 49 of the District Council members elected in 2019 were disqualified on the ground that their oaths to uphold the Basic Law and owe allegiance to the HKSAR were deemed invalid.[44] Many other District Councillors also resigned on their own accord before taking their oaths, because they were concerned that any subsequent disqualification might operate retrospectively such that they would be required to pay back their past salaries.[45]

Beijing's thinking behind the electoral revamp ran counter to its original thinking at the time the Basic Law was drafted. Articles 45 and 68 of the Basic Law regarding the ultimate realisation of universal suffrage, the provisions in Annex II on the progressive reduction in the number of LegCo members elected by the EC and the progressive increase in the number of members elected by universal suffrage in the GCs seemed to indicate that universal suffrage as a mode of election was more democratic than an election by the EC and should therefore be realised over time. In contrast, the electoral revamp of 2021 was ostensibly pursued on the premise that 'Western-style democracy' is not suitable for the HKSAR. The new thinking is that Hong Kong should practise a 'democracy with Hong Kong characteristics'.[46] Otherwise, the dual objectives of OCTS, which include the protection of national sovereignty, security and China's developmental interests as well as the long-term stability and prosperity of Hong Kong, cannot be achieved.

VI. CONCLUSION

The OCTS project in Hong Kong is a constitutional experiment. It rests on a principal paradox: to maintain in the HKSAR a legal system based

[43] See n 20 above.

[44] District Council members were subject to the oath-taking requirement for the first time when the Public Offices (Candidacy and Taking Up Offices) (Miscellaneous Amendments) Ordinance was enacted in 2021.

[45] See n 20 above.

[46] State Council Information Office White Paper, *Hong Kong Democratic Progress Under the Framework of One Country, Two Systems* (December 2021).

on English common law that seeks to protect civil liberties according to international human rights standards, while upholding the interests of Chinese sovereignty and security as understood by a party-state that practises a kind of authoritarian rule that is incompatible with some of the basic values and aspirations shared by many Hong Kong people.

Political tensions and conflicts between the 'pro-China' and 'pro-democracy' camps have stymied the implementation of the Basic Law. Political instability in post-1997 Hong Kong can perhaps be attributed to the inherent contradiction between the 'Two Systems' within OCTS – the authoritarian party-led system on the mainland and a semi-democratic system with some elements of liberal constitutionalism in Hong Kong. In retrospect, it would appear that some of the major difficulties and controversies that the HKSAR has experienced arose because the Basic Law drafters in the late 1980s were too sanguine about the challenges ahead.

For example, in retrospect, the requirement in Article 23 of the Basic Law that the HKSAR should on its own legislate to safeguard China's national security was based on an over-optimistic assessment of the HKSAR government's determination and Hong Kong people's willingness to fulfil this constitutional duty. Moreover, the commitment in the Basic Law to the eventual realisation of democracy by universal suffrage (in the election of the CE and all legislators) resulted in 'an inherently unstable regime, because [the regime] will be taken to task to deliver' on this constitutional promise.[47] Therefore, the political system of the HKSAR – which cannot be changed without the consent of both the central government and (before the 2021 amendments to Annexes I and II to the Basic Law) a two-thirds majority in the HKSAR legislature – is unstable and insufficiently legitimate. In affirming the ultimate goal of universal suffrage, the Basic Law legitimises the struggle for this goal and, in a sense, de-legitimises the existing political system, which falls short of the ideal of universal suffrage.

The OCTS policy achieved some degree of success by securing a smooth handover in 1997 while maintaining Hong Kong's vibrant economy and its status as an international financial centre. However, as time progressed, tensions arising from the coexistence and interaction of the 'two systems' gradually escalated. These tensions were evidenced by the NPCSC's promulgation of Basic Law interpretations, the failed attempt

[47] HC Kuan, 'Escape from Politics: Hong Kong's Predicament of Political Development' (1998) 21 *International Journal of Public Administration* 1423, 1444.

in 2003 to legislate on national security, the social movement in 2012 against the proposed 'national education' curriculum in schools that led to its withdrawal, continuous struggles for democratisation that led to the Occupy Central movement in 2014 and the increased polarisation of Hong Kong's society since then.

After the failure of the Occupy Central movement, some democracy activists in Hong Kong gave up on the hope of achieving democratisation within the framework of OCTS and became advocates of Hong Kong's self-determination or independence. They participated actively in the anti-extradition movement of 2019. Dissatisfaction with an existing system of regional autonomy often leads to outright demands for secession. The case of Hong Kong illustrates this logic at work.

In response, the PRC authorities enacted the HKSAR NSL in 2020 and introduced the electoral overhaul of 2021. While the NSL drew a red line for the 'One Country' component of the OCTS model, the electoral revamp was designed to ensure that only those considered 'patriots' by the central government can continue to govern or participate in the governance of the HKSAR without being hampered by public demands for universal suffrage or accountability through universal suffrage. These developments may be viewed as attempts to assert the absolute precedence of the 'One Country' principle over the 'Two Systems' principle in OCTS, to crush secessionist demands once and for all, and to completely eliminate any risk of Hong Kong being used as a base for subversion against China's socialist regime by 'anti-China' political forces in Hong Kong and overseas. The latter geopolitical consideration is particularly important given the prospect of a Cold War developing between the USA and the PRC.

Before the 2020 developments, the HKSAR's political system has been characterised as a kind of hybrid constitutionalism[48] or liberal authoritarianism[49] in which both liberal and authoritarian elements coexist. The enactment of the NSL, together with the electoral revamp of 2021, have undoubtedly increased the authoritarian elements and reduced the liberal elements in Hong Kong's political and legal system, and re-tilted the balance of OCTS towards the 'One Country' principle. What remains to be seen is how much these authoritarian elements will increase in the future, and what will be the magnitude of this shift towards the 'One Country' principle in the years to come.

[48] EC Ip, *Hybrid Constitutionalism: The Politics of Constitutional Review in the Chinese Special Administrative Regions* (Cambridge University Press, 2019).

[49] Lau Siu-kai, *Huigui hou Xianggang de dute zhengzhi xingtai* [*The Unique Political Form in Post-Handover Hong Kong*] (Commercial Press, 2017).

FURTHER READING

Chan, J and Lim, CL, *Law of the Hong Kong Constitution*, 3rd edn (Sweet & Maxwell, 2021).
Loh, C, *Underground Front: The Chinese Communist Party in Hong Kong*, 2nd edn (Hong Kong University Press, 2018).
Ma, N, *Political Development in Hong Kong* (Hong Kong University Press, 2007).

5

Constitutional Role of the Judiciary

Judicial Independence – Executive-Led Government – Separation of Powers – Constitutional Review – Interpretation of the Standing Committee of the National People's Congress – Margin of Discretion – Principle of Judicial Non-intervention in the Internal Process of the Legislature – Foreign Judges

THE JUDICIARY OF the Hong Kong Special Administrative Region (HKSAR) plays a crucial role in the operation of the constitutional arrangement of 'One Country, Two Systems'. It is the guardian of the constitutional rights of the people of Hong Kong. It also mediates the relationship between the central authorities and the HKSAR by exercising its power to interpret the Basic Law when adjudicating constitutional disputes. In this chapter, we shall begin by looking at the structure and organisation of the court system of the HKSAR. We shall then consider the role of the Hong Kong courts in the constitutional review of local legislation, as well as how the local courts interface with the mainland Chinese legal system and share the power of interpretation of the Basic Law with the central authorities. Finally, we shall consider the position of the judiciary in the context of the HKSAR's unique political system, which combines features of both the principles of 'separation of powers' and 'executive-led government', two legal concepts operative in Hong Kong that we will elaborate upon below.

I. STRUCTURE, ORGANISATION AND COMPOSITION OF HONG KONG'S COURTS

Under the Basic Law, the Hong Kong judiciary is empowered to exercise its judicial powers independently, free from any interference.[1] The power of final adjudication is vested in the Court of Final Appeal (CFA).[2] During adjudication, the Hong Kong courts are authorised to interpret on their own Basic Law provisions that are within the limits of the city's autonomy.[3] The courts may also interpret other provisions of the Basic Law. But, as discussed in chapter two, if a case reaches the CFA and concerns Basic Law provisions regarding affairs which are the responsibility of the Central People's Government, or concerning the relationship between the central authorities and the region, the CFA must seek an Interpretation of the relevant constitutional provision from the Standing Committee of the National People's Congress (NPCSC) if the interpretation of that clause will affect the judgment of the case at hand. Once an Interpretation has been promulgated, the courts will be bound by it.[4] The common law continues to apply in Hong Kong,[5] and the Basic Law expressly authorises local judges to refer to precedents of other common law jurisdictions.[6]

The CFA sits at the apex of the Hong Kong judiciary. Below the CFA in the judicial hierarchy is the High Court of Hong Kong, which comprises the Court of Appeal and the Court of First Instance (CFI). The subordinate courts comprise the District Court, the Magistrates' Courts and specialised tribunals. Notably, the Basic Law only requires the Chief Justice and the Chief Judge of the High Court to be Chinese citizens.[7] Furthermore, foreign judges from other common law jurisdictions are authorised to sit on the CFA as Non-Permanent Judges.[8] The issue of foreign nationals serving on the Hong Kong judiciary has been a recurring bugbear with mainland Chinese commentators. They are concerned that foreign nationals are not sufficiently protective of national interests or are too sympathetic to anti-government dissidents. But to date, the

[1] Basic Law, Art 85 (BL85).
[2] BL82.
[3] BL158.
[4] ibid.
[5] BL8.
[6] BL84.
[7] BL90.
[8] BL82.

Hong Kong government has not announced any plans to reform the judiciary on this front.[9]

The Hong Kong judiciary enjoys significant autonomy from the Hong Kong executive and legislative branches of government. It is the Chief Justice who heads the Hong Kong judiciary.[10] The Chief Justice, the Permanent Judges on the CFA and judges of the High Court and District Courts have security of tenure until retirement.[11] They can only be removed for cause, and only by the Chief Executive upon a recommendation by an independent tribunal and the Legislative Council's endorsement of the removal.[12] To date, no attempts have ever been made to impeach any judge.

The Chief Justice has overall responsibility for the administration of the HKSAR judiciary, and he shapes his bench in two main ways. The first relates to judicial appointments. The Basic Law provides that judges in Hong Kong are appointed by the Chief Executive, on the recommendation of the Judicial Officers Recommendation Commission (JORC).[13] In practice, no judicial appointments have been made without the recommendation of the Commission. Judicial appointments to the CFA, as well as the appointment of the Chief Judge of the High Court, must be endorsed by the Legislative Council.[14] The Legislative Council has so far endorsed all such appointments. The government's views on judicial appointments may be reflected by its appointees on the JORC, particularly the Secretary for Justice. As we will discuss below, national security cases are treated differently: the Chief Executive will appoint 'designated judges' – selected from amongst existing judges – to hear national security cases, but this appointment system has courted controversy. Aside from such appointments, retired CFA judges have disclosed that the government has not otherwise intervened in the process of selection of judges in Hong Kong.[15]

[9] However, it is noteworthy that under the HKSAR's National Security Law, national security cases may only be heard by 'designated judges'. See n 21 below and the reference to ch 2.

[10] Hong Kong Court of Final Appeal Ordinance (CFAO), s 6(2).

[11] The retirement age of CFA judges is 70: see s 14 of the CFAO read with s 13A(1). After the Chief Justice or a Permanent Judge reaches the age of 70, their term may be extended for not more than two periods of three years. CFAO, s 14(2).

[12] BL89 and 90.

[13] BL88.

[14] BL90.

[15] Farewell Sitting for the Honourable Mr Justice Chan PJ (18 October 2013) (2013) 16 HKCFAR 1012, 1019.

In substance, the Chief Justice, who chairs the nine-member JORC, has great latitude in shaping the composition of the bench, especially the crucial CFA. Typically, the JORC comprises the Chief Justice, the Secretary for Justice and seven other members appointed by the Chief Executive (CE): two judges nominated by the Chief Justice; a barrister and a solicitor nominated respectively by the Bar Association and the Law Society; and three lay persons chosen by the CE.

The presence of the Secretary for Justice (SJ) and the government appointees on the JORC would impose ex ante constraints on the Chief Justice to pursue candidates who are perceived by the HKSAR government to be in the political mainstream. But as, in practice, all Permanent Judges of the CFA are promoted from the Court of Appeal, and all Court of Appeal judges are drawn from the CFI, the Chief Justice, who commands the entire Hong Kong judiciary, is in the best position to recruit, evaluate and expedite the promotion of his preferred candidates through the ranks. The lay persons on the JORC, whose memberships are refreshed regularly, are usually drawn from the corporate world and academia (in disciplines other than law itself), and they would simply not have the in-depth knowledge of the Hong Kong judiciary to independently determine which Court of Appeal judges deserve promotion to the CFA. The SJ – typically a barrister (except the first SJ, Ms Elsie Leung, who is a solicitor) – only serves for a term conterminous with the CE who appoints them, and returns to private practice thereafter. Unless the Chief Justice is seeking to promote an individual the government deems politically controversial, the SJ too will be hard-pressed to openly block the promotion of the appellate judges the former wants, especially if the SJ will appear once again as mere counsel before these judges in a few years. Therefore, so long as the Chief Justice does not seek to promote any controversial personalities, he would in all probability get his preferred nominees approved. Furthermore, if the Permanent Judge whom the Chief Justice is seeking to appoint is 70 years old or older, the Chief Justice is not even statutorily required to consult the JORC; the Chief Justice alone decides, subject to the CE's formal approval.[16] Rather extraordinarily, in Hong Kong, a retiring Chief Justice also chairs the JORC that selects his successor.

The Chief Justice can also shape the bench by determining the composition of the CFA panels.[17] The CFA hears substantive appeals in

[16] CFAO, s 14(2)(b).

[17] CFAO, ss 16(1), (2) and (4). See SNM Young, A Da Roza and Y Ghai, 'Role of the Chief Justice' in SNM Young, A Da Roza and Y Ghai (eds), *Hong Kong's Court of Final Appeal: The Development of the Law in China's Hong Kong* (Cambridge University Press, 2014) 230.

panels of five judges.[18] Typically, this will include the Chief Justice, the three Permanent Judges (PJ) of the CFA and a Non-Permanent Judge (NPJ).[19] Although there are both local and overseas NPJs, an overseas NPJ is rostered on the CFA bench in most cases. The overseas NPJs have included concurrent or retired judges from the highest courts in the UK, Australia, New Zealand and Canada. Notably, the Chief Justice alone decides which NPJ hears a particular case; and of all the CFA cases heard to date, overseas NPJs have dissented on only three occasions, and never once in a constitutional law dispute. But that is not to say that the overseas NPJs merely rubber-stamp the CFA's preferred policy agenda. It is just that the chances of an eminent jurist from a Western common law jurisdiction voting against a majority of the CFA, when the latter wants to align itself with liberal Western constitutional practices, are practically nil. The converse may not be true – overseas NPJs may not accord the same level of deference to the local judges if the CFA was seeking to depart from established Western conceptions of human rights.

In view of these two important variables on judicial appointments and composition, the HKSAR's first Chief Justice, Andrew Li, never dissented in the 13 years he served at the helm of the CFA. The second Chief Justice, Geoffrey Ma, who led the CFA from 2010 till early 2021, found himself in the minority only once.[20] Neither of them ever dissented in any constitutional decision. The third and incumbent Chief Justice, Andrew Cheung, who assumed office in January 2021, has not dissented to date.

For cases adjudicated in Hong Kong under the National Security Law (NSL) enacted in June 2020, the CE of Hong Kong will decide on the list of judges (termed 'designated judges' under the NSL) who can hear these national security cases.[21] There are concerns that this system is inconsistent with judicial independence: it is possible that the CE will only designate judges who are politically more 'pro-establishment' and are more likely to render decisions favourable to the government. On the other hand, it has been pointed out that all these 'designated judges' will only be appointed from the pool of pre-existing Hong Kong judges, and the Chief Justice will be consulted prior to the appointment.[22] Furthermore, once the list of designated judges has been decided upon, the specific

[18] CFAO, s 16(3).

[19] CFAO, s 16(1) and BL82.

[20] *T v Commissioner of Police* [2014] 17 HKCFAR 593.

[21] See ch 2's discussion of the NSL in the section on the 'Application of National Laws to the HKSAR'.

[22] NSL, Art 44.

rostering of individual judges for any case is the sole responsibility of the chief judge of the court concerned.[23] Judges who are foreign nationals, including overseas NPJs, are still eligible to be appointed as 'designated judges' to hear these cases.[24] The effect of the NSL's enactment on the operation of Hong Kong's judiciary is unclear, but it is noteworthy that since the passage of the NSL, one Australian and two British NPJs have resigned from the CFA, and another British NPJ has declined a reappointment. On the other hand, Patrick Keane, a former judge of the High Court of Australia, who had also served as Chief Justice of Australia's Federal Court, joined as an NPJ in 2023.[25]

As discussed below, the CFA is not supreme as the NPCSC is empowered under the Basic Law to promulgate an Interpretation that overrules any constitutional interpretation of the courts. However, this is not to say that the courts are politically irrelevant in Hong Kong's constitutional landscape. The Hong Kong judiciary has built up a history of invalidating legislation since the Bill of Rights Ordinance was enacted in the territory in 1991. Like all political practices, judicial practices are path-dependent,[26] such that Hong Kong judges can appeal to history and stare decisis for continuing the practice of enforcing human rights against the Hong Kong government.[27] Furthermore, Beijing will not reverse every decision by the CFA that it dislikes as it does not want to rescind from its commitment to allow the HKSAR to 'exercise a high degree of autonomy and enjoy … independent judicial power',[28] as this would adversely impact on Hong Kong's long-term viability as an international financial centre.

[23] Statement by Chief Justice of Court of Final Appeal, 2 July 2020, www.info.gov.hk/gia/general/202007/02/P2020070200414.htm.

[24] In *HKSAR v Lai Chee Ying* [2021] HKCFA 3, the CFA's first substantive decision on the NSL, the designated CFA judges included, inter alia, two judges of foreign nationality (one PJ and one local NPJ (a retired Hong Kong judge), but no overseas NPJ).

[25] 'Veteran Australian Judge James Spigelman Resigns from Hong Kong's Top Court, Citing National Security Law' *South China Morning Post* (18 September 2020); 'National Security Law: Former British Top Judge to Quit Hong Kong's Highest Court' *South China Morning Post* (4 June 2021) www.scmp.com/news/hong-kong/law-and-crime/article/3136014/national-security-law-britains-former-top-judge-quit; 'UK Judges Withdraw from Hong Kong's Court of Final Appeal' *The Guardian* (30 March 2022) www.theguardian.com/world/2022/mar/30/uk-judges-withdraw-from-hong-kong-court-of-final-appeal; 'Appointment of Non-permanent Judge from Another Common Law Jurisdiction of the Court of Final Appeal' www.info.gov.hk/gia/general/202301/13/P2023011300471.htm.

[26] AS Sweet, 'Path Dependence, Precedent, and Judicial Power' in M Shapiro and AS Sweet, *On Law, Politics, and Judicialization* (Oxford University Press, 2002) 112.

[27] PJ Yap, *Courts and Democracies in Asia* (Cambridge University Press, 2017) 47–48.

[28] BL2.

Unlike the Singapore government, it has not been easy for the HKSAR government to reverse adverse constitutional decisions handed down by their courts. This was apparently the case before the electoral reform of 2021; the impact of this revamp remains to be seen. As discussed in chapter four, before the 2021 electoral overhaul, Legislative Council (LegCo) seats were partly elected by functional constituencies (FCs) and partly by geographical constituencies (GCs). For the FC electoral seats, the individual legislators are accountable electorally only to the voters in their specific sectoral constituencies. For the GC seats, the use of proportional representation before the 2021 electoral revamp led to the electoral success of multiple small parties and individual lawmakers. As the CE is not drawn from any political party, and with the presence of multiple political parties, independents and FC representatives in LegCo, the HKSAR government has to constantly broker different interests among competing political forces when it seeks to pass legislation. While this is not difficult when the government is whipping up support for legislation that Beijing considers imperative, the pro-Beijing lawmakers' interests often diverge from the HKSAR government on issues that are not fundamental to Beijing.

This loose and sometimes fragile coalition between the HKSAR executive government and the pro-Beijing lawmakers has therefore limited the former's ability to command a legislative majority on non-core issues. The political impasse, in turn, provides the Hong Kong judiciary with significant discretion to rule against the government on non-core issues, as we will explain in chapter six.

II. CONSTITUTIONAL REVIEW OF LOCAL LEGISLATION

In the first constitutional decision handed down by the CFA in *Ng Ka Ling v Director of Immigration*,[29] the Court emphatically and unanimously asserted its power to engage in constitutional review of local legislation. This was a fundamental constitutional principle established by the courts in the HKSAR after China's resumption of sovereignty over the city. The CFA also determined that the exercise of this jurisdiction is a matter of obligation, not of discretion. Since *Ng Ka Ling*, the Hong Kong courts have continued to exercise their constitutional jurisdiction to invalidate law that they determine to be contrary to the Basic Law. This will be discussed in greater detail in chapter six.

[29] (1999) 2 HKCFAR 4.

Notably, the Basic Law does not expressly state that the Hong Kong judiciary has this constitutional power. But the CFA justified its actions in the following terms:

> In exercising their judicial power conferred by the Basic Law, the courts of the Region have a duty to enforce and interpret that law … In exercising this jurisdiction, the courts perform their constitutional role under the Basic Law of acting as a constitutional check on the executive and legislative branches of government to ensure that they act in accordance with the Basic Law.[30]

While the CFA did not explicitly cite any Basic Law provision, its position is defensible. The Basic Law provides that 'no law enacted by the legislature of the [HKSAR] shall contravene [the Basic Law]',[31] and it also confers upon the Hong Kong judiciary the power to interpret the Basic Law.[32] Therefore, in exercising this power of constitutional interpretation, the Hong Kong judiciary also possesses the implied duty and power to invalidate any local legislation that contravenes this constitutional instrument.

III. JUDICIAL REVIEW OF THE CENTRAL AUTHORITIES' (NPC/NPCSC) ACTS

In *Ng Ka Ling*, the CFA also declared that the court had a 'duty to declare invalid'[33] any act of the NPC or NPCSC that is inconsistent with the Basic Law. As the CFA explained, the Basic Law was enacted to implement China's commitment – under the Joint Declaration with the British – to preserve its basic policies regarding Hong Kong for 50 years. A fortiori, the courts' jurisdiction to interpret the Basic Law 'necessarily entails the jurisdiction stated above over acts of the National People's Congress and its Standing Committee to ensure their consistency with the Basic Law'.

This legal proposition is highly controversial as it poses a direct challenge to Beijing's sovereignty over the city and the central authorities' interpretive mandate in Hong Kong. By claiming the power to invalidate NPC and NPCSC legislative acts, the CFA was in essence claiming that the Basic Law had the same constitutional status as the

[30] ibid 25.
[31] BL11.
[32] BL158.
[33] *Ng Ka Ling* (n 29) 26.

PRC Constitution, and the Hong Kong judiciary had the concomitant constitutional authority to superintend the legislative actions of the NPCSC. Notably, even the Supreme People's Court in China does not have such power of constitutional interpretation. This power resides exclusively with the NPCSC.[34]

Furthermore, if we examine the terms of the Basic Law, the CFA's position is equally untenable. Article 158(1) of the Basic Law vests the power of interpretation in the Standing Committee of the NPC. Article 158(2) continues by adding that the Standing Committee shall 'authorise' the courts of Hong Kong to interpret, on their own, provisions of the Basic Law that are within the limits of the region's autonomy. Since the power of interpretation granted to the Hong Kong courts is a delegated power from the NPCSC, it is legally untenable for the grantee to possess the powers to override the acts of the grantor.[35] Article 158(3) of the Basic Law confirms this reading:

> If the courts of the Region, in adjudicating cases, need to interpret the provisions of this Law concerning affairs which are the responsibility of the Central People's Government, or *concerning the relationship between the Central Authorities and the Region*, the Courts of the Region shall, before making their final judgments which are non-appealable, seek an interpretation of the relevant provisions from the Standing Committee of the National People's Congress through the Court of Final Appeal of the Region. When the Standing Committee makes an interpretation of the provisions concerned, the courts of the Region, in applying those provisions, *shall follow the interpretation of the Standing Committee*. (emphasis added)

Certainly, the question of whether Hong Kong courts have the authority to invalidate NPC legislative acts concerns 'the relationship between the Central Authorities and the Region'. Insofar as the CFA has a constitutional obligation to seek and abide by an Interpretation from the Standing Committee, it is arguable that the HKSAR judiciary is deprived of the power to invalidate NPC legislative acts that the court considers to be inconsistent with the Basic Law without first seeking an Interpretation from the NPCSC.

In the aftermath of *Ng Ka Ling*, the Hong Kong government swiftly proceeded with a request for the CFA to 'clarify' its decision. The court

[34] 1982 Chinese Constitution, Art 67. See also Q Zhang, *The Constitution of China: A Contextual Analysis* (Hart Publishing, 2012) 135.

[35] PJ Yap, '10 Years of the Basic Law: The Rise, Retreat and Resurgence of Judicial Power in Hong Kong' (2007) 36 *Common Law World Review* 166, 170.

acceded to this request. In a very terse judgment, the CFA in *Ng Ka Ling (No 2)*[36] accepted that NPCSC had the authority to issue a constitutional interpretation under Article 158 of the Basic Law, and this Interpretation would have to be followed by the courts of the HKSAR. But more interestingly, the CFA followed this concession with a veiled reassertion of judicial power: 'the Court accepts that it cannot question, the authority of the National People's Congress or the Standing Committee to do any act which is in accordance with the provisions of the Basic Law and the procedure therein'.[37] What the CFA left deliberately unspoken was the Court's amenability to questioning acts of the NPC or the Standing Committee that it deemed *not* to be in accordance with the Basic Law.

Nevertheless, a weaker version of the clarificatory statement can be defended. The CFA could mean that if the NPCSC does not comply with any explicit procedures laid out in the Basic Law, eg consulting the Basic Law Committee before applying a National Law to Hong Kong[38] or before issuing an Interpretation,[39] those laws passed thereunder would not be a valid exercise of constitutional power and would have no legal force in Hong Kong. But it is also important to note that *all* of Hong Kong's Basic Law Committee members are appointed by the central government in Beijing, and this procedural impediment in reality would have no tangible bite.

Alternatively, the CFA could be taken to mean that the courts can disable themselves from giving effect to NPCSC legislative acts that violate the Basic Law. After all, since the judiciary is a creature of the Basic Law, and so far as Hong Kong judges have to swear allegiance to the Basic Law, the judiciary is disempowered from applying legal principles that violate the source of its powers.[40]

Unlike the CFA, the lower courts in Hong Kong have openly disavowed any judicial role in invalidating NPCSC legislative acts. On 31 August 2014, the NPCSC issued its Decision on electoral reform in Hong Kong. In essence, the Decision allowed for the Election Committee that

[36] (1999) 2 HKCFAR 141.

[37] ibid 142.

[38] BL18.

[39] BL158.

[40] PJ Yap, 'Interpreting the Basic Law and the Adjudication of Politically Sensitive Questions' (2007) 6(3) *Chinese Journal of International Law* 543, 550; see also E Ip, 'Interpreting Interpretations: A Methodology for the Judicial Enforcement of Legislative Interpretations of the Hong Kong Basic Law' [2017] *PL* 552.

currently picks the CE to transition into a nominating committee, and all registered Hong Kong voters would then vote on candidates who have been pre-screened by this nominating committee, which is likely to be dominated by the pro-Beijing camp. Consequently, the Hong Kong government published various proposals on how the HKSAR could introduce electoral reform in accordance with this NPCSC decision. A pro-democracy activist was dissatisfied with the democratic reforms sanctioned by the NPCSC decision and the constitutional proposals introduced, and she took the Hong Kong government to court. Nonetheless, the CFI in *Leung Lai Kwok Yvonne v Chief Secretary for Administration*[41] swiftly refused to grant her leave to seek judicial review. The CFI held emphatically that 'a decision of the NPCSC is not subject to review by the court in Hong Kong, as the court simply has no jurisdiction to do so'. Since the NPCSC had the 'ultimate authority to disapprove' any constitutional proposals endorsed by the Hong Kong legislature, the CFI also ruled that the local government was under no legal duty to consult the people on 'non-viable options' that would contradict NPCSC's stipulated framework for electoral reform.

Similar judicial deference was accorded to NPCSC legislative acts in *Leung Chung Hang Sixtus v President of the Legislative Council*.[42] In that case, the court had to address the constitutionality of a Co-location Arrangement within West Kowloon Station. In furtherance of a seamless high-speed rail link connecting Hong Kong to the mainland, this Co-location Arrangement carved out a Mainland Port Area (MPA) within the West Kowloon Station for mainland immigration personnel to conduct immigration procedures therein, and this MPA would also be placed under mainland jurisdiction. Notably, this Co-location Arrangement was formally approved by an NPCSC decision dated 27 December 2017 before it was passed into law in Hong Kong. While mainland laws would be enforced within the MPA, arguably contrary to Article 18 of the Basic Law, the court once again reaffirmed that Hong Kong courts have no power to determine whether the NPCSC Decision is invalid under Hong Kong laws.

IV. JUDICIAL TREATMENT OF NPCSC INTERPRETATIONS

As elaborated upon in chapter two, Article 158(3) establishes a procedure for a 'judicial reference' (ie reference by the CFA) of certain Basic Law

[41] [2015] HKCFI 929.
[42] [2019] 1 HKLRD 292 (CFI), [2021] HKCA 871.

provisions (termed 'Excluded Provisions' in *Ng Ka Ling*) to the NPCSC for interpretation. Excluded Provisions refer to provisions concerning affairs that are the responsibility of the central authorities or concerning the relationship between the central authorities and the HKSAR. In *Ng Ka Ling*, the government had argued that the Excluded Provisions were engaged and they should be referred to the NPCSC for interpretation. But the CFA held that as the 'predominant provision' to be interpreted in this case was not an Excluded Provision; no reference to the NPCSC was necessary and the CFA thus decided the case on its own.

After the CFA rendered its decision in *Ng Ka Ling* and the related decision on the same day in *Chan Kam Nga*[43] – both cases concerned the constitutional right of abode in Hong Kong of mainland-born children born to Hong Kong permanent residents – the Hong Kong government estimated that *Ng Ka Ling/Chan Kam Nga* would result in a massive influx (1.67 million people over the next 10 years) of mainland Chinese immigrants into Hong Kong and strain the city's healthcare, housing and social welfare system. Therefore, CE Tung Chee-hwa referred the relevant Basic Law provisions to Beijing for interpretation, which in effect was a request for an NPCSC Interpretation to review the CFA's rulings in *Ng Ka Ling/Chan Kam Nga*. In June 1999, the NPCSC promulgated its first-ever Interpretation of the Basic Law.[44] Disagreeing with the CFA, the NPCSC stated that mainland-born children of Hong Kong permanent residents had to first obtain a one-way exit permit from the mainland authorities (in accordance with Article 22(4) of the Basic Law) before they could migrate to Hong Kong. Furthermore, for this right to arise under Article 24(2)(3) of the Basic Law, at least one of the parents had to be a Hong Kong permanent resident at the time of the child's birth. The original parties in the *Ng Ka Ling/Chan Kam Nga* litigations were held not to be affected by this Interpretation, but the rights of all others would be determined by reference to it.

In *Lau Kong Yung v Director of Immigration*,[45] the CFA enforced the NPCSC's First Interpretation against persons who were not parties in the original litigation and affirmed the Director of Immigration's right to issue the removal orders against them. In that case, the CFA affirmed that the NPCSC's power of constitutional interpretation is 'general and unqualified', and its Interpretation on any Basic Law provision is 'binding on the courts of the HKSAR'.[46]

[43] (1999) 2 HKCFAR 82.
[44] See ch 2, s VI.A.
[45] (1999) 2 HKCFAR 300.
[46] ibid 324.

This was a major pronouncement as the CFA herein recognised the free-standing general interpretive mandate that the Standing Committee possessed, an unqualified power the Court had not previously affirmed in *Ng Ka Ling (1)* or *(2)*. There were many options open to the Court. It could have held, as counsel for the abode seekers argued, that the Standing Committee could only issue an Interpretation upon a judicial reference by the Court over a dispute relating to the Excluded Provisions. But, as recognised by the CFA, the authority delegated by Article 158(2) and (3) to the judiciary stems from the general power of interpretation vested in the Standing Committee under Article 158(1). To accept counsel's submission, the Court would be denying the Standing Committee's power to interpret all provisions of the Basic Law save the Excluded Provisions, a position inconsistent with the general power conferred by Article 158(1). Furthermore, accepting this submission would mean that even if the CFA is in breach of its obligation under Article 158(3) to refer an Excluded Provision to the Standing Committee when the conditions for a reference are satisfied, there will be no remedy available to the central authorities.

The CFA in *Lau Kong Yung* held that the Standing Committee's power to interpret the Basic Law extended to all provisions of the Basic Law. On the other hand, Ling Bing has argued that the legislative history of Article 158 lends strong support for the view that the NPCSC 'does not have or at least cannot exercise, the power of interpretation'[47] vis-à-vis Basic Law provisions that are within Hong Kong's autonomy. In support of his view, Ling quotes the Basic Law Drafting Committee in January 1989, when it introduced a draft version of a constitutional clause that was *identical* to the final enacted version of Article 158:

> With respect to the power of interpretation, two major amendments have been made. (1) In order to increase the power of the courts of the HKSAR in interpreting the Basic Law, the second paragraph of Article 169 of the Draft Basic Law for Solicitation of Opinions is amended to read: 'The Standing Committee of the National People's Congress shall authorize the courts of the Hong Kong Special Administrative Region to interpret on their own, in adjudicating cases, the provisions of this Law which are within the limits of the autonomy of the Region.' As a result of this authorisation, the NPCSC *will not interpret those provisions of the Basic Law which are within the*

[47] L Bing, 'Subject Matter Limitation on the NPCSC's Power to Interpret the Basic Law' (2007) 37 *Hong Kong Law Journal* 619, 633.

> *limits of the autonomy of the HKSAR* and which are involved in the adjudication of cases by the courts of HKSAR.[48] (emphasis added)

Notably, in this passage, the Basic Law Drafting Committee expressly disavowed any intention of the NPCSC to interpret constitutional provisions that are within the limits of Hong Kong's autonomy.

Notwithstanding the CFA's recognition of the plenary supremacy of the NPCSC's interpretative power in *Lau Kong Yung*, the Court interestingly announced that parts of the impugned immigration law remained unconstitutional. The Court held that the Interpretation did not affect the Court's earlier ruling on the unconstitutionality of the statutory provision that imposed criminal sanctions retrospectively on parties who entered Hong Kong after the Basic Law came into effect on 1 July 1997 but prior to the enactment of the disputed immigration law on 10 July 1997. Although this judicial manoeuvre had minimal practical impact, its significance lies with the judicial methodology applied. Henceforth, while the CFA would respect and abide by the free-standing interpretive mandate of the NPCSC, its Interpretations would be read narrowly and strictly.

A few years later, in *Director of Immigration v Chong Fung Yuen*,[49] the CFA was confronted with another high-profile right-of-abode litigation. This time, the applicant was a mainland child born in Hong Kong but to parents who were not Hong Kong residents. Chong was herein seeking to assert his right of abode under Article 24(2)(1) of the Basic Law, which expressly provides that Chinese citizens born in Hong Kong before or after the establishment of the HKSAR are Hong Kong permanent residents. This plain, literal reading, however, conflicts with an immigration provision that limits the enjoyment of the right of abode to children born to Hong Kong residents.

But the CFA once again vindicated the child's constitutional right. As the Court explained:

> [T]he courts are bound to give effect to the clear meaning of the [constitutional] language. The courts will not on the basis of any extrinsic materials depart from that clear meaning and give the language a meaning which the language cannot bear.[50]

[48] Report by the Subgroup on the Relationship Between the Central Authorities and the HKSAR on the Amendment of Articles in BLDC Secretariat, *Collection of Documents of the Eighth Plenary Session of the Drafting Committee for the Basic Law of the HKSAR of PRC* (in Chinese), 8–9 (1989). See English translation by Bing (n 47) 631.

[49] (2001) 4 HKCFAR 211.

[50] ibid 225.

One may, however, note that in the 1999 NPCSC Interpretation, the text included a passage which provided that 'the legislative intent of all other categories of Article 24(2) of the Basic Law' had been reflected in the Opinions of the Preparatory Committee for the establishment of the HKSAR. As discussed in chapter one, this Preparatory Committee was established in 1996 by the NPC to make preparations for the establishment of the HKSAR. On 10 August 1996, the Preparatory Committee issued its Opinions on the implementation of Article 24(2) of the Basic Law, and paragraph 1 of the Opinions stated the following:

> Chinese citizens born in Hong Kong as provided in Category (1) of [Article 24(2)] of the Basic Law refer to people who are born during which either one or both of their parents were lawfully residing in Hong Kong, but excluding those who are born to illegal immigrants, overstayers or people residing temporarily in Hong Kong.

In other words, the immigration law at issue reflected the legislative intent of the Preparatory Committee's Opinions, and references to these Opinions were now inserted into the 1999 NPCSC Interpretation.

But the CFA deftly skirted the application of the NPCSC Interpretation by stating that the 1999 Interpretation was targeted at the interpretation of Article 24(2)(3) of the Basic Law – Chinese citizens born on the mainland – while the dispute herein related to Article 24(2)(1) – Chinese citizens born in Hong Kong. Therefore, the NPCSC had not issued a 'binding interpretation' of Article 24(2)(1) for the CFA to apply.

As the CFA explained:

> On the common law approach, which the Court is under a duty to apply in the absence of a binding interpretation by the Standing Committee, the statement in question cannot affect the clear meaning of art.24(2)(1) properly reached, applying the common law approach.[51]

The Court seemed to suggest that the objective of the 1999 Interpretation was directed at resolving the interpretive controversy over Articles 24(2)(3) and 22(4). Therefore, that passage in the Interpretation referencing other categories of Article 24(2) was merely obiter dicta and thus not binding on Hong Kong courts. In doing so, the CFA essentially treated an Interpretation as a judgment, 'drawing an analogy between it and the concept of obiter dictum in the common law tradition'.[52]

[51] ibid 233.

[52] AHY Chen, 'Another Case of Conflict between the CFA and NPC Standing Committee?' (2001) 31 *Hong Kong Law Journal* 179, 185.

One should also note that under Chinese law, legislative interpretations have the force of statutory enactments.[53] It is therefore unclear why the Interpretation was treated not as a statutory enactment, with all provisions binding on the court, but seemingly as a superior court judgment, with only its ratio binding. After all, even under the common law tradition, if the Interpretation were akin to legislation, the courts would not have the power to decide which statutory provisions are obiter and need not be enforced. This is especially puzzling since the Interpretation was passed by the NPCSC – a legislative body.

After the CFA's decision in *Chong Fung Yuen*, a spokesperson for the Legislative Affairs Commission of the NPCSC issued a press statement, pointing out that the CFA's decision was 'not consistent' with the 1999 NPCSC Interpretation and 'expressed concern' about the matter. But no further action was taken by the central authorities, and the Hong Kong government proceeded with a legislative amendment that enforced the CFA's judgment.

V. RETROSPECTIVE EFFECT OF NPCSC INTERPRETATIONS

In 1999, the CFA in *Lau Kong Yung*[54] had to decide on the temporal effect of the NPCSC First Interpretation, and the Court ruled that the Interpretation had retrospective effect. Specifically, the Court ruled that the 1999 Interpretation 'dates from 1 July 1997 when the Basic Law came into effect' and 'declared what the law has always been'.[55]

The CFA's implicit assumption seems to be that NPCSC Interpretations should operate in the same way as common law decisions: when the NPCSC delegates issue an Interpretation, they are acting as common law judges who merely declare what the relevant Basic Law provision has always meant from its inception. Underpinning this assumption is the declaratory theory of judicial decisions pertaining to the judge-made common law and statutory interpretation. The common law is seen as 'an immutable body of doctrine existing from time immemorial',[56] waiting to be discovered and declared by judges who do not make or

[53] AHY Chen, 'The Interpretation of the Basic Law' (2000) 30 *Hong Kong Law Journal* 380, 411–16.

[54] Above n 45.

[55] ibid 326.

[56] *Giannarelli v Wraith* (1988) 165 CLR 543, 584–85.

change it.[57] Therefore, when a new judicial proposition that differs from the previous understanding of the law is announced, the law is revealed but not changed at all. The same approach is applicable when a court adopts an interpretation of a statutory provision (even if different from its previous interpretation), in which case the statutory provision is taken to bear the meaning now adopted by the court from the time of the legislation's enactment.

In 2017, the Appeal Committee of the CFA in *Yau Wai Ching v Chief Executive of the HKSAR*[58] once again reaffirmed the proposition that NPCSC Interpretations apply retrospectively in Hong Kong. This time, the Court had to decide the temporal effect of the NPCSC Interpretation issued on 7 November 2016.

The political context of this dispute can be briefly explained as follows. In the wake of the 2014 'Occupy Central' or 'Umbrella' movement that paralysed key districts in Hong Kong for 79 days, a slew of young pro-democracy protestors were voted into LegCo in 2016. More significantly, some of the newly elected lawmakers had either openly advocated Hong Kong's independence from China or defended Hong Kong's right to democratic self-determination. Less compromising and more confrontational than 'pan-democrats' in the past, two of these lawmakers (Sixtus Leung and Yau Wai-ching) openly derided China at their swearing-in ceremony on 12 October 2016 and even referred to China as 'Sheen-na' – a derogatory term used by the Japanese on the Chinese during the Second World War – and displayed banners advocating Hong Kong's independence. Naturally, the President of LegCo did not accept the validity of the pair's oaths, but he nevertheless allowed them to retake their oaths at the next LegCo Council meeting. However, before Leung and Yau could do so, the Hong Kong government went to court and sought a declaration that the pair had been disqualified from their office by operation of law on 12 October 2016 when they declined to take the requisite oath of office, and the LegCo President was therefore disempowered from readministering their oaths.

Three days after the CFI finished hearing this case but before it delivered judgment, the NPCSC issued an Interpretation of Article 104 of the Basic Law.[59] The Interpretation inter alia provides that 'If the oath taken is determined as invalid, no arrangement shall be made for retaking

[57] *Kleinwort Benson Ltd v Lincoln City Council* [1999] 2 AC 349, 358.
[58] (2017) 20 HKCFAR 390.
[59] See ch 2, s VI.E.

the oath'. The Interpretation effectively pre-empted the courts and the LegCo President from taking a different approach.

Both the CFI and the Court of Appeal concluded that the errant legislators-elect had been automatically disqualified from assuming their offices when they declined to take their oath properly.[60] The CFI held that the disqualification flowed from the existing statutory requirements codified in the Oaths and Declarations Ordinance even if there had been no NPCSC Interpretation, while the Court of Appeal applied the Interpretation in reaching its decision. And the Appeal Committee of the CFA subsequently refused the lawmakers leave to appeal. According to the CFA, the Interpretation 'declares what the law is and has always been since the coming into effect of the Basic Law on 1 July 1997',[61] and 'there is no warrant for revisiting' this proposition.

One should note that under Chinese law, there is no categorical rule that legislative interpretations by the NPCSC have retrospective effect. Article 50 of the PRC Law on Legislation simply states that NPCSC Interpretations 'have the same effect as laws', but it does not expressly provide for the retrospective effect of such Interpretations.[62]

Given that an NPCSC Interpretation is a legislative act of a legislative body, it is arguable that the presumption against retrospectivity of legislation should also apply. According to this common law presumption, unless a contrary intention appears, a legislative provision is presumed not to operate retrospectively,[63] that is, to impair vested rights acquired under then-existing laws or to create a new obligation, duty or disadvantage in relation to past events,[64] regardless of whether it is 'penal in the sense of punishment'.[65]

One must note the central difference between the 1999 NPCSC Interpretation and the 2016 one. When the CFA in *Lau Kong Yung* declared that a 1999 NPCSC Interpretation applied retrospectively, it was dealing with an Interpretation that *expressly* stated so. In contrast,

[60] *Chief Executive of the Hong Kong Special Administrative Region v President of the Legislative Council* [2017] 1 HKLRD 460; *Chief Executive of HKSAR v President of Legislative Council* [2016] 6 HKC 417.

[61] *Yau Wai Ching* (n 58) [35].

[62] H Zhu and AHY Chen, 'The Oath-Taking Cases and the NPCSC Interpretation of 2016: Interface of Common Law and Chinese Law' (2019) 49 *Hong Kong Law Journal* 381, 403.

[63] F Bennion and O Jones (eds), *Bennion on Statutory Interpretation*, 6th edn (Sweet & Maxwell, 2013) 291; *Spread Trustee Co Ltd v Hutcheson* [2012] 2 AC 194 (Privy Council) [65].

[64] *Yew Bon Tew v Kenderaan Bas Mara* [1983] 1 AC 553 (Privy Council) 558–59.

[65] *Re School Board Election for the Parish of Pulborough* [1894] 1 QB 725 (Court of Appeal) 737.

the 2016 Interpretation is silent on its temporal effect. It is arguable that if the NPCSC had intended to make the Interpretation retrospective, it could have easily expressed its intention in the text. For example, the NPCSC's 1999 Interpretation expressly provides that whilst it does not affect the legal rights acquired by the parties under *Ng Ka Ling*, 'the question whether any other person fulfils the conditions prescribed by Article 24(2)(3) of the Basic Law… shall be determined by reference to this Interpretation', thus implying that the First Interpretation was intended to have retrospective effect. In contrast, the 2016 Interpretation does not include a provision on its temporal effect. Nor do the NPCSC's Explanations on the Draft Interpretation evince any unambiguous intention that the Interpretation applies retrospectively. Therefore, one can argue that the presumption against retrospectivity is not displaced, and if the 2016 Interpretation is viewed as a piece of legislation, it should not be applied to events that predated its announcement.[66]

Nevertheless, in *Yau Wai Ching*, the Appeal Committee of the HKCFA simply deemed the legal distinction between the 1999 and 2016 NPCSC Interpretations 'not reasonably arguable' and refused leave for appeal. Interestingly, six months after *Yau Wai Ching* was decided, Robert Tang – a then-Permanent Judge of the HKCFA – in an extrajudicial address at Oxford University voiced his disagreement with the HKCFA brethren on this issue: 'the Court of Final Appeal may if it wishes to do so reconsider the point in a full court of five judges after full argument. The 2016 Interpretation may provide a good opportunity to do so.'[67]

It should be noted that Robert Tang PJ was not assigned to the CFA's Appeal Committee panel that decided *Yau Wai Ching*.

VI. CONSTITUTIONAL SIGNIFICANCE OF THE NPCSC'S POWER OF INTERPRETATION

In countries around the world that have constitutional arrangements which enshrine provincial or territorial autonomy within the state – whether they take the form of devolution or federalism – there will usually be a judicial forum for the resolution of constitutional questions

[66] PJ Yap and E Chan, 'Legislative Oaths and Judicial Intervention in Hong Kong' (2017) 47 *Hong Kong Law Journal* 1, 12–14.

[67] R Tang, 'Dr Mok Hing Yiu Memorial Lecture: One Country, Two Systems: Basic Law, Common Law and the Rule of Law' (St Hugh's College, Oxford, 22 February 2018) [47].

and jurisdictional disputes arising from the country's practice of territorial autonomy. The judicial forum usually takes the form of a highly respected court at the apex of the national judicial system, such as a national supreme court or constitutional court. The court is usually staffed by highly respected judges, who decide on constitutional questions and jurisdictional disputes by issuing well-reasoned judgments after careful consideration of the legal arguments put forward by all parties concerned.

Examples of such courts include the US Supreme Court, the Supreme Court of Canada, the High Court of Australia, the Indian Supreme Court and the Federal Constitutional Court of Germany. Each of these courts serves as the guardian of the constitution and is responsible for the impartial interpretation and application of the law, including the law that governs the relationship between the national (or federal) government and the local (or provincial) one.

A distinguishing feature of the devolved arrangement under 'One Country, Two Systems' in the HKSAR is that the authority of the Hong Kong courts to interpret the Basic Law is subject to the overriding authority of the NPCSC to promulgate an Interpretation at any time. This means that although the HKSAR courts have exclusive power to try cases and to apply the law to the cases before them, they do not have exclusive power to interpret the Basic Law. This also means that, unlike other countries, it is not the national supreme court, but the national legislature that resolves any jurisdictional disputes and questions on autonomy. This unique system of constitutional power-sharing between the NPCSC of the PRC and the HKSAR courts may be considered a product of the 'marriage' between Hong Kong's common law-based legal system and the socialist legal order in the PRC.

Apart from the procedure provided in Article 158(3) for a judicial reference by CFA to the NPCSC (*Congo* case),[68] the NPCSC's power of interpretation may also be exercised to overrule the CFA after it has adjudicated on an issue (*Ng Ka Ling*), or even before the Hong Kong court decides a case involving the interpretation of the Basic Law so as to pre-empt the court's decision (*Yau Wai Ching*). This means that the authority of the courts of the HKSAR to interpret and apply the Basic Law is subordinated to and subject to the overriding authority and free-standing power of the NPCSC to issue an interpretation of any provision of the Basic Law at any time. This is a crucial limitation on

[68] (2011) 14 HKCFAR 95 & 395. See ch 2, s VI.D.

the competence and authority of the Hong Kong judiciary to adjudicate cases in accordance with the Basic Law and the laws of the HKSAR.

Furthermore, the NPCSC is not a judicial institution but is instead a 'supreme organ of state power' of the PRC that is subject to the leadership of the Chinese Communist Party. The NPCSC is not considered by a significant section of the Hong Kong public, including many members of the legal community, to be an impartial, legitimate and trustworthy guardian of the city's autonomy or interpreter of its Basic Law rights. This may be considered a crucial flaw in the devolved arrangement under 'One Country, Two Systems'.

On the other hand, one may also note that the NPCSC has stayed its hand on constitutional disputes solely within Hong Kong's autonomy. Furthermore, in the absence of any relevant interpretation of the Basic Law by the NPCSC, all questions on the interpretation of the Basic Law litigated before the Hong Kong courts are decided by its local courts. Furthermore, it is noteworthy that the NPCSC has so far issued only three interpretations over litigated cases: one interpretation that overrules the Hong Kong court's interpretation of the Basic Law (*Ng Ka Ling*); one interpretation that pre-empts the Hong Kong court's decision (*Lau Wai Ching*); and one interpretation requested by the Hong Kong court in accordance with the 'judicial reference' procedure (*Congo* case).

VII. 'SEPARATION OF POWERS' OR 'EXECUTIVE-LED GOVERNMENT'?

There is a recurring debate on whether the 'separation of powers' model of government underpins Hong Kong's constitutional system or the SAR has an 'executive-led government' instead. Notably, neither phrase is found in the Basic Law. The debate is constitutionally significant insofar as it reflects the divergent views of the central authorities and many members of the Hong Kong legal community.

'Executive-led government' in the HKSAR is the political narrative promoted by mainland Chinese officials and scholars. They argue that the Chinese phrase for 'separation of powers' (*sanquan fenli*, 三權分立), which literally translates as 'separate establishment of three powers', is not an accurate description of the HKSAR's political system.[69]

[69] PY Lo and AHY Chen, 'The Judicial Perspective of "Separation of Powers" in the Hong Kong Special Administrative Region of the People's Republic of China' (2018) 5 *Journal of International and Comparative Law* 337, 355.

When the Basic Law was being drafted in the 1980s, Deng Xiaoping, China's paramount leader and architect of the 'One Country Two Systems' model, on 16 April 1987 informed members of the Basic Law Drafting Committee that 'it would not be appropriate for [Hong Kong's system] to be a total copy of [the UK and the USA] with, for example, the separation of the three powers'.[70] Since then, mainland officials and scholars have avoided using the term 'separate establishment of the three powers' to characterise Hong Kong's political system. Instead, Ji Pengfei, Chairman of the Basic Law Drafting Committee, stated the official position as follows when he explained the draft Basic Law to the session of the National People's Congress that formally enacted the Basic Law in April 1990:[71] 'The executive authorities and the legislature should regulate each other as well as co-ordinate their activities.' The CE of the HKSAR, as the head of the SAR and its government who is accountable to the Central People's Government and the SAR, 'must have real power which, at the same time, should be subject to some restrictions'.

Within the Basic Law, the constitutional allocation of powers is provided for in Article 2 and fleshed out in subsequent Articles: the HKSAR is vested with executive power (Article 16) and legislative power (Article 17), and its courts with 'independent judicial power' (Article 19). Chapter IV of the Basic Law sets out the political structure of the HKSAR and lays out the constitutional powers of the CE, the executive authorities, the legislature and the judiciary in separate sections of the chapter. This structural division of power has impressed upon scholars and lawyers trained in the Western or common law tradition that the Basic Law provides for 'a clear and sharp separation between the executive and the legislature in Hong Kong', and 'The separation of the judiciary from the executive and the legislature (and its independence) is secured through various devices'.[72]

In the 1990s and particularly after the handover in 1997, mainland Chinese legal scholars and members of the former Basic Law Drafting Committee characterised the political system of the HKSAR as an 'executive-led government' (*xingzheng zhudao* 行政主導, also translated as 'executive dominance').[73] This phrase underscores the pivotal role of

[70] Deng Xiaoping, *Deng Xiaoping on the Question of Hong Kong* (New Horizon Press, 1993) 55.

[71] See www.basiclaw.gov.hk/en/basiclawtext/images/basiclawtext_doc10.pdf.

[72] Y Ghai, *Hong Kong's New Constitutional Order*, 2nd edn (Hong Kong University Press, 1999) 263.

[73] W Shuwen (ed), *Introduction to the Basic Law of the Hong Kong Special Administrative Region*, 2nd edn (Law Press China and Joint Publishing (HK) Co Ltd, 2009) 345–50; X Weiyun, *On the Hong Kong Basic Law* (Peking University Press, 2003) 640–44.

the HKSAR's CE, who is vested with gubernatorial powers under the Basic Law and, more importantly, is also accountable to both the Central People's Government and the HKSAR.[74]

In June 2007, Wu Bangguo, Chairman of the NPCSC, reaffirmed the official line by stating that a key characteristic of the HKSAR's political system is its 'executive-led government', with the CE as the core (*yi xingzheng zhangguan wei hexin de xingzheng zhudao*, 以行政長官為核心的行政主導).[75]

Subsequently, in June 2014, the Information Office of the State Council in China published a White Paper on 'The Practice of the "One Country, Two Systems" Policy in the Hong Kong Special Administrative Region'.[76] The White Paper emphasised the central authorities' 'comprehensive/overall jurisdiction' (*quanmian guanzhi quan*, 全面管治權) over the HKSAR. The new phrase, 'comprehensive/overall jurisdiction', builds on discourse in mainland China that the central authorities have only delegated power (*shouquan*, 授權) to the SAR and have not divided it (*fenquan*, 分權) between the central authorities and the SAR.[77]

A recent iteration of the Chinese position was presented by the Hong Kong and Macau Affairs Office of the PRC State Council and the Liaison Office of the Central People's Government in the HKSAR in two separate statements in September 2020. The statements emphasised that Hong Kong has an executive-led government, practises the separate administration of three powers (*sanquan fenzhi*, 三權分置, alternatively translated as 'separate location of three powers') and is vested with judicial independence, but not judicial supremacy.[78]

On the other hand, the Hong Kong courts have only recognised that the Basic Law enshrines an executive-led government on two occasions, and not once by the CFA. In *Leung Kwok Hung v President of Legislative*

[74] BL43.

[75] W Bangguo, 'The Principal Feature of Hong Kong's Political System Is That It Is Executive-Led' (香港政治体制的最大特点是行政主导), speech on 6 June 2007, www.npc.gov.cn/zgrdw/npc/wbgwyz/hyhd/2007-06/06/content_366599.htm.

[76] http://english.gov.cn/archive/white_paper/2014/08/23/content_281474982986578.htm.

[77] C Jie, 'Jurisprudential Basis for the New Constitutional Order of Hong Kong: Separation of Powers or Delegation of Powers' (2017) 5 *China Legal Science* 56–83.

[78] 香港中联办发言人：香港特别行政区行政主导的政治体制由其宪制地位所决定 (www.xinhuanet.com/gangao/2020-09/07/c_1126463870.htm); 'Liaison Office of Central Government in HKSAR Clarifies Hong Kong's Political System as "Executive-Led"' (www.xinhuanet.com/english/2020-09/07/c_139349893.htm); 国务院港澳办发言人：关于香港特别行政区实行"三权分立"的说法必须纠正" (www.xinhuanet.com/gangao/2020-09/07/c_1126463856.htm).

Council,[79] the CFI upheld the constitutionality of a Legislative Rule of Procedure, which prohibited legislators from proposing any legislative amendment that had a charging effect, on the ground that 'Hong Kong has an Executive-led Government. It is the function of the Chief Executive to lead the Government, to decide on Government policies and to approve the introduction of motions regarding revenues or expenditure to the Legislative Council.' Similarly, in *Leung Kwok Hung v Secretary for Justice*,[80] the Court of Appeal upheld the Chief Executive in Council's powers to enact regulations on any occasion of public danger, and in doing so acknowledged that 'the Government is very much an executive-led government'.

In contrast, the Hong Kong judiciary has regularly affirmed that the 'separation of powers' principle is vested in the Basic Law. As the CFA emphasised in *Chong Fung Yuen*: 'under a common law system which includes a separation of powers, the interpretation of laws once enacted is a matter for the courts. So it is with the Basic Law.'[81]

The 'separation of powers' principle has been regularly invoked by the courts to ensure that each branch of government does not interfere with each other's discharge of its constitutional functions.

First, pursuant to this 'separation of powers' principle, the executive may not interfere with judicial functions. In *Yau Kwong Man v Secretary for Security*,[82] the CFI invalidated a statutory provision that, inter alia, authorised the CE to impose a minimum and unspecified term of imprisonment on minors convicted of murder, as the impugned law unconstitutionally interfered with the Court's judicial powers.

Second, the 'separation of powers' principle also means that the judiciary will accord a margin of discretion to the legislature or the executive when the courts rule on the constitutionality of rights-infringing laws. In determining how wide the margin of discretion should be, the courts would examine 'The content and features of the impugned measure, the identity and constitutional role of its originator and any special competence possessed by such person'.[83] This deference rests on the relative informational or institutional advantages the political branches of government have over policy issues like national security and resource

[79] *Leung Kwok Hung v President of the Legislative Council* [2007] 1 HKLRD 387. See also the discussion on legislative filibuster in ch 3, s VI.C.

[80] [2020] HKCA 192, [92]. The Court of Appeal's decision was largely affirmed on appeal to the CFA ([2020] HKCFA 42). See also ch 3, s II.B.

[81] *Chong Fung Yuen* (n 49) 225.

[82] [2002] 3 HKC 457.

[83] *Hysan Development v Town Planning Board* (2016) 19 HKCFAR 372, [114].

allocation. Deference was accorded to the legislature when the CFA upheld the statutory imposition of mandatory life imprisonment for murder on the basis that such sentences were not manifestly disproportionate. Town planning decisions that restrict property rights would 'in general only be susceptible to constitutional review if the Court is satisfied that they are manifestly without reasonable foundation'.[84]

In 2017, the CFA in *Kwok Cheuk Kin v Secretary for Constitutional and Mainland Affairs*[85] announced that a 'wider' margin of appreciation ought to be accorded to electoral laws as they involve 'political or policy considerations' and the courts are generally not equipped to determine political questions. On the facts, the CFA upheld a law that disqualifies a legislator from running in the by-election held to fill a vacancy consequent on that member's resignation. The law was passed in 2012 after five pro-democracy legislative councillors from different GCs resigned – as a collective act of political protest – mid-term in 2010 to trigger city-wide by-elections for their seats. The focus of the electoral challenge centred on whether the electoral restriction was proportionate. The CFA accepted that it was legitimate for the government to deter resignations that were intended to trigger by-elections, especially since this political exercise cost HK$126 million in public expenditure. Furthermore, the electoral restriction was deemed proportionate as 'some leeway should be permitted to the Legislature to determine what would be an appropriate way of dealing with the perceived mischief'. The 'political question' doctrine as articulated in the *Kwok* case is potentially the most consequential development of the 'separation of powers' principle by the Hong Kong courts.

Third, the judiciary has determined that the 'separation of powers' principle also includes a principle of judicial non-intervention in the internal process of LegCo. This principle of non-intervention was first affirmed by the CFA in *Leung Kwok Hung v President of the Legislative Council (No 1)*.[86] On the facts in *Leung Kwok Hung*, two lawmakers had attempted to filibuster a legislative Bill by moving over 1300 amendments at the relevant LegCo debate. After 33 hours of debate, the President of LegCo relied on rule 92 of the Rules of Procedure of the Legislative Council (RoP) – which provides that, in any matter not provided for in the RoP, the practice and procedure to be followed in LegCo shall be as decided by the President – to end the debate.

[84] ibid [129].
[85] [2017] 20 HKCFAR 353.
[86] (2014) 17 HKCFAR 689.

The central issue before the CFA in *Leung Kwok Hung* was whether Article 73(1) of the Basic Law, which empowers LegCo to 'enact, amend or repeal laws in accordance with the provisions of this [Basic] Law and legal procedures', requires Hong Kong courts to exercise jurisdiction to ensure compliance with the RoP in LegCo's law-making process. Critically, the CFA noted that Article 73(1) of the Basic Law does not address the question of whether any non-compliance with the 'legal procedures' in the legislative process would invalidate the law that was enacted after such non-compliance. Since Article 73(1) of the Basic Law is ambiguous on this point, the Court held that the constitutional provisions therein do not displace the common law principle of judicial non-intervention. Where this principle applies, the judiciary will only determine whether the legislature or its President has a particular power – in this case, the LegCo's President's power to terminate a legislative debate – and the Court will not further exercise jurisdiction to determine 'the occasion or the manner of exercise' of such powers by LegCo or its President. On this basis, the CFA in *Leung Kwok Hung* determined that the President of LegCo had the power to terminate a debate, as this was inherent in his power granted under Article 72(1) of the Basic Law to 'preside over meetings'. However, it was not for the Court to consider whether that power was exercised properly or whether the impugned decision to close the debate was an unauthorised making of a rule of procedure.

On the other hand, in *Yau Wai Ching*, the Appeal Committee of the CFA held that 'the principle of non-intervention cannot apply in respect of the court's duty to rule on the question of compliance with the constitutional requirements of [Basic Law, Article] 104'. As discussed earlier, the constitutional dispute centred on whether the courts have jurisdiction to enforce the adverse consequences against lawmakers after they declined to take a valid LegCo oath upon assuming office. According to the CFA, Article 104 of the Basic Law

> gives rise to a constitutional duty on members of LegCo to take an oath to swear to uphold the Basic Law and to swear allegiance to the Hong Kong Special Administrative Region. This is clear from the terms of [Basic Law, Article] 104 itself but is reinforced by para.2 of the [2016 NPCSC] Interpretation.[87]

[87] *Yau Wai Ching* (n 58) [21].

But one should note that Article 104 merely requires office-holders, upon the assumption of office, to swear an oath of allegiance. The Basic Law is silent on whether it should be for the judiciary to enforce any non-compliance. The relevant 2016 NPCSC Interpretation is also silent on this issue as no mention is made about the judiciary. In other words, the Basic Law and the NPCSC Interpretation are ambiguous on whether Hong Kong courts are required to adjudicate on the adverse consequences that follow from an invalid LegCo oath or whether the matter should be left to the President of LegCo to decide.

Previously, the CFA in *Leung Kwok Hung* invoked this principle of non-intervention in the internal affairs of LegCo when it refused to determine whether the President of LegCo had lawfully invoked his power to terminate a legislative filibuster.[88] The CFA justified its decision on the basis that Article 73(1) of the Basic Law is ambiguous on whether any non-compliance with the 'legal procedures' in the legislative process would invalidate any legislation passed.[89] Then, any perceived irregularity with the internal process of the legislature was a procedural question for the President of LegCo alone to resolve.

On the other hand, the Appeal Committee of the CFA subsequently held in *Yau Wai Ching* that it was simply 'untenable' that this principle of non-intervention would apply to another internal process of the legislature – the President of LegCo's decision to grant newly elected LegCo members the opportunity to retake the requisite legislative oath after they bungled their first attempt. Even though Article 104 is equally ambiguous on whether it is for the Hong Kong courts or the President of LegCo to resolve this legal procedure, the Court herein summarily decided that it was for the judiciary alone to adjudicate on whether lawmakers had duly taken their legislative oaths and to remove any errant lawmakers 'automatical[ly]'. Alternatively, it is arguable that the *Leung* and *Yau* cases can be distinguished on the basis that in *Leung*, the question of whether the LegCo President could terminate a debate after a lengthy filibuster was a procedural one pertaining to LegCo's internal operations, while in *Yau*, the issue was whether the LegCo members concerned had been disqualified by operation of law, which was not a matter pertaining to LegCo's internal operation and procedure.

[88] *Leung Kwok Hung* (n 86).
[89] ibid [38].

VIII. CONCLUSION: COEXISTENCE OF 'SEPARATION OF POWERS' AND 'EXECUTIVE-LED GOVERNMENT'

Regarding the debate over the 'executive-led government' principle and the 'separation of powers' principle, the better view is the one adopted by the CFI in *Leung Kwok Hung v President of the Legislative Council*.[90] In this case, both concepts were endorsed, underscoring how they are not mutually exclusive concepts, but can coexist under the Basic Law.

As we have discussed above, it is axiomatic that the Basic Law intended the executive branch of government to be the dominant organ of policy formulation and implementation in the HKSAR.[91] Furthermore, unlike most elected legislatures in the world, the powers of the executive are enhanced, as Hong Kong lawmakers – individually or collectively – are constitutionally prohibited from introducing any Bill relating to 'public expenditure or political structure or the operation of the government'; nor may they introduce 'Bills relating to government policies' unless the written consent of the CE is first obtained.[92]

Nevertheless, the Basic Law has also vested powers upon the executive, the legislature and the judiciary in separate sections of the Basic Law. More importantly, judicial power is vested only in the judiciary and the courts shall 'exercise judicial power independently, free from any interference'.[93] This structural division of labour within the Basic Law has been recognised by the CFA in *Leung Kwok Hung v President of the Legislative Council (No 1)*.[94] Therefore, it is also evident that each of the executive, the legislature and the judiciary has its own constitutionally assigned roles and functions.

Viewed in this light, and subject to the overriding authority of the NPCSC to promulgate interpretations of the Basic Law, the Hong Kong judiciary is engaged in a constitutional dialogue with the other co-ordinate branches of government on rights interpretation. This model of government celebrates a model of 'judicial penultimacy'[95] whereby courts are engaging in a continuing colloquy with the political institutions, and with society at large, and participating in a dynamic process

[90] [2007] 1 HKLRD 387, [66]–[67].
[91] BL62.
[92] BL74.
[93] BL85.
[94] *Leung Kwok Hung* (n 86) [27].
[95] M Perry, 'Protecting Human Rights in a Democracy: What Role for the Courts?' (2003) 38 *Wake Forest Law Review* 635, 673.

in which constitutional meanings have evolved conversationally and are not perfected unilaterally.[96]

FURTHER READING

Chen, AHY and Lo, PY, 'Hong Kong's Judiciary under One Country, Two Systems' in HP Lee and M Pittard (eds), *Asia Pacific Judiciaries: Independence, Impartiality and Integrity* (Cambridge University Press, 2018) 145.

Lo, PY and Chen, AHY, 'The Judicial Perspective of "Separation of Powers" in the Hong Kong Special Administrative Region of the People's Republic of China' (2018) 5 *Journal of International and Comparative Law* 337.

Yap, PJ, 'Interpreting the Basic Law and the Adjudication of Politically Sensitive Questions' (2007) 6(3) *Chinese Journal of International Law* 543.

Yap, PJ, '10 Years of the Basic Law: The Rise, Retreat and Resurgence of Judicial Power in Hong Kong' (2007) 36 *Common Law World Review* 166.

Young, SNM, Da Roza, A and Ghai, Y (eds), *Hong Kong's Court of Final Appeal: The Development of the Law in China's Hong Kong* (Cambridge University Press, 2014).

[96] PJ Yap, *Constitutional Dialogue in Common Law Asia* (Oxford University Press, 2015).

6

Constitutional Rights

Hong Kong Bill of Rights Ordinance – International Covenant on Civil and Political Rights – Judicial Use of Comparative Law – Proportionality Analysis – Chief Justice Andrew Li – Chief Justice Geoffrey Ma – Chief Justice Andrew Cheung

THE CONSTITUTIONAL RELATIONSHIP between the Hong Kong Special Administrative Region (HKSAR) and the central authorities has been examined in the preceding chapters and an overview of the political system given. In this chapter, we turn to the subject of fundamental rights, and analyse how constitutional rights are protected and interpreted in Hong Kong. The chapter begins by exploring the interrelationship between the Basic Law and the Hong Kong Bill of Rights Ordinance (BORO), and the operative scope of a reservation made over the International Covenant on Civil and Political Rights (ICCPR) vis-à-vis immigration matters. This chapter also examines how the courts have used comparative law and engaged in proportionality analysis during rights adjudication. Finally, the constitutional record of the Court of Final Appeal (CFA) under the respective tenure of each Chief Justice will be analysed in turn.

I. THE BASIC LAW AND THE HONG KONG BILL OF RIGHTS ORDINANCE

Fundamental rights in Hong Kong are protected by its Basic Law and the BORO. Before the Basic Law came into force in 1997 and prior to China's resumption of sovereignty over Hong Kong, the BORO was passed in 1991 by the colonial legislature to 'bring home' the rights and the corresponding rights-protecting obligations the British government acceded to in 1976 when it ratified the ICCPR and extended its application to Hong Kong.[1] The passage of the BORO was, in particular, triggered by the military crackdown of student demonstrators in Tiananmen Square over the summer of 1989.

Article 39 of the Basic Law provides that 'the provisions of the ICCPR … as applied to Hong Kong [by the UK] shall remain in force and shall be implemented through the laws of the HKSAR'. The relevant ICCPR rights have been statutorily codified in Hong Kong as BORO rights. In addition, fundamental rights are also expressly enshrined in chapter III of the Basic Law (entitled 'Fundamental Rights and Duties of the Residents'). The Basic Law thus expressly and concurrently confers constitutional status on a wide range of rights. Some of these rights include the right to free expression, the right to assembly, the right to equality, the freedom of religious belief, and the right against arbitrary arrest and imprisonment. With regard to those rights expressly and concurrently protected in both the ICCPR/BORO and the Basic Law, the invalidation of any rights-incompatible legislative provision is uncontroversial as it is expressly stated that the Basic Law prevails over conflicting statutory provisions.[2]

On the other hand, there are several BORO rights that are not expressly protected in the Basic Law. The BORO explicitly protects a person's right to a fair hearing in civil cases,[3] but this right is not expressly mentioned in the Basic Law. Some BORO rights are more circumscribed in the Basic Law. The BORO protects a person's right against torture and cruel, inhuman or degrading treatment or punishment,[4] but the Basic Law only expressly prohibits torture;[5] there is a general right to privacy under the BORO,[6] but the Basic Law only expressly protects the privacy of one's communication.[7]

Originally, section 3(2) of the BORO provided that 'All pre-existing legislation that does not admit of a construction consistent with this

[1] See R Swede, 'One Territory–Three Systems? The Hong Kong Bill of Rights' (1995) 44 *International & Comparative Law Quarterly* 358. At the same time as the enactment of the BORO, a corresponding amendment was made to the Letters Patent – the constitutional instrument of colonial Hong Kong – for the purpose of giving constitutional force to the ICCPR as applied to Hong Kong. See A Byrnes and J Chan (eds), *Public Law and Human Rights: A Hong Kong Sourcebook* (Butterworths, 1993) 18–26, 215–17.

[2] Basic Law, Art 8.

[3] BORO, Art 10.

[4] BORO, Art 3.

[5] Basic Law, Art 28.

[6] BORO, Art 14.

[7] Basic Law, Art 30.

Ordinance is, to the extent of the inconsistency, repealed', and section 4 of the BORO stated that

> [a]ll legislation enacted on or after the commencement date [of the BORO] shall, to the extent that it admits of such a construction, be construed so as to be consistent with the International Covenant on Civil and Political Rights as applied to Hong Kong.

But, significantly, a few months before China resumed sovereignty over Hong Kong, the Standing Committee of the National People's Congress (NPCSC), in its Decision dated 23 February 1997 on 'the treatment of the laws previously in force in Hong Kong in accordance with Article 160 of the Basic Law', determined, inter alia, that sections 3 and 4 of the BORO would no longer be adopted as laws in Hong Kong after the handover on 1 July 1997.[8] This was an expression of China's unyielding resolve that only the Basic Law could reign supreme over all other Hong Kong laws.

A. *Ng Kung Siu* and Article 39 of the Basic Law

Interestingly, after the handover, the CFA in the landmark decision of *HKSAR v Ng Kung Siu*[9] decided that, pursuant to Article 39 of the Basic Law, legislative provisions that are inconsistent with the BORO provisions are, to the extent of the inconsistency, invalidated. This decision marked a very significant development.

Ng Kung Siu was a case concerning flag desecration. On the facts, the defendants were charged for desecrating the national and regional flags, contrary to section 7 of the National Flag and National Emblem Ordinance and section 7 of the Regional Flag and Regional Emblem Ordinance, respectively. The central issue turned on whether the above restrictions were consistent with the freedom of expression entrenched under Article 27 of the Basic Law and Article 16 of the BORO. The CFA eventually upheld both laws on the basis that the statutory restrictions were reasonable, taking into account the uniqueness of the national and regional flags in reinforcing national unity and territorial integrity,

[8] Decision of the Standing Committee of the National People's Congress on Treatment of the Laws Previously in Force in Hong Kong in accordance with Article 160 of the Basic Law of the Hong Kong Special Administrative Region of the People's Republic of China (adopted at the Twenty-Fourth Session of the Standing Committee of the Eighth National People's Congress on 23 February 1997).

[9] (1999) 2 HKCFAR 442.

and that the restrictions were limited as they only banned one mode of expression such that the same message could be expressed via other means.[10]

More significantly, the CFA also ruled that the BORO 'in fact provides for the incorporation of the provisions of the ICCPR into the laws of Hong Kong', and to be compliant with Article 39 of the Basic Law, any 'restriction on either freedom [protected in the Basic Law or the BORO] cannot contravene the provisions of the ICCPR'.[11] In other words, Article 39 has been interpreted as meaning that the relevant provisions of the ICCPR and the corresponding provisions in BORO have the same constitutional force as the Basic Law itself, and can override laws that are inconsistent with these rights provisions.[12]

Insofar as a BORO right is *concurrently* and expressly protected in the Basic Law, *Ng Kung Siu*'s pronouncement is uncontroversial. On the other hand, if any legislative provision is invalidated because it violates rights found *exclusively* in the BORO, the CFA would arguably be in effect rejecting the legislative repeal of sections 3 and 4 of the BORO; and the CFA would be conferring quasi-constitutional status on these statutory rights too.[13]

Ostensibly, the CFA relied on Article 39 of the Basic Law for this legal manoeuvre. Specifically, paragraph 1 of this Article states that 'The provisions of the International Covenant on Civil and Political Rights … as applied to Hong Kong shall remain in force and shall be implemented through the laws of the Hong Kong Special Administrative Region'. Paragraph 2 of Article 39 further provides that 'The rights and freedoms enjoyed by Hong Kong residents shall not be restricted unless as prescribed by law. Such restrictions shall not contravene the provisions of the preceding paragraph of this Article'. Note that the text of Article 39 does not explicitly provide for the direct enforcement of ICCPR rights in Hong Kong or the concomitant judicial invalidation of any conflicting statutory provisions. Only those ICCPR rights *concurrently* and expressly protected in the Basic Law enjoy that constitutional status, and only by virtue of Articles 8 and 11 of the Basic Law,

[10] ibid 456.

[11] ibid 455.

[12] AHY Chen, 'International Human Rights Law and Domestic Constitutional Law: Internationalisation of Constitutional Law in Hong Kong' (2009) 4 *National Taiwan University Law Review* 237, 246; S Young, 'Restricting Basic Law Rights in Hong Kong' (2004) 34 *Hong Kong Law Journal* 109, 116.

[13] See PJ Yap and F Chung, 'Statutory Rights and De Facto Constitutional Supremacy in Hong Kong? (2019) 17 *International Journal of Constitutional Law* 836.

which establish the supremacy of the Basic Law over all other legal rules. For those ICCPR rights not found in the Basic Law, Article 39 merely prohibits any restrictions from contravening any local implementation of the ICCPR, which has been achieved through the BORO, an ordinary law.

The BORO is an ordinance consisting of 14 sections; section 8 contains the 'Hong Kong Bill of Rights' (BOR), which consists of 23 Articles. The Ordinance, particularly the BOR, is basically a faithful replication of those substantive ICCPR obligations acceded to by the UK government on behalf of Hong Kong in 1976, which the Chinese government also agreed to abide by after the handover. However, it should be noted that the ICCPR itself also does not provide for the judicial enforcement of these rights, nor does it empower courts to invalidate any conflicting legislation. (Even today in the UK, a signatory of the ICCPR as well as the European Convention on Human Rights, its Supreme Court does not have the formal power to strike down legislation that is incompatible with the UK's Human Rights Act 1998.)

Article 2 of the ICCPR merely obligates state parties to ensure that 'any person whose rights or freedoms as herein recognized are violated shall have an effective remedy'. The February 1997 Decision of the NPCSC mentioned above would ostensibly suggest that the remedy chosen by China after it resumed sovereignty over Hong Kong was to allow only ICCPR rights concurrently and expressly protected in the Basic Law to prevail over local legislation, while removing those judicial powers to invalidate pre-BORO legislation for violating exclusive BORO rights[14] and interpret post-BORO legislation in a BORO-friendly manner.[15]

Therefore, in *Ng Kung Siu*, with this expansive interpretation of Article 39, the CFA was clawing back power the judiciary lost with the statutory repeal purportedly made by the NPCSC Decision. It should be noted that the repeal of these interpretative provisions in the BORO was passed by China *before* the handover and that these legislative changes were timed to take effect when the Basic Law came into force on the HKSAR's Establishment Day. Therefore, it is inconceivable that the CFA's reading of Article 39 would have reflected the original intentions of China when the latter framed the Basic Law.

The CFA's judicial manoeuvre in *Ng Kung Siu* had little practical impact on constitutional rights that are already expressly protected

[14] BORO, s 3(2).
[15] BORO, s 4.

in the Basic Law, as the supremacy clauses enshrined under Articles 8 and 11 of the Basic Law would always deem statutory restrictions that violate Basic Law rights unconstitutional, even in the absence of the BORO. This was indeed the case in *Ng Kung Siu* as the CFA was therein addressing the freedom of expression, a right protected both in Article 16 of the BOR and Article 27 of the Basic Law.

However, the CFA's expansive reading of Article 39 had momentous implications on another category of rights not at issue in this appeal, ie exclusive BORO rights – rights found *only* in the BORO and not expressly stipulated in the Basic Law – as this move implicitly reinstated sections 3 and 4 of the BORO, which had been removed by the NPCSC Decision in February 1997. Henceforth, based on the CFA's expansive reading of Article 39 of the Basic Law, HKSAR courts can also rely on this constitutional provision to strike down legislation that conflicts with these exclusive BORO rights too.

B. Article 39 of the Basic Law Post-*Ng Kung Siu*

This was exactly what the CFA did a decade later in *Lam Siu Po v Commissioner of Police*. In that case, a police constable contended that a blanket ban on professional legal representation at his disciplinary hearing violated his right to a fair hearing under Article 10 of the BOR. Notably, this statutory right is not expressly found in the Basic Law, but the CFA ruled that 'Article 39 of the Basic Law gives constitutional force to Article 10 [of the BOR]'.[16] The Court further ruled that the blanket exclusion of legal representation by the relevant subsidiary legislation was deemed unfair, in light of the severity of the charge and the potential penalty, and the impugned provisions were thus invalidated.

Furthermore, the lower courts of the HKSAR have also proceeded to invalidate post-BORO legislation that violates exclusive BORO rights, thereby expanding upon the original powers conferred under section 4 of the BORO, which had previously only allowed the judiciary to give a remedial interpretation to – but not invalidate – rights-conflicting laws enacted *after* the passage of the BORO.

In *Wong Hin Wai v Secretary for Justice*,[17] the applicants were on bail pending appeal against their convictions and sentences of imprisonment

[16] (2009) 12 HKCFAR 237, [60].
[17] [2012] 4 HKLRD 70.

for public order offences. Under section 39(1)(b)(i) of the Legislative Council Ordinance, they were disqualified from standing for Legislative Council elections unless they had finished serving their sentences before the end of the nomination period. The central issue of the case turned on whether this electoral restriction constituted an unlawful curtailment of their right to stand for election.

Article 26 of the Basic Law stipulates that 'Permanent residents of the Hong Kong Special Administrative Region shall have the right to vote and the right to stand for election in accordance with law'. It is thus noteworthy that the Basic Law explicitly adopts a 'by law' clause for electoral rights. A 'by law' clause is a constitutional provision that allows the scope of its protection and extent of implementation to be determined by ordinary legislation.[18] As the methods for electing Legislative Council members can be amended to realise the ultimate goal of universal suffrage stipulated in Article 68 of the Basic Law, the Basic Law intentionally avoided constitutionalising a fixed electoral arrangement and instead explicitly delegated these constitutional questions to future legislatures. However, Article 21 of the BOR confers additional electoral rights: Hong Kong permanent residents shall have the right 'to take part in the conduct of public affairs, directly or through freely chosen representatives', and the right 'to vote and to be elected at genuine periodic elections which shall be by universal and equal suffrage'. Not only is the right to participate in public affairs broader in scope than the rights to vote and to stand for election, Article 21 of the BOR prohibits any 'unreasonable restrictions' on the BORO right, which stands in contrast with Article 26 of the Basic Law's requirement that the restriction be only 'in accordance with law.'

The impugned blanket ban in *Wong Hin Wai* was introduced in 1997 as the government ostensibly wanted to prevent escaped convicts from holding office in the legislature.[19] In the view of the Court of First Instance (CFI), there was a disconnect between barring escaped convicts from elections and banning all persons with unserved jail terms from electoral office, and this measure was therefore not proportionate.[20] Therefore, the CFI invalidated the law as it violated Article 21 of the BOR, read with Articles 26 and 39 of the Basic Law.[21]

[18] R Dixon and T Ginsburg, 'Deciding Not to Decide: Deferral in Constitutional Design' (2011) 9(3–4) *International Journal of Constitutional Law* 636.

[19] [2012] 4 HKLRD 70, [57].

[20] ibid [95]–[96].

[21] ibid [104].

In *Secretary for Justice v Chan Wah*, the CFA even enforced the BORO against private actors, even though the Ordinance only binds state action.[22] This dispute arose over village elections in the New Territories. Only an indigenous villager – defined as 'a person who was in 1898 a resident of an established village in Hong Kong or who is descended through the male line from that person'[23] – was traditionally entitled to vote and stand as a candidate in the Village Representatives (VR) election. In *Chan Wah*, non-indigenous villagers challenged this electoral practice on the ground that it denied their right to participate in village affairs as protected under Article 21(a) of the BOR. Noting that the VR represent the entire village in liaising with the government, and the role they play extends beyond the village level up to the Legislative Council, the CFA concluded that the VR were engaged in the conduct of public affairs. Furthermore, since the VR represent the village as a whole, the CFA determined that the exclusion of non-indigenous inhabitants from the VR election was an unreasonable curtailment of their Article 21(a) BOR right and was thus unconstitutional.[24] It is noteworthy, however, that there was no legislation governing the VR election, as it was only a customary practice within these villages to limit voting to indigenous villagers. Nevertheless, the CFA asserted state action on the basis that the government's approval was needed before the elected VR could formally take office.[25]

II. EFFECT OF ICCPR RESERVATIONS AND SECTION 11 OF THE BORO

Immigration restrictions are hotly contested in Hong Kong. Nevertheless, section 11 of the BORO states: 'As regards persons not having the right to enter and remain in Hong Kong, this Ordinance does not affect any immigration legislation governing entry into, stay in and departure from Hong Kong, or the application of any such legislation.'

The CFA has routinely taken the view that section 11 of the BORO was intended to give effect to one of the reservations laid down by the UK government when it ratified the ICCPR and made it applicable to Hong Kong.

[22] BORO, s 7.
[23] Government Rent (Assessment and Collection) Ordinance (Cap 515), s 2.
[24] (2000) 3 HKCFAR 459, 474.
[25] ibid 471.

Specifically, this reservation (the Reservation) is worded as follows:

> The Government of the United Kingdom reserve the right to continue to apply such immigration legislation governing entry into, stay in and departure from the United Kingdom as they may deem necessary from time to time and, accordingly, their acceptance of Article 12 (4) [of the ICCPR] and of the other provisions of the Covenant is subject to the provisions of any such legislation as regards persons not at the time having the right under the law of the United Kingdom to enter and remain in the United Kingdom. The United Kingdom also reserves a similar right in regard to each of its dependent territories.[26]

The Reservation was apparently intended to prevent a British subject from the British colonies or dependencies from claiming a right to enter the UK on the basis of Article 12(4) of the ICCPR,[27] that is, as 'his own country'.

But transplanted to Hong Kong, this narrow reading of the Reservation would make little sense as Hong Kong – in 1976 or at any other time – has never been threatened by an influx of British subjects from other British colonies or dependencies who might, but for the Reservation, be able to claim a right to enter Hong Kong as their 'own country'.[28]

While seeking to avoid rendering the Reservation otiose in Hong Kong, the CFA in *Ubamaka v Secretary for Security* proceeded to give a broad reading of the Reservation instead. Within the Hong Kong context, the CFA ruled that the Reservation was 'aimed at preventing illegal immigrants from … relying on a range of potentially applicable ICCPR rights'.[29]

On the other hand, Michael Ramsden has argued for a narrower reading of the Reservation. Instead of applying to all immigration matters, Ramsden argues that the Reservation, within the HKSAR context, should be limited to limiting the rights of mainland Chinese nationals from claiming the right to enter Hong Kong under Article 12(4) of the ICCPR as their 'own country'.[30] This narrower

[26] https://treaties.un.org/Pages/ViewDetails.aspx?chapter=4&clang=_en&mtdsg_no=IV-4&src=IND#EndDec.

[27] Art 12(4) of the ICCPR reads: 'No one shall be arbitrarily deprived of the right to enter his own country.'

[28] *Ubamaka v Secretary for Security* (2012) 15 HKCFAR 743, [64].

[29] ibid [65]. See also the text accompanying n 127 below for a discussion of another aspect of the *Ubamaka* case.

[30] M Ramsden, 'Reviewing the United Kingdom's ICCPR Immigration Reservation in Hong Kong Courts' (2014) 63 *ICLQ* 635, 656.

reading of the Reservation would also be consistent with Articles 22 and 24 of the Basic Law, which spell out the constitutional conditions under which a mainland Chinese resident may gain the right of abode in Hong Kong.

This narrower reading is also compelling because it is consistent with another reservation to Article 13[31] of the ICCPR, which is specific to Hong Kong:

> The Government of the United Kingdom reserve the right not to apply Article 13 in Hong Kong in so far as it confers a right of review of a decision to deport an alien and a right to be represented for this purpose before the competent authority.

If the CFA is right that the Reservation on Article 12(4) ICCPR was intended to apply to *all* immigration matters in Hong Kong, then this specific reservation on Article 13 of the ICCPR, which expressly applies to Hong Kong and bars the right to a hearing and legal representation for deportations of immigrants, would be rendered redundant and otiose.[32]

In *Ghulam Rbani v Secretary for Justice*, the CFA further ruled that section 11 of the BORO – even though it was a mere statutory provision – 'operates at the constitutional level and qualifies the scope and effect'[33] of Basic Law rights.

According to the CFA:

> [I]n giving constitutional status to the Hong Kong Bill of Rights Ordinance including s.11, BL art.39 gives constitutional status to a specific exception to relevant provisions of the Hong Kong Bill of Rights in relation to persons not having the right to enter and remain in Hong Kong and in respect of immigration legislation governing entry into, stay in and departure from Hong Kong, or the application of such legislation.[34]

The CFA therefore converts a statutory exception, which can always be repealed by ordinary legislation, to a constitutional exception that can disapply constitutional rights directly. Henceforth, section 11 of

[31] Art 13 of the ICCPR reads: 'An alien lawfully in the territory of a State Party to the present Covenant may be expelled therefrom only in pursuance of a decision reached in accordance with law and shall, except where compelling reasons of national security otherwise require, be allowed to submit the reasons against his expulsion and to have his case reviewed by, and be represented for the purpose before, the competent authority or a person or persons especially designated by the competent authority.'

[32] Ramsden (n 30) 655.

[33] (2014) 17 HKCFAR 138, [94].

[34] ibid [97].

the BORO would preclude illegal overstayers from enforcing constitutional rights curtailed by or inconsistent with immigration legislation. The CFA in the same case also held that section 11 would not prevent the overstayers from relying on any common law right against arbitrary arrest or detention, specifically the *Hardial Singh* common law principles that regulate the government's statutory power of administrative detention.[35]

Interestingly, while section 11 of the BORO does not override the application of *common law* rights in the immigration context, the CFA in *Comilang Milagros Tecson v Director of Immigration* decided that section 11 can override *constitutional* rights in the immigration context even if those rights are not covered in the BORO but are expressly provided for in the Basic Law:

> Although s.11 [of the BORO] in terms only applies textually to the rights set out in HKBORO, by necessary implication it limits the application of cognate rights in the [Basic Law] whether they are invoked directly or in connection with the enjoyment of another right.[36]

According to the CFA, all constitutional rights 'must be interpreted as a coherent whole, consistently with s.11 [of the BORO]'.[37] Therefore, non-residents of Hong Kong could not, in arguing that they had a right to remain in the city, rely on the constitutional right of abode – a right not included in the BORO – to circumvent section 11's foreclosure of the BORO and other 'cognate rights in the Basic Law (here the family unity rights)'.[38]

III. JUDICIAL USE OF COMPARATIVE LAW

In Hong Kong, judges routinely refer to comparative law during constitutional adjudication. This is not unusual because the Basic Law expressly authorises local judges to refer to precedents of other common law jurisdictions,[39] and foreign judges are also eligible to serve as Non-Permanent Judges (NPJs) on the CFA.[40]

[35] ibid [98], [106].
[36] (2019) 22 HKCFAR 59, [61].
[37] ibid [30].
[38] ibid [69].
[39] Basic Law, Art 84. For further details, see ch 5 of this volume.
[40] Basic Law, Art 82.

As Sir Anthony Mason NPJ once wrote: 'Comparative law has a natural attraction for a common law court of final appeal, especially a newly-established court which has not developed its own corpus of jurisprudence.'[41]

In *Shum Kwok Sher v HKSAR*, the CFA held that, in interpreting the Basic Law and the BORO,

> the Court may consider it appropriate to take account of the established principles of international jurisprudence as well as the decisions of international and national courts and tribunals on like or substantially similar provisions in the ICCPR, other international instruments and national constitutions.[42]

Aside from constitutional case law from leading common law jurisdictions like the UK, Australia, Canada, South Africa and New Zealand, the CFA has also looked to the European Court of Human Rights (ECtHR) and the United Nations Human Rights Committee (UNHRC) for guidance. Vis-à-vis the ECtHR, the CFA has held that the Strasbourg decisions 'are of high persuasive authority';[43] the General Comments of the UNHRC also 'provide influential guidance as to how the ICCPR is applied'.[44] Post-1997, the courts have been even more receptive of international and comparative legal materials during rights adjudication than they were during colonial times, and this development has led to the 'internationalisation of constitutional law'[45] in Hong Kong.

Occasionally, the CFA had to choose between the positions of different foreign tribunals when their rights jurisprudence differed from one another. In *Lam Siu Po v Commissioner of Police*,[46] the CFA had to determine whether civil servants were entitled to a 'fair hearing', enshrined in Article 10 of the BOR, at their disciplinary proceedings. In particular, the CFA had to decide whether Article 10 should align with the ECtHR decision in *Eskelinen v Finland*,[47] which included disciplinary hearings of civil servants within the protective ambit of the comparable Article 6(1) of the European Convention on Human Rights (ECHR), or mirror

[41] A Mason, 'The Place of Comparative Law in Developing the Jurisprudence on the Rule of Law and Human Rights in Hong Kong' (2007) 37 *Hong Kong Law Journal* 299, 302.

[42] (2002) 5 HKCFAR 381, [59].

[43] *Koon Wing Yee v Insider Dealing Tribunal* (2008) 11 HKCFAR 170, [27].

[44] ibid [101].

[45] See Chen, 'International Human Rights Law' (n 12).

[46] (2009) 12 HKCFAR 237.

[47] (2007) 45 EHRR 43.

the General Comments of the UNHRC,[48] which excluded disciplinary proceedings of civil servants from the coverage of Article 14(1) of the ICCPR, upon which Article 10 of the BOR is based.

Ribeiro PJ, on behalf of the unanimous Court, opined: 'I pause to note that the HRC has evidently fallen behind the European court in developments in this area … I would respectfully adopt in preference the Eskelinen approach as the more principled.'[49]

On the other hand, in *ZN v Secretary for Justice*, the CFA rejected ECtHR jurisprudence when it ruled that Article 4 of the BOR does not prohibit human trafficking generally for the purpose of exploitation, nor does it prohibit human trafficking for the purposes of servitude and forced or compulsory labour.[50] It may be noted that the ECtHR in *Rantsev v Cyprus and Russia*[51] had determined that Article 4 of the ECHR, which is *in pari materia* with Article 4 of the BOR, prohibits human trafficking generally, but the CFA was unpersuaded. According to the CFA, the ECtHR's 'broad brush approach' to incorporating human trafficking generally as a prohibited conduct 'ignores the separate concepts of slavery, servitude and forced or compulsory labour'.[52]

IV. PROPORTIONALITY ANALYSIS

In the twenty-first century, proportionality analysis (PA) – in its varied manifestations and permutations – has emerged as the most ubiquitous legal doctrine relied upon by judges in rights adjudication.[53] With its genesis in German law, this PA doctrinal device has diffused globally across Europe to the anglophone common law jurisdictions (eg the UK, Canada and New Zealand), mixed legal systems that are rooted in the common law (eg Israel and South Africa), and parts of Latin America and Asia, including Hong Kong.[54] Notably, unlike most charters of rights, neither the Basic Law nor the BORO enshrines a general limitation clause on rights. PA in Hong Kong is therefore largely judicially constructed.

[48] General Comment No 32 (90th Session) (2008) 15(1) IHRR 1.
[49] *Lam Siu Po* (n 46) [90].
[50] (2020) 23 HKCFAR 15, [80].
[51] (2010) 51 EHRR 1.
[52] *ZN* (n 50) [61].
[53] AS Sweet and J Mathews, *Proportionality Balancing and Constitutional Governance: A Comparative and Global Approach* (Oxford University Press, 2019).
[54] PJ Yap (ed), *Proportionality in Asia* (Cambridge University Press, 2020).

When Hong Kong was still under British rule, the Court of Appeal in *R v Sin Yau Ming*[55] invalidated for the first time a law in Hong Kong for violating the BORO. On the facts, statutory provisions which presumed that the accused were drug traffickers if they were found in possession of certain amounts of prohibited drugs were deemed to have disproportionately restricted their right to the presumption of innocence until proven guilty. Whilst the Canadian *Oakes*[56] test on PA was cited favourably in this case, PA in colonial Hong Kong lacked structure. This was a consequence of the Privy Council, in a case on appeal from Hong Kong, warning against 'follow[ing] the somewhat complex process now established in Canada', so that when Hong Kong courts determine whether a legislative restriction is justified, 'the tests which have been identified in Canada do not need to be applied rigidly or cumulatively'.[57]

In its first PA decision post-handover, the CFA in *Ng Kung Siu* also retained the colonial aversion to structured proportionality (SP). Therein, when determining the constitutionality of a statutory ban on flag desecration, the CFA merely assessed whether there was a legitimate aim for the law and whether the law was necessary. Specifically, proportionality was only invoked when the Court was engaging in the 'necessity' analysis, and the discussion was brief. The impugned legislation was swiftly upheld on the basis that it served the goals of nation-building under the 'One Country, Two Systems' constitutional model, and that the law only imposed a 'limited restriction'[58] as only one mode of expression was prohibited, leaving persons with the freedom to express the same message by other means. Subsequently, in *Solicitor v Law Society of Hong Kong*, the CFA invoked PA to invalidate a law for the first time in the HKSAR's history. An ouster clause that barred the CFA from hearing all appeals from the Solicitors' Disciplinary Tribunal was struck down on the basis that the nature and extent of the blanket prohibition was not reasonably proportionate to the legitimate purpose of regulating the scope of the CFA's jurisdiction.[59]

A three-stage PA was finally endorsed by the CFA for rights adjudication in *Leung Kwok Hung v HKSAR*. Citing with approval the Privy

[55] [1992] 1 HKCLR 127.

[56] *R v Oakes* [1986] 1 SCR 103.

[57] *Attorney General of Hong Kong v Lee Kwong-Kut* [1993] AC 951, [1993] 2 HKCLR 186, 200.

[58] *HKSAR v Ng Kung Siu* (1999) 2 HKCFAR 442, 461.

[59] (2003) 6 HKCFAR 570, [40].

Council's decision in *De Freitas v Permanent Secretary of Ministry of Agriculture, Fisheries, Lands and Housing*,[60] the CFA formulated its proportionality test in the following terms:

> (1) the restriction [on the relevant constitutional right] must be *rationally connected* with one or more of the *legitimate purposes*; and (2) the means used to impair the right … must be no more than is *necessary* to accomplish the legitimate purpose in question.[61] (emphasis added)

While framed as a two-stage analysis, this structured test encompasses the three stages of PA: the 'legitimacy' of the purpose for which the constitutional right is restricted; a 'rational connection' between such legitimate purpose and the means by which the right is restricted; and the 'necessity' of the restriction. Nevertheless, unlike *De Freitas*, the Hong Kong courts would not examine whether a legislative objective is 'sufficiently important'[62] to justify a rights derogation. Hitherto, in Hong Kong, it would suffice if the government's purpose or aim was legitimate. On the facts, a law which imposed a requirement on persons to notify the police prior to a public demonstration was deemed proportionate as the government had to be given time to take reasonable and appropriate measures to enable lawful assemblies to take place peacefully; the notification requirement only applied to public demonstrations that consisted of more than 30 persons; the Police Commissioner had to act proportionately when deliberating on the notified demonstration and within tight statutory time limits; and his discretion was subject to judicial review.[63]

Finally, in *Hysan Development v Town Planning Board*, the CFA added a fourth step to its PA:

> [W]here an encroaching measure has passed the three-step test, the analysis should incorporate a fourth step asking whether a reasonable balance has been struck between the societal benefits of the encroachment and the inroads made into the constitutionally protected rights of the individual, asking in particular whether pursuit of the societal interest results in an unacceptably harsh burden on the individual.[64]

The CFA's judgment in *Hysan* was replete with references to the contemporary jurisprudence of the Supreme Court of the UK, and the CFA also

[60] [1999] 1 AC 69.
[61] (2005) 8 HKCFAR 229, [36].
[62] ibid [38].
[63] ibid [92].
[64] (2016) 19 HKCFAR 372, [135].

noted how *De Freitas* – the Privy Council decision on which the CFA had relied for its three-stage PA – has been cast aside as 'deficient in omitting reference to the fourth step'.[65] On the facts in *Hysan*, the CFA determined that planning restrictions imposed by the Town Planning Board on the private property rights of land owners/developers had to be subject to this four-step proportionality assessment.

However, integrated within PA is a margin of appreciation that the CFA accords to the relative informational or institutional advantages the political branches of government have over policy issues like national security and resource allocation.[66] In determining how wide the margin of discretion should be, the court would examine 'The content and features of the impugned measure, the identity and constitutional role of its originator and any special competence possessed by such person'.[67] In *Hysan*, after noting that town planning is a polycentric exercise that involves the careful consideration of competing views, the CFA blunted the force of this new-found proportionality oversight by determining that if such governmental restrictions in a particular case are unassailable on traditional judicial review grounds, these limitations would in general only be susceptible to constitutional review if the court is satisfied that they are 'manifestly without reasonable foundation'.[68] Johannes Chan has argued that this bifurcated framework relegates a 'residual or supplementary'[69] status to PA's fourth step, while Alec Stone Sweet criticises this framework for allowing courts to simply apply the fourth step 'within step three (necessity) to determine outcomes'.[70]

The CFA has also opined in *Kwok Cheuk Kin v Secretary for Constitutional and Mainland Affairs* that election law involves political or policy considerations, and the court is not in a position, or equipped, to determine the necessity of these electoral restrictions. Therefore, the CFA would simply defer to the legislature on 'matters of political judgment and assessment'.[71] On the facts, the CFA upheld a law that

[65] ibid [66].
[66] ibid [117]–[118].
[67] ibid [114].
[68] ibid [129].
[69] J Chan, 'Proportionality after Hysan: Fair Balance, Manifestly without Reasonable Foundation and Wednesbury Unreasonableness' (2019) 49 *Hong Kong Law Journal* 265, 268.
[70] AS Sweet, 'The Necessity of Balancing: Hong Kong's Flawed Approach to Proportionality, and Why It Matters' (2020) 50 *Hong Kong Law Journal* 541, 544.
[71] (2017) 20 HKCFAR 353, [55]. See also the discussion of this case in the text accompanying n 175 below.

disqualifies a legislator from running in a by-election that is intended to fill the vacancy consequent on that member's resignation.

V. CFA DURING CHIEF JUSTICE ANDREW LI'S TENURE

A. Central–HKSAR Constitutional Relations

Andrew Li served as the HKSAR's first Chief Justice of the CFA from July 1997 to September 2010. The early years of the Andrew Li Court were notable for constitutional controversies over the status and applicability of NPCSC legislative acts in Hong Kong.

As discussed more fully in chapter five, in the CFA's first constitutional decision of *Ng Ka Ling v Director of Immigration*,[72] the Court vindicated the constitutional right of abode of children born on the mainland to Hong Kong Permanent Residents by invalidating HKSAR immigration laws that required these children to obtain the requisite exit permits to leave the mainland before they could exercise the right of abode in Hong Kong. In *Chan Kam Nga v Director of Immigration*,[73] a judgment issued on the same day as *Ng Ka Ling*, the CFA also invalidated a statutory bar that excluded a child who was born before at least one of the parents had acquired the right of permanent residency in Hong Kong from claiming the right of abode by descent in Hong Kong. Both rulings were soon reversed by the NPCSC in the 1999 Interpretation.[74] The original parties in the two litigations were not affected by this Interpretation, but the rights of all others would be determined by reference to it.

In *Lau Kong Yung v Director of Immigration*, the CFA enforced the 1999 Interpretation against persons who were not parties in the earlier right of abode litigation and affirmed the Director of Immigration's right to issue removal orders against them. In that case, the CFA accepted that the NPCSC's power of Basic Law interpretation is 'binding on the courts of the HKSAR'.[75] Interestingly, in *Lau Kong Yung*, the CFA also held that the 1999 Interpretation was silent on the immigration law's second

[72] (1999) 2 HKCFAR 4.

[73] (1999) 2 HKCFAR 82.

[74] The Interpretation by the Standing Committee of the National People's Congress of Articles 22(4) and 24(2)(3) of the Basic Law of the Hong Kong Special Administrative Region of the People's Republic of China (adopted at the Tenth Session of the Standing Committee of the Ninth National People's Congress on 26 June 1999).

[75] (1999) 2 HKCFAR 300, 324.

basis for infirmity, namely that it attempted to impose criminal sanctions retrospectively on parties who entered Hong Kong after the Basic Law came into effect on 1 July 1997 but prior to the enactment of the disputed law by the HKSAR legislature on 10 July 1997. Since this ground was 'not affected by the Interpretation',[76] the Court held that the retrospective provision remained invalid.

Subsequently, in *Director of Immigration v Chong Fung Yuen*, the CFA held that the NPCSC Interpretation is only 'binding'[77] vis-à-vis the Basic Law provisions that the NPCSC had specifically interpreted in the text of the Interpretation. And the CFA was not obliged to apply parts of the NPCSC Interpretation that expressed an opinion on other Basic Law provisions that were not at issue in the said Interpretation. By doing so, the CFA in this case was able to confer the constitutional right of abode in the HKSAR on children born in Hong Kong to mainland parents who were visitors or tourists in Hong Kong at the time of the children's birth.

B. Law and Order

On law-and-order issues, the Li Court was relatively conservative. In *Lau Cheong v HKSAR*, the CFA upheld the constitutionality of a mandatory life sentence for all persons convicted of murder. The Court held that the imposition of a uniform punishment was not 'manifestly disproportionate'[78] and arbitrary, even though the moral probity of a mercy killer may differ from that of a sadist.

In the same vein, the CFA in *So Wai Lun v HKSAR* also upheld the constitutionality of a penal code which criminalised the conduct of a male (to the exclusion of a female) for the same act engaged by both when the male engages in unlawful sexual intercourse with a female under the age of 16. Notably, this law imposes absolute liability on the offender as the *mens rea* of the perpetrator is irrelevant. In the Court's view:

> Where the legislature has enacted an absolute offence, the judiciary will not strike down the offence merely on the basis of a view that it would be preferable for the offence to admit of a defence of belief or reasonable belief [that the female in this case was aged 16 or above].[79]

[76] ibid 327.
[77] (2001) 4 HKCFAR 211, 233.
[78] (2002) 5 HKCFAR 415, [123].
[79] (2006) 9 HKCFAR 530, [37].

In *Leung Kwok Hung v HKSAR*, the CFA ruled that the Police Commissioner's power to ban or impose conditions on notified public processions in the interests of public order (*ordre public*) was unconstitutional. Specifically, the Court held that the term 'public order (ordre public)' (which the Public Order Ordinance reproduced from Article 21 of the ICCPR, which guarantees the freedom of assembly) was too imprecise, as it did not provide 'an adequate indication of the scope of the discretion with a degree of precision appropriate to the subject matter'.[80] The majority therefore severed the term 'ordre public' from 'public order' in the 'law and order' sense, and upheld the rest of the Public Order Ordinance. It should be noted, however, that the CFA merely obliterated one vague concept from the impugned regulatory scheme, leaving other statutory bases for police intervention untouched, eg national security, public safety, and the protection of rights and freedoms of others. The Commissioner of Police therefore continues to retain a host of at-large broad powers to prohibit or restrain the organisation of public processions on those equally vague grounds.[81] However, the Court did suggest in obiter that the police's statutory discretion to restrict public assembly for the purpose of protecting 'the rights and freedoms of others' was 'of such wide and imprecise import'[82] that this ground too may be unconstitutional, but the CFA did not decide this point.

Nevertheless, credit must be given to the Li Court in *Yeung May Wan v HKSAR* for upholding the constitutional right of a small group of peaceful protestors to demonstrate outside the Liaison Office of the Central People's Government in Hong Kong.[83] The peaceful demonstrators were convicted in the magistracy for obstructing a public place and assaulting the police upon arrest. Notably, the demonstrators belonged to a religious sect known as the Falun Gong, which has been under intense persecution on the mainland since 1999. The CFA quashed their convictions on the basis that the obstruction posed by the peaceful demonstrators was a 'reasonable' use of the pavement, as the facts indicated that there was still 'ample room for pedestrians as well as office workers safely to pass and to gain access'[84] to the Liaison Office building.

[80] (2005) 8 HKCFAR 229, [76].

[81] See J Brabyn, 'Leung Kwok Hung and Others through the Hong Kong Courts' (2006) 36 *Hong Kong Law Journal* 83.

[82] *Leung Kwok Hung* (n 80) [88].

[83] AHY Chen, 'Constitutional Adjudication in Post-1997 Hong Kong' (2006) 15(3) *Pacific Rim Law & Policy Journal* 627, 667.

[84] (2005) 8 HKCFAR 137, [47].

Since the 'obstruction' was a reasonable use of public space, the police's arrests of those demonstrators were thus illegal; the demonstrators were therefore justified in resisting the unlawful arrest.[85]

In *Prem Singh v Director of Immigration*, the CFA also invalidated a statutory clause that required an applicant for permanent residency to be 'not subject to any limit of stay'[86] imposed by the immigration authorities before he was eligible for the right of abode. This legislative requirement was ruled inconsistent with Article 24(2)(4) of the Basic Law as the latter only requires foreign nationals to have 'ordinarily resided in Hong Kong for a continuous period of not less than seven years and have taken Hong Kong as their place of permanent residence'. The CFA accepted that the Director could exclude foreign nationals from entering Hong Kong at his own discretion and could withdraw their permission to stay after entry, but the Court held that 'the discretionary removal of a limit of stay forms no part of the permanence requirement'.[87] Nevertheless, the CFA also decided that imprisonment – aside from *de minimis* overnight jail sentences for contempt of court – during the qualifying period would not be considered *ordinary* residence for the purpose of Article 24(2)(4).[88]

The Li Court also invented new constitutional remedies that were not expressly provided for in the Basic Law. But it is noteworthy that these judicial innovations were created to blunt the force of otherwise unconstitutional criminal legislation and to prevent it from losing effect immediately.

In *HKSAR v Lam Kwong Wai*, the CFA held that the Basic Law conferred on the courts 'implied powers'[89] to give a remedial interpretation to an otherwise unconstitutional law so that the impugned legislation could continue to apply, instead of being invalidated with immediate effect. On the facts, the impugned law required an accused charged with the possession of an imitation firearm to prove he had a lawful excuse. The lower court had invalidated the law as this provision was inconsistent with the presumption of innocence, a constitutionally protected right. On appeal, the CFA agreed that this law was a disproportionate restriction of this constitutional liberty, but decided that this law could nonetheless be upheld by reading down

[85] ibid [112].
[86] Immigration Ordinance, Sch 1, para 1(5) (Cap 115).
[87] (2003) 6 HKCFAR 26, [63].
[88] ibid [76].
[89] (2006) 9 HKCFAR 574, [78].

the persuasive/legal burden of proof imposed on the accused to an evidential burden to produce exculpatory evidence.[90] Other penal laws that imposed a legal burden of proof on the defendant were also read down by the CFA so that they now only place an evidential onus on the accused.[91]

Furthermore, in *Koo Sze Yiu v Chief Executive of the HKSAR*, the CFA held that the courts had the 'inherent jurisdiction'[92] to suspend a declaration of invalidity so that an unconstitutional law can continue to be enforced while the government prepares to enact corrective legislation. The impugned statutory provision in the Telecommunications Ordinance was invalidated in the lower courts as it allowed the Chief Executive, whenever they considered that public interest so required, to order the interception or disclosure to the government of any telecommunications. In the same case, an Executive Order that authorised and laid out the administrative procedures for the conduct of covert surveillance was also struck down. Upon further appeal, the unconstitutionality of the laws was accepted by the government, and the CFA was asked only to determine the appropriate remedy. Concerned that an immediate invalidation of the impugned procedures would unduly hamper legitimate interception and covert surveillance activities, the CFA suspended the declarations of invalidity, and allowed for the legislation and the Executive Order to be enforced in the interim, pending legislative change.

The most extraordinary remedy created by the CFA was the one in *Koon Wing Yee v Insider Dealing Tribunal*, where the Court recognised the power to invalidate a legislative provision that was constitutional. On the facts, the CFA determined that prosecutions for insider dealing offences before the Insider Dealing Tribunal (IDT) would be viewed as criminal, and not civil, in nature,[93] because the statutory penalty – the disgorgement of 300 per cent of the defendants' profits – was punitive in nature. But once the proceedings before the IDT were deemed criminal in nature, it naturally followed that section 33(6) of the Securities (Insider Dealing) Ordinance (SIDO), which compelled persons under investigation to answer questions posed to them under the said

[90] ibid [54].
[91] *HKSAR v Hung Chan Wa* (2006) 9 HKCFAR 614; *HKSAR v Ng Po On* (2008) 11 HKCFAR 91.
[92] (2006) 9 HKCFAR 441, [35].
[93] (2008) 11 HKCFAR 170, [49].

legislation, would violate their right against self-incrimination.[94] The consequence of this judicial determination would logically lead to the immediate invalidation of the impugned section 33(6), and the government would lose these investigatory powers under the said Ordinance. In an unusual move, the CFA acceded to the government's request of invalidating section 23(1)(c) of the SIDO instead – the penalty provision that authorised the disgorgement of 300 per cent of the defendants' profits, which was itself constitutional.[95] This case will be examined more closely in chapter seven.

C. Declarations of Invalidity

Post-*Chong Fung Yuen*, the most progressive constitutional rulings issued by the Andrew Li Court did not provoke any major controversy – despite the invalidation of laws – as they did not impact core concerns of the Central People's Government or the HKSAR government. But these decisions were nevertheless constitutional milestones in Hong Kong.

In *Solicitor v Law Society of Hong Kong*,[96] the CFA invalidated a finality provision in the Legal Practitioners Ordinance, which completely ousted the CFA's jurisdiction over all orders issued by the Solicitors Disciplinary Tribunal, on the basis that the impugned provision was inconsistent with the power of final adjudication vested in the Court.[97] The impugned law only allowed an appeal to the Court of Appeal. With this important decision, the CFA was able to gain supervisory control over the docket of its lower courts.

A bankruptcy provision was also invalidated in *Official Receiver v Chan Wing Hing* on the basis that the law disproportionately restricted a bankrupt's constitutional right to travel. On the facts, the impugned provision had required a bankrupt to notify his trustee of his travel itinerary prior to any trip outside of Hong Kong, otherwise the relevant period of his bankruptcy, which counts toward the discharge of his bankruptcy, would not continue to run during his absence. According to the majority, the sanction was disproportionate as it applied irrespective of the reason for the bankrupt's failure to notify, and no discretion was vested in the

[94] BOR, Art 11(2)(g).
[95] *Koon Wing Yee* (n 93) [110].
[96] (2003) 6 HKCFAR 570.
[97] Basic Law, Art 82.

court to disapply the sanction or mitigate its consequences in meritorious circumstances.[98]

In *Secretary for Justice v Yau Yuk Lung*, the CFA invalidated a statutory provision that targeted homosexual buggery in public. Even though sexual orientation was not an expressly protected class in the Basic Law or in the BORO, the Court ruled that all differentiations on the basis of sexual orientation must also be justified by the government.[99] Given that the government was unable to explain why homosexuals alone were subject to the statutory offence, the law was invalidated as it did not serve 'any legitimate aim'.[100] This monumental decision paved the way for a series of lesbian, gay, bisexual and transgender (LGBT) victories under Chief Justice Geoffrey Ma's stewardship of the CFA.

Finally, in *Lam Siu Po v Commissioner of Police*, the CFA invalidated those regulations that imposed a blanket ban on legal representation at the disciplinary hearings of police constables because the impugned rules violated the right to a fair hearing protected under Article 10 of the BOR. In deciding what Article 10 would mandate, the CFA opined that the 'well-developed common law principles of procedural fairness supply the answer'.[101] In other words, the CFA elevated the common law norms of procedural fairness to the constitutional level in situations where Article 10 is applicable. Previously, such common law norms were subject to legislation (including subsidiary legislation), but these norms are now given constitutional force and can override inconsistent legislation.[102]

VI. CFA DURING CHIEF JUSTICE GEOFFREY MA'S TENURE

Geoffrey Ma served as the HKSAR's second Chief Justice of the CFA from September 2010 to January 2021. Unlike the early years of the Andrew Li Court, the CFA with Geoffrey Ma at the helm avoided major constitutional controversies and preserved the central government's core interests in Hong Kong. On the other hand, the Court's most confrontational and progressive constitutional rulings pertain only to issues that Beijing cares less for – the CFA's supervisory control over the lower

[98] (2006) 9 HKCFAR 545, [47]–[49].
[99] (2007) 10 HKCFAR 335, [20].
[100] ibid [27].
[101] (2009) 12 HKCFAR 237, [137].
[102] Chen, 'International Human Rights Law' (n 12) 261.

courts, LGBT rights, bankruptcy reform and welfare entitlements. Nevertheless, these judicial decisions are of immense constitutional significance in Hong Kong. On domestic law and order issues, there have also been modest liberal developments as the CFA more regularly recasts otherwise restrictive laws in a more rights-friendly manner. On electoral restrictions, the Ma Court has signalled its willingness to defer to the government, uphold what is most essential to the core positions of the government, but equally ensuring that the unsuccessful claimants are not completely excluded by the outcome. These issues will now be explored in turn.

A. Central-HKSAR Constitutional Relations

In *Democratic Republic of the Congo v FG Hemisphere Associates LLC (No 1)*, the CFA in a 'provisional'[103] ruling determined that: (i) the determination of the applicable law of state immunity in Hong Kong constitutes an act of state falling within Article 19(3) of the Basic Law;[104] (ii) the HKSAR could not, as a matter of legal or constitutional principle, adhere to a doctrine of state immunity that was at variance with the PRC's, and therefore the doctrine of absolute immunity as practised in the Chinese mainland should apply too in Hong Kong;[105] and (iii) the CFA had a duty to refer the interpretation of Articles 13[106] and 19(3) of the Basic Law to the NPCSC, as these provisions concern respectively foreign affairs within the responsibility of the Central People's Government and the relationship between the central authorities and the HKSAR, and their interpretation was necessary for the adjudication of this case in question.[107]

As discussed in chapter two, *Congo* marked the first time the CFA initiated a judicial reference on a Basic Law provision to the NPCSC for interpretation. The decision was also groundbreaking because it overruled Hong Kong's long-standing practice since its colonial days of

[103] (2011) 14 HKCFAR 95, [183].

[104] Art 19(3) of the Basic Law provides: 'The courts of the Hong Kong Special Administrative Region shall have no jurisdiction over acts of state such as defence and foreign affairs.'

[105] *Congo* (n 103) [183(a)].

[106] Art 13(1) of the Basic Law provides: The Central People's Government shall be responsible for the foreign affairs relating to the Hong Kong Special Administrative Region.

[107] *Congo* (n 103) [183(c)].

applying a restrictive theory of state immunity, which had carved out an exception to state immunity for commercial transactions that states undertook.

But this result was inevitable. The PRC's Ministry of Foreign Affairs had placed three letters before the Hong Kong courts – twice in the lower courts and once before the CFA – insisting that the local judiciary must enforce the absolute theory of state immunity as practised in the rest of the PRC. If the CFA had ruled against the PRC's resolute stance, this would have been a Pyrrhic victory as the NPCSC would simply overrule the Court's ruling once again.[108]

One should also note that giving Hong Kong preferential treatment in this regard would undermine the PRC's consistent position of adhering to the absolute theory of state immunity in international law.[109] More importantly, most of the disputed transactions in the *Congo* case were not really 'commercial' in nature. On the facts, the plaintiff – FG Hemisphere – was trying to implead the Democratic Republic of the Congo (DRC) and attach funds originating from the PRC earmarked for a development scheme negotiated between the PRC and the DRC. China has pledged billions of dollars in investments or loans in Africa and Asia to boost its political influence in the regions and on the international stage.[110] If absolute immunity in Hong Kong were rejected, some of the PRC's state-owned and state-backed enterprises, with significant resources in this city and (as was the case in *Congo*) engaged in transactions with foreign governments, might have their assets that had been earmarked for these loans/investments siphoned off by international vulture funds, thereby impeding the PRC's foreign policy strategy abroad.

Possibly mindful of the public outcry that broke out when the Li Court had previously adopted a broad and liberal interpretation of the constitutional right of abode in *Ng Ka Ling* and *Chong Fung Yuen*, the CFA in *Vallejos v Commissioner of Registration* decided not to judicially expand the class of migrants that could acquire permanent residence. Herein, the CFA determined that foreign domestic helpers as a class had

[108] As in *Ng Ka Ling*, and as provided for in Art 158(3) of the Basic Law, an NPCSC Interpretation rendered *after* the CFA decided this case would not overturn the CFA's decision as far as the litigants in the case were concerned, as the NPCSC Interpretation would only be binding on HKSAR courts in all future cases.

[109] *Congo* (n 103) [290].

[110] M Pei, 'A Play for Global Leadership' (2018) 29 *Journal of Democracy* 37; Z Zhu, *China's New Diplomacy: Rationale, Strategies and Significance* (Ashgate Publishing, 2010) 25–27.

not 'ordinarily resided'[111] in Hong Kong and therefore could not – like other foreign nationals who reside and work in Hong Kong – acquire the right of abode under Article 24(2)(4) of the Basic Law after living seven continuous years in the city. Had the CFA ruled for the migrant workers, there would definitely have been an NPCSC Interpretation that reversed it, as the government counsel so warned.[112] But at the same time, the CFA reaffirmed the approach adopted in *Chong Fung Yuen*, and viewed the relevant passage on Article 24(2)(4) of the Basic Law in the text of the NPCSC's 1999 Interpretation as 'extrinsic materials'[113] which did not need to be relied on in this case. In *Gutierrez v Commissioner of Registration*, the CFA also held that children of these foreign domestic helpers – even if born in Hong Kong – may not acquire permanent residence unless the children have the subjective intention to establish a permanent home in Hong Kong and have objectively taken action to achieve that.[114] The facts that the Filipino child had no home in the Philippines and spoke no Tagalog would not suffice.[115]

In *Yau Wai Ching v Chief Executive of the HKSAR*,[116] the Appeal Committee of the CFA once again reaffirmed the proposition in *Lau Kong Yung* that NPCSC Interpretations apply retrospectively from the time the Basic Law took effect in Hong Kong. As discussed more fully in chapter five, the Appeal Committee of the CFA agreed with the lower courts that the 2016 Interpretation could be retrospectively enforced, and the errant lawmakers were automatically disqualified from assuming their offices when they refused to recite the requisite oath of office.

B. Law and Order

The most significant law-and-order ruling handed down by Ma CJ was also the CFA's final substantive constitutional law ruling before Ma's retirement. In *Kwok Wing Hang v Chief Executive in Council*, the CFA had to decide on whether the Chief Executive in Council (CEIC) can invoke the Emergency Regulations Ordinance (ERO) to make regulations on any occasion of public danger, and whether the Prohibition on Face

[111] Basic Law, Art 24(2)(4).
[112] (2013) 16 HKCFAR 45, [97].
[113] ibid [96].
[114] (2014) 17 HKCFAR 518, [37].
[115] ibid [51].
[116] (2017) 20 HKCFAR 390.

Covering Regulation (PFCR) – the subsidiary legislation enacted pursuant to the ERO – was constitutional.[117]

The context of this litigation has been discussed in previous chapters. For most of 2019, Hong Kong was rocked by civil unrest. The protests originally arose in opposition to the government's attempt to pass an extradition law that would allow for Hong Kong residents to be extradited to other countries and jurisdictions, including mainland China, Macau and Taiwan, to face trial for alleged serious offences committed there. Even though the Bill was eventually withdrawn, the unrest continued as protestors pressed on for other demands, including amnesty for arrested protestors and an independent inquiry into alleged police brutality. Notably, many protestors wore masks during the protests to prevent identification and to shield themselves from the effects of the tear gas and pepper spray used regularly by the police. In response to the escalating street violence, the CEIC invoked the ERO to enact the PFCR, which banned facial covering in public assemblies.

Notably, section 2(2)(g) of the ERO stipulates that regulations made by the CEIC on 'an occasion of emergency or public danger' may provide for and have the effect of 'amending any enactment, suspending the operation of any enactment and applying any enactment with or without modification'. Section 2(4) of the ERO further provides that

> [a] regulation … shall have effect notwithstanding anything inconsistent therewith contained in any enactment; and any provision of an enactment which may be inconsistent with any regulation … shall … have no effect so long as such regulation … remain in force.

The upshot of these two provisions would be that, on its face, the ERO would have allowed the CEIC to pass regulations that override all BORO rights.

But the CFA in the *Kwok Wing Hang* case neutralised the draconian effects of the ERO by ruling that any regulations enacted pursuant to the ERO must not restrict any 'fundamental rights protected under the ICCPR and the BORO as guaranteed under Article 39 of the Basic Law unless the regulations satisfy the prescribed by law requirement and proportionality analysis'.[118] In short, because of Article 39 of the Basic Law, regulations made under the ERO cannot be used to 'override the HKBORO'.[119]

[117] See also the discussion of this case in ch 3, s II above.
[118] [2020] HKCFA 42, [69].
[119] ibid [73].

Nevertheless, when examining the proportionality of the PFCR, the CFA overturned the lower court's decision to invalidate the PFCR's ban on facial covering at lawful peaceful assemblies. For the CFA, it was proportionate even to ban facial covering at these authorised assemblies:

> [T]here is no simple dichotomy between peaceful and violent protesters and that it is important to give effect to the preventative and deterrent nature of the prohibition. Resort to police powers to order a dispersal when a fluid situation is deteriorating is too late and of little practical efficacy in the factual circumstances surrounding the making of the PFCR.[120]

In the CFA's view, it is proportionate to dampen the emboldening effect of a facial covering at all assemblies, especially since the 'desire for anonymity, does not lie at the heart of the right to peaceful assembly. It is still possible to demonstrate peacefully without wearing a facial covering.'[121]

On other law-and-order issues, there have been modestly liberal developments. The Ma Court has actively engaged in what is termed 'dialogic review'.[122] Instead of deeming an impugned legislative or executive practice unconstitutional per se, the CFA more regularly enforces constitutional rights in a way that leaves sufficient decisional space to the legislature or allows the legislature to disagree using the ordinary legislative process. Furthermore, the CFA, being very attentive to potential governmental backlash, regularly strategically blunts the force of its liberal decisions ex ante so as to secure ex post compliance or acquiescence from the government. These cases will be examined below.

(i) Mitigation of Absolute Liability Offences

Previously in *So Wai Lun v HKSAR*, the CFA – during Li CJ's tenure – had been sympathetic to the legislature's imposition of absolute liability for serious crimes, even if it might be preferable 'for the offence to admit of a defence of belief or reasonable belief'.[123] On the facts, the Li Court refused to invalidate a penal provision that omitted a *mens rea* requirement for the offence of unlawful sexual intercourse with a minor to be established.

[120] ibid [129].
[121] ibid [134].
[122] See PJ Yap, *Constitutional Dialogue in Common Law Asia* (Oxford University Press, 2015) 93–96.
[123] (2006) 9 HKCFAR 530, [37].

But the Ma Court has begun to sow seeds of change. In *Kulemesin v HKSAR*, the CFA held that where the offence-creating penal provisions were silent or ambiguous as to the *mens rea*, 'the more serious the offence in terms of penalty and social obloquy, the less likely it is that the presumption of *mens rea* will be held to have been supplanted'.[124] Where a serious offence carrying severe penalties was involved, the CFA held that the following alternative regime on *mens rea* could apply:

> [T]he prosecution need not set out to prove *mens rea*, but if there is evidence capable of raising a reasonable doubt that the defendant may have acted or omitted to act in the honest and reasonable belief that the circumstances *or likely consequences* of his conduct were such that, if true, liability would not attach, he must be acquitted unless the prosecution proves beyond reasonable doubt the absence of such exculpatory belief or that there were no reasonable grounds for such belief ...[125]

One must note what the CFA was doing here: in essence, the Court was construing an ambiguous penal statute in ways that advanced substantive values of due process. But at the same time, the principles enunciated by the Court are mere common law 'clear-statement' rules that leave it open for the legislature to override the Court's interpretive presumptions by ordinary legislation if it so wishes. In other words, the Legislative Council can simply disagree and statutorily remove the 'due diligence' defence in express terms if it so chooses. But until the legislature does so, the CFA has imposed a new 'default rule' that enhances criminal due process for the accused charged with serious crimes.

To this end, the CFA in *HKSAR v Choi Wai Lun* determined that a penal provision that criminalised indecent assault on a minor did not impose absolute liability but merely absolved the prosecution from proving '*mens rea* as to the girl's age, but the accused has a good defence if he can prove on a balance of probabilities that he honestly and reasonably believed that the girl was 16 or over'.[126]

(ii) Prohibition against Cruel, Inhuman or Degrading Treatment or Punishment (CIDTP) is Non-derogable

In *Ubamaka v Secretary for Security*, the CFA, for the first time, read down an ouster clause pertaining to BORO rights. Notably, section 5(1)

[124] (2013) 16 HKCFAR 195, [59].
[125] ibid [83(b)].
[126] (2018) 21 HKCFAR 167, [70].

read with section 5(2)(c) of the BORO provides that Article 3 of the Bill of Rights, which prohibits CIDTP, is non-derogable even in times of a public emergency that threatens the life of the nation. Notwithstanding section 5, section 11 of the BORO provides that, 'As regards persons not having the right to enter and remain in Hong Kong, [the BORO] does not affect any immigration legislation governing entry into, stay in and departure from Hong Kong, or the application of any such legislation'. Interestingly, in addressing the apparent conflict between sections 5 and 11 of the BORO, the CFA decided that 'precedence'[127] must be given to the absolute character of the Article 3 right. Henceforth, section 11 must be read as qualified by section 5, and section 11 would apply in immigration cases 'except insofar as the non-derogable and absolute rights protected by BOR art.3 are engaged'.[128]

While the CFA refused to allow section 11 of the BORO to immunise immigration laws from the prohibition against CIDTP, the Court strategically blunted the impact of its decision by setting 'a very high threshold'[129] that has to be surmounted before a claimant can actually benefit from this CIDTP protection. The CFA held that in order to benefit from this Article 3 protection, a person claiming that he is at risk of being subjected to CIDTP if deported from Hong Kong pursuant to the immigration legislation must demonstrate that: '(i) the ill-treatment which he would face if expelled attains what has been called "a minimum level of severity"; and (ii) that he faces a genuine and substantial risk of being subjected to such mistreatment'.[130] On the facts of this case, the CFA held that the claimant's severe mental and psychological blow at the prospect of facing another trial abroad, and potential imprisonment for an offence for which he had already been convicted and served a sentence in Hong Kong, would not meet the threshold requirements for establishing CIDTP.

Ubamaka concerned the deportation of foreign nationals with criminal records – a typical high-stakes decision for the Hong Kong government. Nevertheless, while the CFA drew a line in the sand by refusing to exempt immigration practices from the BORO's ban on CIDTP and conferred constitutional protection on these statutory rights, the CFA also dialogically blunted the potential impact of its decision by raising the bar for a successful CIDTP claim, thereby assuring the

[127] (2012) 15 HKCFAR 743, [115].
[128] ibid.
[129] ibid [172].
[130] ibid.

government that it was not opening the floodgates to a litany of unmeritorious claims. In *GA v Director of Immigration*,[131] the CFA extended the principles established in *Ubamaka* to the review of the government's general prohibition against mandated refugees and screened-in torture claimants obtaining paid employment in Hong Kong, so that these claimants must be allowed to work if they would face a substantial and imminent risk of inhumane or degrading treatment otherwise.

(iii) Extension of Constitutional Rights for Non-residents

Ghulam Rbani v Secretary for Justice is another extraordinary decision. In essence, the CFA had to address whether the government's power of detaining non-residents pending removal under the Immigration Ordinance was subject to any applicable principle of law barring arbitrary or unlawful detention. The applicant – a serial overstayer – had argued inter alia that his detention was unlawful as it was in violation of Article 28 of the Basic Law (read with Article 41). Notably, the constitutional right against arbitrary or unlawful arrest, detention or imprisonment enshrined in Article 28 is only expressly conferred on Hong Kong residents, and the applicant was not one. It is also noteworthy that the Basic Law mostly confers constitutional rights on its residents. For non-residents, they merely have the constitutional 'right to a fair trial by the judicial organs without delay and shall be presumed innocent until convicted';[132] and pursuant to Article 41, they shall 'in accordance with law' enjoy the rights and freedoms of Hong Kong residents.

But the CFA emphatically rejected the notion that the words 'in accordance with law' in Article 41 permit the legislature, 'simply by passing legislation',[133] to deprive non-residents of constitutional rights. As the CFA reasoned, if that had been the Basic Law's intention, Article 41 would not have been included at all. Furthermore, the CFA went on to state that 'The object of BL art. 41 is to extend the Chapter III constitutional guarantees to persons in Hong Kong who are not residents'.[134] Obviously, the drafting history of the Basic Law would clearly indicate that the framers never intended to confer an identical bundle of constitutional rights on residents and non-residents alike, and the CFA in all likelihood knew this. If left unmitigated, the CFA's broad reading

[131] (2014) 17 HKCFAR 60, [45].
[132] Basic Law, Art 87.
[133] (2014) 17 HKCFAR 138, [93].
[134] ibid.

of Article 41 would have neutralised section 11 of the BORO. If non-residents now had the constitutional right against arbitrary detention, the statutory ouster clause, which insulated all immigration practices from rights review, would be in jeopardy. Hence, the CFA swiftly executed its next nifty move. Section 11, despite being a mere statutory provision, 'operates at the constitutional level and qualifies the scope and effect of BL art.41'.[135] In essence, the CFA converts a statutory exception, which can always be repealed by ordinary legislation, to a constitutional derogation that disapplies constitutional rights directly.

By constitutionalising the statutory ouster expressed in section 11, the CFA preserved the government's primary concern of insulating the core pillars of the immigration regime from rights review. But since section 11 only pertains to immigration matters, the CFA could then rule that this ouster clause does *not* preclude non-residents from enforcing the swathe of constitutional rights – contained in Chapter III of Basic Law – that the CFA was now conferring on non-residents 'in respect of legislation other than "immigration legislation"'.[136] Furthermore, the CFA also determined that section 11 would also *not* preclude these non-residents from relying on any common law right against arbitrary arrest or detention, specifically the *Hardial Singh* common law principles[137] that regulate the government's statutory power of administrative detention. On the facts, the CFA held that the applicant's detention was excessive by 10 days and was inconsistent with the *Hardial Singh* principles.

As discussed earlier, in *Comilang Milagros Tecson v Director of Immigration*, the CFA also ruled that non-residents could not, in arguing that they were entitled to remain in the city, rely on the constitutional right of abode – a right not included in the BORO – to circumvent section 11's foreclosure of the BORO and other 'cognate rights in the Basic Law (here the family unity rights)'.[138]

(iv) Rewriting the Impugned Law under the Guise of Upholding it

In *HKSAR v Fong Kwok Shan Christine*, an administrative by-law that ostensibly imposed a blanket prohibition on signs and messages, including signs or messages on items of clothing of persons in the public/press gallery of the Legislative Council, was read down by the CFA, so that

[135] ibid [94].
[136] ibid [98].
[137] ibid [22]–[23].
[138] (2019) 22 HKCFAR 59, [69].

the impugned by-law would only apply to 'conduct which amounts to behaving in a disorderly manner'.[139] In the same vein, in *HKSAR v Wan Thomas*, prison rules that limited visits to 'friends' of inmates were construed by the CFA to include companies that deliver meals and magazines to them, such that employees of these companies were acquitted of defrauding officers of the Correctional Services Department when they had represented themselves as the inmates' friends.[140] Note that the visitors in question did not have any pre-existing personal relationship with the inmates and had never met them.[141] But in view of its 'proper construction'[142] of the prison rules, the CFA held that it was unnecessary to determine whether they were inconsistent with the BORO.

(v) Non-retrospectivity of Harsher Criminal Sentences

In 2018, the CFA unanimously freed the student leaders of the 'Occupy Central' movement – a mass street protest that partially shut down Hong Kong's financial district for 79 consecutive days – for public order offences they committed in the lead up to the road blockades.[143] The Court of Appeal had imposed a custodial sentence that ranged from six to eight months of imprisonment. Specifically, the Court of Appeal announced a new list of factors that the courts should consider when determining the appropriate sentence for unlawful assembly involving violence,[144] and held that community service orders or suspended prison sentences imposed by the magistrate were manifestly inadequate. On appeal, the CFA agreed that the Court of Appeal was right to issue a new sentencing guideline on unlawful assemblies involving violence, but as the custodial sentences imposed by the Court of Appeal on the offenders were significantly more severe than the range established by past judicial practice, the CFA held that these guidelines could not be retrospectively applied to the offenders.[145] This was indeed a wise solution. The CFA stood up for a cardinal due process principle that an offender should not suffer a heavier punishment than was prescribed at the time the offence was committed; the government was equally appeased by the fact that

[139] (2017) 20 HKCFAR 425, [107].
[140] *HKSAR v Wan Thomas* (2018) 21 HKCFAR 214.
[141] ibid [19].
[142] ibid [50].
[143] *Secretary for Justice v Wong Chi Fung* (2018) 21 HKCFAR 35.
[144] *Secretary for Justice v Wong Chi Fung* [2018] 2 HKLRD 699, [135].
[145] *Wong Chi Fung* (n 143) [126].

future unlawful assemblies involving violence will be 'subject to the new guidelines'.[146]

C. Express Findings of Unconstitutionality

Continuing the trends of the Andrew Li Court in its later years, the Geoffrey Ma Court's express findings of unconstitutionality were reserved for decisions that did not encroach on Beijing's core concerns or impede the HKSAR government's ability to maintain law and order. Where the political stakes are lowest, the CFA is confident that any potential backlash would be least severe, and the CFA can therefore assert its authority more decisively and give a more generous interpretation of the Basic Law. These express findings of unconstitutionality all pertained to judicial orders that the HKSAR government would grudgingly enforce, even if it might not agree with the Court on the merits.

As discussed earlier, the Li Court had invalidated a finality provision in the Legal Practitioners Ordinance, which completely ousted the CFA's jurisdiction over all orders issued by the Solicitors Disciplinary Tribunal on the basis that the impugned provision was inter alia inconsistent with the power of final adjudication vested in the CFA.[147] In the same vein, the Ma Court in *Mok Charles v Tam Wai Ho*[148] invalidated another finality provision in the Legislative Council Ordinance, which provided that, in the case of an election petition questioning the election of a member to the Legislative Council, the decision of the Court of the First Instance shall be final.

In the same vein, relying on a series of Li Court's precedents,[149] the Ma Court in *Lee To Nei v HKSAR* read down a legal burden of proof imposed on the defendant such that the accused would only have the evidential burden to adduce credible evidence that the elements for his liability were not satisfied, and where such evidence existed, the legal onus would remain on the prosecution to prove the accused's guilt beyond reasonable doubt.[150]

Previously, the Li Court had invalidated a bankruptcy law provision on the basis that it disproportionately restricted a bankrupt's

[146] ibid [135].
[147] *Solicitor v Law Society of Hong Kong* (2003) 6 HKCFAR 570.
[148] (2010) 13 HKCFAR 762.
[149] *HKSAR v Lam Kwong Wai* (2006) 9 HKCFAR 574; *HKSAR v Hung Chan Wa* (2006) 9 HKCFAR 614; *HKSAR v Ng Po On* (2008) 11 HKCFAR 91.
[150] (2012) 15 HKCFAR 162, [52].

constitutional right to travel.[151] Similarly, the Ma Court in *Official Receiver v Zhi Charles* invalidated another bankruptcy provision, which stated that when a bankrupt left Hong Kong before the commencement of his bankruptcy, the relevant period of his bankruptcy would be suspended until he returned to Hong Kong and notified his trustee of his return. As the sanction imposed by the bankruptcy provision applied regardless of whether the bankrupt was willing to co-operate with his trustee or whether the bankrupt was unable to return because of illness, impecuniosity or incarceration,[152] the CFA held that this provision too was a disproportionate restriction on his constitutional right to travel and therefore unconstitutional.

The Ma Court also advanced the progressive LGBT agenda established by the Li Court and ruled in favour of transsexual marriage in 2013. In *W v Registrar of Marriages*,[153] the CFA determined that the Registrar of Marriages, in applying the existing matrimonial legislation in Hong Kong that prohibited a post-operative male-to-female transsexual from marrying (a male) in the capacity of her acquired gender, had violated her constitutional right to marriage. Next, in *QT v Director of Immigration*,[154] the CFA upended the Immigration Department's discriminatory practice of limiting spousal dependant visas to expatriates who were in heterosexual marriages, and extended persons in same-sex civil partnerships (entered into abroad) equal access to these visas. Finally, in *Leung Chun Kwong v Secretary for Civil Service*, the CFA ruled that it was unconstitutional for the Civil Service to deny spousal benefits to same-sex couples married overseas and for the Inland Revenue Department to prohibit these couples from electing for joint-tax assessment when both benefits were conferred on married heterosexual couples. While the CFA accepted that the government was entitled to protect the traditional family constituted by heterosexual marriage, the CFA was 'unable to accept the proposition that heterosexual marriage would be undermined by the extension of [these] benefits to same-sex married couples … Heterosexual marriage is not promoted by the differential treatment in question'.[155]

Similarly, gender stereotypes were ameliorated when the prison authorities' long-standing policy of requiring male inmates to keep

[151] *Official Receiver v Chan Wing Hing* (2006) 9 HKCFAR 545.
[152] (2015) 18 HKCFAR 467, [55].
[153] (2013) 16 HKCFAR 112.
[154] (2018) 21 HKCFAR 324.
[155] (2019) 22 HKCFAR 127, [72].

a 'sufficiently close'[156] haircut – while females were exempted – was ruled to be a violation of the Sex Discrimination Ordinance (SDO). In *Leung Kwok Hung v Commissioner of Correctional Services*, the CFA held that this differential treatment based on conventional standards of appearance in society simply does not have any reasonable connection with custodial discipline, especially since the government did not explain 'why individual choice should be denied to male prisoners but not female ones, and what this selective denial of choice has to do with a de-emphasis on individuality'.[157] While this decision was reached under the SDO, the CFA also held that the 'outcome would not be different'[158] under the constitutional right to equality.

In *Kong Yunming v Director of Social Welfare*, the CFA invalidated the Hong Kong government's policy that required all recipients of the Comprehensive Social Security Assistance Scheme (CSSA) to have been a Hong Kong resident for at least seven years. Specifically, the CFA's 'stroke of genius'[159] was in its adoption of the social welfare entitlements as at 1 July 1997 as the baseline for constitutional protection,[160] so that all governmental restrictions below this baseline have to be justified using PA. (Prior to the handover in 1997, residents were eligible for CSSA welfare after living in the city for a year.) Rather oddly, the CFA concluded that there was no rational nexus between the increased residency requirement and the government's avowed legitimate aim of ensuring the long-term sustainability of the welfare system.[161] Notably, the CFA relied on the statistics for the fiscal year 2001–02 as its example, and noted that if the seven-year rule had been in effect then, the government would have saved less than HK$764 million out of a total CSSA expenditure of HK$14.4 billion that year.[162] According to the CFA, such 'relatively insignificant level of savings … severely undermines'[163] the suggestion that the seven-year rule was rationally connected to the avowed legitimate aim of safeguarding the sustainability of the social security system. To be fair, the

[156] Correctional Services Standing Order 41-05.
[157] *Leung Kwok Hung* [2020] HKCFA 37, [49].
[158] ibid [56].
[159] A Chen, '"A Stroke of Genius" in *Kong Yunming*' (2014) 44 *Hong Kong Law Journal* 7.
[160] *Kong Yunming v Director of Social Welfare* (2013) 16 HKCFAR 950, [35].
[161] For a contrary view, see PJ Yap and T Wong, 'Public Welfare and the Judicial Over-enforcement of Socio-economic Rights in Hong Kong' (2014) 44 *Hong Kong Law Journal* 41.
[162] *Kong Yunming* (n 160) [94]–[95].
[163] ibid [96].

fact that there was about HK$764 million dollars of savings suggests that a rational connection can be established between the law and the legislative aim. In fact, one may note that in the fiscal year 2012–13 – the fiscal year that immediately preceded the CFA decision of *Kong Yunming* – the HK government actually spent about HK$19 billion on CSSA.[164] Post-*Kong Yunming*, in the fiscal year 2016–17, the CSSA expenditure ballooned to approximately HK$22 billion.[165] Regardless of whether one agrees that the cost imposition of HK$764 million (or even HK$3 billion – the increased expenditure from HK$19 billion to HK$22 billion) a year would just be a 'relatively insignificant' drain on the city's coffers, *Kong Yunming* marked a monumental decision as the CFA has decisively conferred the constitutional right of social welfare on all residents who have lived in Hong Kong for at least a year.

D. Constitutionality of Electoral Restrictions

Equally significant is the Ma Court's strategic efforts to 'trim' the excesses of the HKSAR government's policy choices on electoral restrictions. 'Trimming' has been defended by Cass Sunstein as a heuristic for judges to attend carefully to competing positions and attempt to steer between the poles when reaching a particular legal result.[166] Judges 'trim' either by striking a middle path or by preserving what is most essential to competing reasonable positions, so that political conflict is reduced and people who hold competing positions do not feel humiliated or excluded by the outcome.[167]

In *Leung Chun Ying v Ho Chun Yan Albert*, the CFA upheld the constitutionality of a statutory provision that restricted a failed candidate in the Chief Executive race to only seven days to lodge an election petition after the result was declared,[168] and thus overruled the lower court's decision to read-in a judicial discretion to extend time. In the lower court, the seven-day limit was deemed unconstitutional as the government could not discharge its burden of justifying how a short

164 Social Welfare Department, 'Social Welfare Services in Figures 2014' (2014) 5, https://web.archive.org/web/20150924112329/www.swd.gov.hk/doc/res_stat/swdfig2014.pdf.

165 Social Welfare Department, 'Social Welfare Services in Figures 2017' (2017) 5, www.swd.gov.hk/storage/asset/s/296/en/swdfig2017.pdf.

166 C Sunstein, 'Trimming' (2009) 122 *Harvard Law Review* 1049, 1051.

167 ibid 1053.

168 Chief Executive Election Ordinance (Cap 569), s 34(1).

time bar as such was proportionate. Specifically, the lower court applied *Mok Charles v Tam Wai Ho*,[169] discussed above, where the CFA had invalidated a statutory restriction that barred the CFA from hearing any appeal over Legislative Council electoral disputes. In disagreement with the lower court, the CFA in *Leung Chun Ying* now insisted that its prior *Charles Mok* decision could be distinguished:

> No useful guidance can be obtained from *Charles Mok* … In that case, the court was faced with a total absence of any appeal in election petition proceedings … This is not the same situation in the present case where a comparison had to be made between time limits.[170]

While the CFA was certainly right that *Charles Mok* could be distinguished on the basis that the Court was therein addressing a statutory clause that ousted the CFA's jurisdiction completely, it is important to note that in *Charles Mok*, the Court required the government to demonstrate how the legislative restriction at issue was proportionate, in particular how it was 'no more than is necessary'[171] to accomplish the legitimate aims of the restriction. To be consistent, the CFA in *Leung Chun Ying* could have required the government to prove how this tight seven-day time bar was necessary, especially since returns for election expenses in the Chief Executive elections do not have to be lodged until 30 days after the publication of the election result, so it would be well past the seven-day deadline before any illegal conduct in this regard could be discovered and raised in a timely election petition.[172]

However, in *Leung Chun Ying*, the CFA did *not* mention, let alone apply, the proportionality analysis. Instead, the proportionality test applied in *Charles Mok* was turned on its head when the CFA decided to accord significant deference to the legislative choice, instead of requiring the government to discharge its burden of proof and demonstrate how the rights derogation at issue was proportionate:

> Elections, however, also involve political and policy considerations and it is in these areas where the legislature is involved. The determination that seven days is the appropriate limit for the lodging of election petitions is one that does involve considerations other than legal ones. A due margin of appreciation should be accorded in the present case.[173]

[169] (2010) 13 HKCFAR 762.
[170] *Leung Chun Ying v Ho Chun Yan, Albert* (2013) 16 HKCFAR 735, [47(3)].
[171] *Charles Mok* (n 169) [28].
[172] *Leung Chun Ying* (n 170) [48].
[173] ibid [45].

By sweeping aside the proportionality analysis, the CFA was thus free to downplay the possible excessiveness of the seven-day time bar.

But, in perhaps the most important part of this judgment, the CFA then suggested an alternative mode of electoral redress: persons who were *not* candidates in the Chief Executive election, and hence were unaffected by the seven-day time bar that applied only to the election candidates, could still launch separate judicial review proceedings against the election result.[174] In other words, while the candidates themselves were time-barred after seven days, their surrogates were still free to seek judicial review and challenge the validity of the election after that time. There is essentially no substantive difference in result between (i) allowing the Court to exercise a discretion to extend the seven-day time bar for candidates lodging election petitions and (ii) authorising their third-party surrogates or any other person to seek leave to bring judicial review proceedings to litigate the very same electoral issue. But in ruling as it did, the CFA reached a decision that upheld the impugned law – thereby avoiding a potential conflict with the government – whilst preserving its oversight over electoral matters.

Next, in *Kwok Cheuk Kin v Secretary for Constitutional and Mainland Affairs*, the CFA upheld a law that disqualifies a legislator from running in the by-election held to fill a vacancy consequent on that member's resignation. The law was passed in 2012 after five pro-democracy legislative councillors from different geographical constituencies resigned, as a collective act of political protest, mid-term in 2010 to trigger city-wide by-elections for their seats, claiming that the by-elections could serve as a 'de facto referendum' on their views on democratic reforms.

The focus of the electoral challenge centred on whether the electoral restriction was proportionate. The CFA once again reaffirmed that 'Where electoral laws involve political or policy considerations, a wider margin of appreciation ought generally to be accorded'.[175] The Court agreed that it was legitimate for the government to deter resignations with a view to triggering by-elections, especially since this political exercise cost HK$126 million in public expenditure in 2010.[176] Furthermore, this electoral restriction was deemed no more than necessary as 'some leeway should be permitted to the Legislature to determine what would be an appropriate way of dealing with the perceived mischief'.[177]

[174] ibid [49].
[175] *Kwok Cheuk Kin v Secretary for Constitutional and Mainland Affairs* (2017) 20 HKCFAR 353, [42].
[176] ibid [9].
[177] ibid [55].

Interestingly, counsel for the applicant had raised concerns that this law was overbroad insofar as it had also barred legislative councillors who had resigned due to poor health but recovered in time for the by-election. But the CFA parried this concern by stating that, pursuant to Article 79(2) of the Basic Law,[178] ailing legislators would have a 'valid reason' to be absent from the Legislative Council (LegCo) meetings and could *not* be disqualified from office,[179] and therefore have no reason to resign from office. This judicial manoeuvre extraordinarily neutralised Article 79(1) of the Basic Law, which authorised the President of LegCo to disqualify a LegCo member if 'he or she loses the ability to discharge their duties as a result of serious illness or other reasons'. It is also noteworthy that the CFA made no mention of Article 79(1) at all, let alone square its reading of Article 79(2) with Article 79(1).

VII. CFA DURING CHIEF JUSTICE ANDREW CHEUNG'S TENURE

Chief Justice Andrew Cheung assumed leadership of the CFA in January 2021. As of early 2023, when this volume was completed, the CFA has decided only three substantive constitutional decisions. In *HKSAR v Lai Chee Ying*, the CFA determined, on the basis of Article 42(2) of Hong Kong's National Security Law (NSL), that the requirements for bail under the NSL are 'more stringent'[180] than the position under the ordinary criminal law, where a presumption in favour of bail exists. But the Court also ruled *against* the government when the former concluded that the bail conditions should *not* be presumptively excluded from consideration when judges decide whether to grant bail under the NSL.[181] Notably, the CFA also accepted that the NSL had been validly promulgated in the HKSAR by the NPCSC in accordance with Article 18(3) of the Basic Law. The CFA further opined that 'there is no power to hold any provision of the NSL to be unconstitutional or invalid as incompatible with the Basic Law and Bill of Rights',[182] but it is unclear

[178] Art 79 of the Basic Law reads: 'The President of the Legislative Council of the Hong Kong Special Administrative Region shall declare that a member of the Council is no longer qualified for the office under any of the following circumstances: … (2) When he or she, with no valid reason, is absent from meetings for three consecutive months without the consent of the President of the Legislative Council.'

[179] *Kwok Cheuk Kin* (n 175) [58].

[180] [2021] HKCFA 3, [53(b)].

[181] ibid [57].

[182] ibid [42].

whether this pronouncement was intended as a definitive ruling on the constitutionality of the NSL or was merely premised on the concession from the accused's counsel that he was not challenging the constitutionality of any provision of the NSL.[183] In *HKSAR v Ng Hau Yi*,[184] the Appeal Committee of the CFA also confirmed that sedition – an offence prohibited under section 10(1)(c) of the Crimes Ordinance – also qualifies as an offence endangering national security and therefore the more stringent threshold for the grant of bail stipulated under the NSL would equally apply to this offence.

The second substantive constitutional law judgment handed down by the Andrew Cheung Court pertained to the constitutionality of the Small House Policy (SHP) in Hong Kong. Under this controversial policy, every male indigenous villager – descended through the patrilineal line from a resident in 1898 of a recognised village in the New Territories – is allowed to build a small house on a suitable site in his own village. Female indigenous villagers do not enjoy this housing benefit, nor do non-indigenous villagers.

In *Kwok Cheuk Kin v Director of Lands*,[185] the applicant argued that the SHP was discriminatory. At the heart of this constitutional dispute is the interpretation of Article 40 of the Basic Law: 'The lawful traditional rights and interests of the indigenous inhabitants of the "New Territories" shall be protected by the Hong Kong Special Administrative Region.' In this case, the CFA decided that anti-discrimination laws could not be relied upon to subvert the SHP as the SHP is a traditional right and interest within Article 40 of the Basic Law, which 'qualifies and limits'[186] the application of the Court's equality jurisprudence. Ergo, non-beneficiaries – women and non-indigenous villagers – of the SHP may *not* bring constitutional challenges against the operation of this policy. But at the same time, the CFA interestingly did not accept that the rights of SHP beneficiaries were constitutional in nature. Instead, an eligible SHP applicant only has 'a right to have his application dealt with in accordance with the criteria laid down in the government's public statements of the current [Small House] Policy, subject to a lawfully exercised administrative discretion of the Lands Department'.[187] The CFA did not explain this stance; it merely asserted so. Ergo, subject to the

[183] ibid [33].
[184] [2021] HKCFA 42.
[185] [2021] HKCFA 38.
[186] ibid [43].
[187] ibid [45].

rules of administrative justice, the government is free to modify and even repeal the SHP if it so chooses in the future. In other words, Article 40 does not confer a constitutional right on the SHP beneficiaries; it merely insulates the SHP – if in existence – from a constitutional challenge.

Finally, in early 2023, the CFA unanimously ruled that it was unconstitutional for the Commissioner of Registration to require female-to-male transgender persons to undergo full sex reassignment surgery before they could alter their gender markers on Hong Kong Identity Cards.[188] The Court ruled that the impugned Commissioner's Guidelines was a disproportionate infringement on transgender persons' right to privacy protected under Article 14 of the Bill of Rights as the requirement for full sex reassignment surgery did not 'represent the only workable, objective and verifiable criterion for altering the gender marker'.[189]

Besides these constitutional law rulings, the Andrew Cheung Court also handed down two landmark criminal law decisions that have immense due process implications. In *HKSAR v Leung Tin Kei*,[190] the CFA unanimously decided that the common law doctrine of joint enterprise cannot be used to impose liability on a defendant as a principal offender for the offences of unlawful assembly or rioting if the defendant was not physically present at the unlawful or riotous assembly. Next, in *HKSAR v Chan Chun Kit*,[191] the CFA also ruled unanimously that a six-inch plastic cable tie is not an 'instrument fit for unlawful purposes' that is prohibited under the Summary Offences Ordinance. As the penal legislation expressly lists 'crowbar, picklock, skeleton key'[192] as statutory examples, the CFA ruled that the *ejusdem generis* rule of statutory interpretation would limit an 'instrument fit for unlawful purposes' to only instruments fit for gaining unlawful access to premises, vehicles or objects.[193]

As CJ Andrew Cheung's tenure only commenced in 2021, it would be premature at this stage to assess his legacy. But one hopes that the CFA he now leads would continue the commendable approach adopted by his predecessors where the judges were described as 'neither too proud nor too humble'[194] (*bukang bubei*, 不亢不卑) when determining the constitutional and legal limits of governmental power.

[188] *Q v Commissioner of Registration* [2023] HKCFA 4.
[189] ibid [103].
[190] [2021] HKCFA 37.
[191] [2022] HKCFA 15.
[192] Summary Offences Ordinance, s 17.
[193] *Chan Chun Kit* (n 191) [28].
[194] Chen, 'Constitutional Adjudication in Post-1997 Hong Kong' (n 83) 629.

VIII. CONCLUSION

The fundamental jurisprudential conundrum that the CFA faces is how it can preserve the judiciary as a separate and independent branch of government, respected both locally and internationally, whilst quelling any concerns from the mainland that, if left unleashed, Hong Kong courts would turn the city into another 'renegade province' in the south.

If the Hong Kong courts are too aggressive in invalidating legislation, this might trigger a backlash that takes the form of an Interpretation from the NPCSC.[195] On the other hand, if the judges are too deferential towards the HKSAR government, the Basic Law would be reduced to a mere hollow shell that only protects constitutional rights on paper but not in practice.

The Geoffrey Ma Court, and the Andrew Li Court in its later years, were careful about upholding the core interests of the central authorities and the HKSAR government in the city. On these high-stakes decisions, the Court and the government would be in lockstep. But the Court has been equally jealous about protecting its own powers of adjudication, and has taken pains to preserve this constitutional prerogative. On the other hand, for rights controversies with lower stakes, the CFA has deliberately avoided the austerity of tabulated legalism, as the judges were probably confident that, in these instances, the political backlash against their rulings would be minimal. These cases therefore provide the best opportunity for the Court to intervene aggressively, advance the development of human rights, and signal to the public and global community that the Hong Kong judiciary remains separate and independent.

For better or for worse, this has been the CFA's solution to the jurisprudential conundrum of preserving civil liberties in this new age where the Court regularly chooses 'the middle path'[196] between confrontation with and subservience to Beijing.

Almost 300 years ago, Lord Mansfield once exhorted judges as follows: 'We must not regard political consequences; how formidable soever they might be: if rebellion was the certain consequence, we are

[195] In the worst-case scenario, the NPCSC may, by promulgating an Interpretation, strip the HKSAR courts of their power to review the compatibility of local legislation (or at least pre-1997 legislation) with the Basic Law. It is noteworthy that immediately after the Court of First Instance in the *Kwok Wing Hang* case held that the ERO was at least partially unconstitutional (insofar as it conferred legislative powers on the CEIC on occasions of 'public danger'), a spokesman for the Legislative Affairs Commission of the NPCSC questioned the court's authority to declare pre-1997 statutory provisions unconstitutional. See AHY Chen, 'Constitutional Controversies in the Aftermath of the Anti-extradition Movement of 2019' (2020) 50 *Hong Kong Law Journal* 609, 610–11.

[196] Chen (n 194).

bound to say "*fiat justitia ruat cælum*" [let justice be done, though the heavens fall].'[197]

Whilst the flagrant judicial disregard of political consequences may have been possible under the common law centuries ago, this approach is no longer prudent in post-colonial Hong Kong, where the present legal landscape is the offspring of an unusual marriage of two bedfellows with distinctively different characters. If the CFA is blind to the political fallout of its decisions, it is likely that NPCSC Interpretations will be routinely used to censure the Court and fetter its powers. The CFA, aware that it is the branch of government most predisposed institutionally to safeguarding the HKSAR's autonomy, can only successfully defend the old legal traditions it has inherited by accepting the new political structures it now operates within.

As the eminent Hong Kong constitutional scholar, Peter Wesley Smith, once wrote:

> [T]he Basic Law, with all its imperfections, must be made to work, and it cannot be made to work if judges and lawyers close their eyes to 'political fallout' and in the process, deny the constitution's character as a compromise between incompatible systems of law.[198]

APPENDIX: LIST OF CFA CASES WITH EXPRESS FINDINGS OF UNCONSTITUTIONALITY

Table 1 Andrew Li as Chief Justice (1997–2010)[a]

Number	Case name	Legal provision(s)/policy
1	*Ng Ka Ling v Director of Immigration* (1999) 2 HKCFAR 4	Immigration Ordinance: s 2A(1), s 2AA(1)(a), s 53D(3)(a), para 1(2)(b) of Sch 1 Immigration (Amendment) (No 3) Ordinance: s 1(2) Immigration Regulations: the second sentence in Form No 12 in Sch 1 Paras A(1) and B of the Notice dated 11 July 1997 and published in the Gazette on 16 July 1997 (G No (E) 21 of 1997)

(continued)

[197] *R v Wilkes* (1770) 4 Burr 2527, 2562.

[198] PW Smith, 'Judicial Autonomy under Hong Kong's Basic Law' in R Ash (ed), *Hong Kong in Transition: One Country, Two Systems* (Routledge Curzon, 2003) 172.

Table 1 *(Continued)*

Number	Case name	Legal provision(s)/policy
2	*Chan Kam Nga v Director of Immigration* (1999) 2 HKCFAR 82	Immigration Ordinance: para 2(c) in Sch 1 (introduced by the Immigration (Amendment) (No 2) Ordinance 1997)
3	*Director of Immigration v Chong Fung Yuen* (2001) 4 HKCFAR 211	Immigration Ordinance: para (2)(a) of Sch 1
4	*Gurung Kesh Bahadur v Director of Immigration* [2002] 2 HKLRD 775	Immigration Ordinance: application of s 11(10) to non-permanent residents with valid permits[b]
5	*Prem Singh v Director of Immigration* (2003) 6 HKCFAR 26	Immigration Ordinance: para 3(1)(c) in Sch 1, read with para 1(5)(b) of the said Schedule
6	*Solicitor v The Law Society of Hong Kong* (2003) 6 HKCFAR 570	Legal Practitioners Ordinance: s 13(1)
7	*Leung Kwok Hung and Others v HKSAR* (2005) 8 HKCFAR 229	Public Order Ordinance: ss 14(1), 14(5), 15(2)
8	*Koo Sze Yiu v Chief Executive of the HKSAR* (2006) 9 HKCFAR 441	Executive Order: Law Enforcement (Covert Surveillance Procedure) Order Telecommunications Ordinance: s 33
9	*Official Receiver v Chan Wing Hing* (2006) 9 HKCFAR 545	Bankruptcy Ordinance: s 30A(10)(b)(i)
10	*HKSAR v Lam Kwong Wai* (2006) 9 HKCFAR 574	Firearms and Ammunition Ordinance: s 20(1) read with s 20(3)(c)[b]
11	*HKSAR v Hung Chan Wa* (2006) 9 HKCFAR 614	Dangerous Drugs Ordinance: ss 47(1) and 47(2)[b]
12	*HKSAR v Ng Po On* (2008) 11 HKCFAR 91	Prevention of Bribery Ordinance: s14(4) read with 24[b]

(continued)

Table 1 *(Continued)*

Number	Case name	Legal provision(s)/policy
13	*Secretary for Justice v Yau Yuk Lung* (2007) 10 HKCFAR 335	Crimes Ordinance: s 118F(1)
14	*Koon Wing Yee v Insider Dealing Tribunal* (2008) 11 HKCFAR 170	Securities (Insider Dealing) Ordinance: s 23(1)(c)
15	*Lam Siu Po v Commissioner of Police* (2009) 12 HKCFAR 237	Police (Discipline) Regulations: Regulations 9(11) and 9(12)

[a] Table 1 excludes *Secretary for Justice v Chan Wah* (2000) 3 HKCFAR 459. In this case, the unconstitutional practice derives not from any governmental law or policy, but a customary practice within the villages.

[b] Statutory provisions in which the CFA expressly or implicitly applies a remedial interpretation to the impugned law after an express finding of unconstitutionality.

Table 2 Geoffrey Ma as Chief Justice (2010–21)

Number	Case name	Legal provision(s)/policy
1	*Mok Charles Peter v Tam Wai Ho* (2010) 13 HKCFAR 762	Legislative Council Ordinance: s 67(3)
2	*Lee To Nei v HKSAR* (2012) 15 HKCFAR 162	Trade Descriptions Ordinance: s 26(4)[a]
3	*W v Registrar of Marriages* (2013) 16 HKCFAR 112	Matrimonial Causes Ordinance: s 20(1)(d)[a] Marriage Ordinance: s 40[a]
4	*Kong Yunming v Director of Social Welfare* (2013) 16 HKCFAR 950	Comprehensive Social Security Assistance Seven-years Residence Requirement
5	*Official Receiver v Zhi Charles* (2015) 18 HKCFAR 467	Bankruptcy Ordinance: s 30A(10)(a)
6	*QT v Director of Immigration* (2018) 21 HKCFAR 324	Immigration Policy on Spousal Dependant Visa: Exclusion of Same-Sex Civil Partnerships

(continued)

Table 2 *(Continued)*

Number	Case name	Legal provision(s)/policy
7	*Leung Chun Kwong v Secretary for Civil Service* (2019) 22 HKCFAR 127	Civil Service's Decision to Exclude Married Same-Sex Spouse from Spousal Benefits Inland Revenue Ordinance: ss 2 and 10[a]
8	*Leung Kwok Hung v Commissioner of Correctional Services* [2020] HKCFA 37	Correctional Services Standing Order 41–05

[a] Statutory provisions in which the CFA applies a remedial interpretation to the impugned law after an express finding of unconstitutionality.

Table 3 Andrew Cheung as Chief Justice (2021–)

Number	Case name	Legal provision(s)/policy
1	*Q v Commissioner of Registration* [2023] HKCFA 4	Commissioner of Registration's Guidelines on Amendment to the HKID Card Gender Marker

FURTHER READING

Abeyratne, R, 'More Structure, More Deference?: Proportionality in Hong Kong' in PJ Yap (ed), *Proportionality in Asia* (Cambridge University Press, 2020) 25.

Chen, AHY, 'Constitutional Adjudication in Post-1997 Hong Kong' (2006) 15(3) *Pacific Rim Law & Policy Journal* 627.

Chen, AHY, 'International Human Rights Law and Domestic Constitutional Law: Internationalisation of Constitutional Law in Hong Kong' (2009) 4 *National Taiwan University Law Review* 237.

Chen, AHY and Lo, PY, 'Basic Law Jurisprudence of the Court of Final Appeal' in SNM Young, A Da Roza and Y Ghai (eds), *Hong Kong's Court of Final Appeal: The Development of the Law in China's Hong Kong* (Cambridge University Press, 2014).

Ramsden, M, 'Reviewing the United Kingdom's ICCPR Immigration Reservation in Hong Kong Courts' (2014) 63 *International and Comparative Law Quarterly* 635.

Yap, PJ, '10 Years of the Basic Law: The Rise, Retreat and Resurgence of Judicial Power in Hong Kong' (2007) 36 *Common Law World Review* 166.

Yap, PJ and Chung, F, 'Statutory Rights and De Facto Constitutional Supremacy in Hong Kong?' (2019) 17 *International Journal of Constitutional Law* 836.
Yap, PJ, 'Twenty Years of the Basic Law: Continuity and Changes in the Geoffrey Ma Court' (2019) 49 *Hong Kong Law Journal* 209.
Young, S, 'Restricting Basic Law Rights in Hong Kong', (2004) 34 *Hong Kong Law Journal* 109.

7

Constitutional Remedies

Advisory Review – Judicial Invalidation – Remedial Interpretation – Prospective Overruling – Provisional Determination – Severance – Suspension Order

IN THE PREVIOUS chapter, we examined the constitutional rights mechanism in the Hong Kong Special Administrative Region (HKSAR) and discussed how human rights are protected by the courts. Rights can only be effectively enforced if there exists a system of effective remedies that courts can grant when rights are violated. This chapter thus analyses the constitutional remedies that have been used by the Hong Kong courts. These remedies are categorised as follows, and will be examined in turn: (i) invalidation of unconstitutional laws; (ii) advisory review or provisional determination; (iii) remedial interpretation; (iv) Suspension Order or a delayed declaration of invalidity of an unconstitutional law; and (v) invalidation of a statutory provision that is in itself constitutional.

I. INVALIDATION OF UNCONSTITUTIONAL LAWS

In Hong Kong, when a law is declared unconstitutional, the standard practice is for the court to invalidate the law with immediate effect. According to the Court of Final Appeal (CFA) in *Ng Ka Ling v Director of Immigration* – the Court's first constitutional decision – the 'exercise of this jurisdiction is a matter of obligation, not of discretion so that if inconsistency is established, the courts are bound to hold that a law or executive act is invalid at least to the extent of the inconsistency'.[1]

[1] (1999) 2 HKCFAR 4, 25.

The unconstitutional law – whether it is a legislative or regulatory provision – is henceforth 'null and void',[2] and will be 'of no effect'.[3]

Where only a portion of the impugned provision is unconstitutional, the Court may sever the unconstitutional parts of the law from the constitutional elements. As the CFA opined in *Ng Ka Ling*: 'The test [for severance] is whether the constitutional parts are distinct from the unconstitutional parts so that what is unconstitutional may be severed from what is constitutional leaving what is constitutional intact.'[4]

On the facts, the CFA decided inter alia that it was unconstitutional for the government to statutorily require mainland-born persons residing on the mainland, who acquired by operation of law Hong Kong Permanent Residency on 1 July 1997 when the Basic Law came into force, to obtain a 'one-way exit permit' from the mainland authorities before they could enjoy the constitutional right of abode in Hong Kong. This unconstitutional precondition was excised from the immigration law, leaving the unobjectionable parts in place.[5]

Similarly, in *Leung Kwok Hung v HKSAR*, when the CFA decided that the Commissioner of Police's statutory discretion to prohibit or impose conditions on notified public assemblies and processions for the purpose of 'public order (*ordre public*)' was constitutionally imprecise, the remedy chosen by the Court was 'to sever public order from "public order (*ordre public*)"'.[6] This is because 'public order in the law and order sense, that is, the maintenance of public order and prevention of public disorder',[7] is sufficiently certain. Endorsing the test applied by the Privy Council on an appeal from Hong Kong,[8] the CFA opined:

> The real question is whether what remains is so inextricably bound up with the part declared invalid that what remains cannot independently survive or, as it has sometimes been put, whether on a fair review of the whole matter it can be assumed that the legislature would have enacted what survives without enacting the part that is ultra vires at all.[9]

With this judicial severance, only 'public order' remains in the legislation.

[2] ibid 46.
[3] *Lam Siu Po v Commissioner of Police* (2009) 12 HKCFAR 237, [169(b)].
[4] *Ng Ka Ling* (n 1) 37.
[5] ibid 37–38. As discussed in previous chapters, the CFA's ruling in this regard was subsequently reversed by the NPCSC.
[6] (2005) 8 HKCFAR 229, [83].
[7] ibid [82].
[8] *Ming Pao Newspapers Ltd & Others v A-G of Hong Kong* [1996] AC 907.
[9] *Leung Kwok Hung* (n 6) [84].

II. ADVISORY REVIEW OR PROVISIONAL DETERMINATION

In *Ng Ka Ling*, the CFA also determined that the CFA has no jurisdiction to engage in an advisory review of the Basic Law. According to the Court, Article 158(2) of the Basic Law only vests the courts with the power of constitutional interpretation when they are 'adjudicating cases'. A fortiori, the CFA reasoned: 'It follows that the courts have no such power when not engaged in adjudicating cases. This reflects the well established principle in our system that the courts' role is adjudicative and not advisory.'[10]

Despite the above pronouncement, the CFA in *Democratic Republic of the Congo v FG Hemisphere Associates LLC (No 1)* declared that it had the jurisdiction to make a 'provisional'[11] determination of the meaning of various Basic Law provisions. This provisional determination can be made alongside its legal obligation to refer those provisions to the Standing Committee of the National People's Congress (NPCSC) for interpretation. The CFA provisionally held that: (i) the determination of the applicable doctrine of state immunity in Hong Kong constituted an act of state falling within Article 19(3) of the Basic Law; and (ii) Hong Kong could not, as a matter of legal or constitutional principle, adhere to a doctrine of state immunity that was at variance with the PRC's, and therefore the doctrine of absolute immunity as practised in the PRC should also apply in Hong Kong.[12]

Notably, the CFA's earlier caution in *Ng Ka Ling* against an advisory opinion was *not* cited in this decision. Instead, the CFA in the *Congo* decision now opined the following:

> [Article 158 of the Basic Law] was not intended to preclude this Court from expressing its view on a question of interpretation which it is bound to refer and does refer to the NPCSC. The language of art.158(3) plainly permits this Court to express its view on the question. What art.158(3) precludes is the making of a final judgment before a reference is made in a case where a reference is required.[13]

In other words, when a reference to the NPCSC is required, Article 158(3) of the Basic Law only expressly bars a final judgment from the CFA before the NPCSC responds to the reference. The Court is not precluded

[10] *Ng Ka Ling* (n 1) 30.
[11] (2011) 14 HKCFAR 95, [183].
[12] ibid [183(a)].
[13] ibid [398].

from offering a provisional or advisory opinion, which the NPCSC may take into account when making its interpretation on the matter.

III. REMEDIAL INTERPRETATION

A remedial interpretation (RI) of an impugned law occurs when the court reads in words or reads down the legal effect of statutory language without invalidating the legislation. In essence, this interpretive power creates 'a practical power of law reform (in substance, a legislative power)'[14] for the judiciary. Notably, this power is not set out in the Basic Law, but in *HKSAR v Lam Kwong Wai* the CFA declared that such powers can be 'implied'[15] and have been implicitly conferred by the Basic Law as 'necessary to make effective the exercise of judicial power'.[16]

RI is defended on the basis that the legislature would prefer 'its legislative provision to have a valid, even if reduced, operation than to have no operation at all, so long as the valid operation is not fundamentally or essentially different from what it enacted'.[17] In this way, the courts would interfere less with the exercise of legislative power than they would if the impugned law was completely invalidated with immediate effect. Previously, in *Ng Ka Ling*, the CFA held that the immediate invalidation of an unconstitutional legislative provision was 'a matter of obligation, not of discretion'.[18] In *Lam Kwong Wai*, the CFA refined this resolute stance by stating that 'only in the event that such [remedial] interpretation is not possible, will the Court proceed to make a declaration of contravention, entailing unconstitutionality and invalidity'.[19]

In the HKSAR, the courts have used RI in three different ways, but the substantive effect on the impugned law in all three circumstances is the same – the legal meaning of the pre-existing impugned text is judicially changed.

In the first mode, the court explicitly states that the law, as enacted, is unconstitutional, and expressly adopts RI to modify the text of the impugned legislation or alter its operative scope.

[14] P Sales and R Ekins, 'Rights-Consistent Interpretation under the Human Rights Act 1998' (2011) 127 *LQR* 217, 224.

[15] [2006] 9 HKCFAR 574, [78].

[16] ibid [70].

[17] ibid [77].

[18] *Ng Ka Ling* (n 1) 25.

[19] *Lam Kwong Wai* (n 15) [78].

This method was applied by the CFA in *Lam Kwong Wai*.[20] On the facts, the impugned law required an accused charged with the possession of an imitation firearm to prove he had a lawful excuse.[21] The CFA held that this law was a disproportionate restriction of the accused's constitutional right to a presumption of innocence, but decided that this law could nonetheless be upheld by reading down the persuasive/legal burden of proof imposed on the accused to an evidential burden to produce some exculpatory evidence.[22] Subsequently, other penal laws that imposed a legal burden of proof on the defendant were also explicitly read down by the CFA so that they now only place an evidential onus on the accused.[23]

On another occasion, instead of reading down the operative meaning of the statutory language, the CFA simply read down the operative scope of the law. In *Gurung Kesh Bahadur v Director of Immigration*, the CFA was confronted with the constitutionality of section 11(10) of the Immigration Ordinance, which stated that the permission given to a person (who is not a Hong Kong Permanent Resident) to land or remain in Hong Kong would 'expire immediately after his departure'. The CFA held that this was a total abrogation of the constitutional right to travel of a non-permanent resident whose limit of stay in Hong Kong remained valid throughout his travel period.[24] But instead of invalidating this unconstitutional law, the CFA held that section 11(10) would simply no longer apply to non-permanent residents whose limit of stay in Hong Kong was 'still current at the time of re-entry'.[25]

The lower courts have been more aggressive in this explicit use of RI. Notably, a penal provision in Hong Kong provided that 'A man who commits buggery with a man under the age of 16 … shall be liable on conviction … to imprisonment for life',[26] while the statutory cap for heterosexual intercourse with minors is five years' imprisonment.[27] To remedy this discriminatory measure against male homosexuals, the Court of First Instance read new sentencing caps into the pre-existing

[20] ibid.
[21] Firearms and Ammunition Ordinance, s 20(1), read with s 20(3)(c).
[22] *Lam Kwong Wai* (n 15) [54].
[23] *HKSAR v Hung Chan Wa* (2006) 9 HKCFAR 614; *HKSAR v Ng Po On* (2008) 11 HKCFAR 91; *Lee To Nei v HKSAR* (2012) 15 HKCFAR 162.
[24] [2002] 2 HKLRD 775, [38].
[25] ibid [39].
[26] Crimes Ordinance (CO), s 118C.
[27] ibid s 124.

law: 'imprisonment for 5 years if the buggery is committed with a boy under the age of 16 but is of or above the age of 13'.[28]

But the distinctive honour of having issued the lengthiest express RI goes to the Court of Appeal in *HKSAR v Yu Lik Wai*.[29] In this case, the impugned statutory provision[30] allowed law enforcement agents to withhold intercepted covert surveillance communication from the defendant, and even 'marginaliz[ed] the role of the prosecutor in the disclosure process'.[31] This was held to be a disproportionate and unconstitutional interference with 'elements of a fair trial'.[32] However, instead of invalidating this law, the Court ruled that the statutory provision would henceforth foist a duty on law enforcement agents to disclose intercepted covert surveillance communication to the prosecution and it was for the prosecution to decide whether that communication was of assistance to the defence, instead of entrusting law enforcement agents alone with this power.[33] Notably, the following italicised words were added to the impugned statutory provision to make it constitutional:

> any information obtained pursuant to a relevant prescribed authorization and continuing to be available to the department concerned *shall be provided to the prosecution so that it may consider whether the information* might reasonably be considered capable of undermining the case for the prosecution against the defence or of assisting the case for the defence. Where, *in respect of such information that is disclosed to it, the prosecution is of the view that it might reasonably be considered capable of undermining the case for the prosecution against the defence or of assisting the case for the defence* it shall then disclose the information to the judge in an ex parte hearing that is held in private.[34]

Such 'strained interpretation'[35] of impugned legislative provisions in substance creates a legislative power for the judiciary. But where the requisite changes needed to the law do not require the government to

[28] *Yeung Chu Wing v Secretary for Justice* [2019] HKCFI 1431, [34]–[35]. The CFI's approach was approved by the Court of Appeal in an unrelated case of *HKSAR v Yeung Ho Nam* [2020] 1 HKLRD 91, [44]–[48].

[29] [2019] HKCA 135, [2019] HKCA 1093. These are two separate judgments concerning the same case; the later judgment confirms and cross-references the RI first proposed in the earlier one.

[30] Interception of Communications and Surveillance Ordinance (Cap 589), s 61.

[31] [2019] HKCA 135, [163].

[32] ibid [179].

[33] ibid [234].

[34] See *HKSAR v Yu Lik Wai* [2019] HKCA 135, [233]; *HKSAR v Yu Lik Wai* [2019] HKCA 1093, [49].

[35] *Lam Kwong Wai* (n 15) [77].

deliberate over a range of complex constitutional options that implicate polycentric concerns, such piecemeal reforms writ small undertaken by the judges themselves may also be more expedient and effective, especially if there is a backlog of more important Bills on the legislative agenda. This might explain why, in these above-mentioned lower court cases, it was the government that sought RI as the preferred remedy after the impugned law was deemed unconstitutional.

The second way that courts engage in RI occurs when they construe legislation consistently with constitutional guarantees without expressly stating that the impugned law as enacted is unconstitutional and without expressly using the term RI. In *Yeung May Wan v HKSAR*, the CFA had to interpret section 50 of the Police Force Ordinance. On its face, the section provided two alternative statutory bases for the exercise of the power of arrest: (i) where the officer reasonably believes that the arrested person *will be charged* with a relevant offence; and (ii) where the officer reasonably suspects that person *of being guilty* of a relevant offence. However, the CFA opined that if the law permitted a person to be arrested even if there was no reasonable suspicion that the person had committed any relevant offence but merely where the arresting officer believed that the person in question would be charged, section 50 would open the door to arbitrary arrest.[36] Therefore, section 50 had to be construed consistently with the Basic Law's constitutional guarantees against arbitrary arrest, and the statutory clause that permitted a police officer to apprehend a person 'who he reasonably believes will be charged' was reinterpreted so that the police officer may only apprehend a person 'who he reasonably believes will be charged *on the basis of a reasonable suspicion that the arrested person is guilty of the offence to be charged*' (emphasis added).[37]

Similarly, in *HKSAR v Chow Nok Hang*, a public order provision that criminally sanctioned a person who acted 'for the purpose of preventing the transaction of the business for [a] public gathering'[38] was interpreted so that it now only applies when the offender's 'purpose is to make it impossible in practical terms to hold or continue with the gathering; or, at least, to interrupt the gathering for such a duration or by using such means as substantially to impair the intended transaction of business'.[39] Herein, the remedial reading of the law was justified on

[36] *Yeung May Wan v HKSAR* (2005) 8 HKCFAR 137, [62].
[37] ibid [66].
[38] Public Order Ordinance, s 17B(1).
[39] (2013) 16 HKCFAR 837, [58].

the basis that the restriction on the constitutional right to freedom of assembly should be narrowly construed, and where the statutory provision can 'properly be given a range of meanings, the Court inclines towards adopting a meaning which preserves a wider ambit for the relevant rights'.[40]

This implied use of RI was also applied in *Kwok Wing Hang v Chief Executive in Council* when the CFA had to address the constitutionality of the Emergency Regulations Ordinance (ERO). Notably, the ERO on its face stipulated that regulations passed pursuant to the ERO by the Chief Executive in Council (CEIC) 'shall have effect notwithstanding anything inconsistent therewith contained in any enactment',[41] and these regulations 'shall continue in force until repealed by order of the [CEIC]'.[42] This would prima facie mean that any of these emergency regulations can override the Hong Kong Bill of Rights Ordinance (BORO) – an enactment – and these emergency regulations may not even be repealed by the Legislative Council (LegCo). But the CFA held that Article 73(1) of the Basic Law vests legislative power in LegCo, and therefore the court would 'adopt a construction which does not contravene Article 73(1)',[43] so that 'any regulations made under the ERO are subject to the scrutiny and control of LegCo, just like any other subsidiary legislation'.[44] Furthermore, the Court held that any regulations passed under the ERO must comply with the BORO because the fundamental rights protected under the BORO are 'guaranteed under Article 39 of the Basic Law',[45] and the ERO must be 'construed in such a way as to be compatible with the Basic Law'.[46] Therefore, any regulation passed under the ERO that restricts BORO rights, like any rights-restricting legislation passed by LegCo, is subject to constitutional review by the courts to determine whether the law is constitutionally precise and proportionate.

Implied RI is most strategically deployed when an express judicial finding of unconstitutionality would trigger public disquiet or governmental backlash. By incrementally adjusting the meaning of the statutory text on its own, instead of openly deeming the legislation in question unconstitutional, the court diffuses potential political opposition, whilst

[40] ibid [60].
[41] ERO, s 2(4).
[42] ibid s 2(3).
[43] [2020] HKCFA 42, [62].
[44] ibid [65].
[45] ibid [69].
[46] ibid [79].

quietly modifying the operational meaning of the flawed law to achieve greater constitutional compliance.

The final way courts engage in RI occurs when the judiciary adopts a statutory construction that is more rights-friendly, without superimposing Basic Law rights on the legislation. In short, this covert variety of RI is adopted under the guise of statutory interpretation.

In *HKSAR v Fong Kwok Shan Christine*, an administrative by-law that imposed a blanket prohibition on signs and messages, including signs or messages on items of clothing worn by persons in the public/press gallery of LegCo, was read down by the CFA so that the impugned by-law would only apply in the context of 'conduct which amounts to behaving in a disorderly manner'.[47] According to the CFA, section 12(3) of LegCo's Administrative Instructions for Regulating Admittance and Conduct of Persons was aimed at conduct that amounted to behaving in a disorderly manner, and did not prohibit messages on T-shirts that were not brandished intrusively. But if we examine the text of section 12(3) closely, the by-law actually uses the word 'or' to separate each sub-clause that justifies non-admission.

According to section 12(3):

> An officer of the Council may refuse admission to a press or public gallery
>
> (i) to any person displaying any sign, message or banner, or
> (ii) to any person displaying any sign or message on any item of clothing, or
> (iii) to any person who, in the opinion of an officer of the Council, may so display any sign, message or banner, may so display any sign or message on any item of clothing *or may otherwise behave in a disorderly manner*. (emphasis added)

The use of the word 'or' suggests that each ground for justifying non-admission was separate and may be applied disjunctively. But with a sleight of hand, the CFA converted a separate independent sub-clause into a general limitation that restricts the operation of all the other independent clauses.

The CFA further claimed that such a statutory construction was reinforced by section 8(3) of the Legislative Council (Powers and Privileges) Ordinance, which authorises the President of LegCo to pass Administrative Instructions for 'the purpose of maintaining the security of the precincts of the Chamber, ensuring the proper behaviour and decorum of persons therein and for other administrative purposes'.

[47] (2017) 20 HKCFAR 425, [107]. See ch 6, s VI.

In the Court's view, a blanket prohibition on signs or messages in the present case would be an ultra vires exercise of the President's power, and the Court would therefore choose a rule of construction that implements the legislative purpose instead.[48] In essence, this is an argument about the law's disproportionality dressed up as a rule of statutory construction. In reality, the Court was engaging in a covert constitutional review, and the operative scope of the law was read down under the guise of 'ordinary common law principles of [statutory] construction'.[49] However, as the Court openly admitted, the same conclusion would have been reached had the Court used RI explicitly.

Similarly, in *HKSAR v Wan Thomas*, a prison rule that limited visitation rights to 'friends' of inmates was construed by the CFA to include companies engaged by inmates' relatives or friends to deliver meals and magazines to them, so that employees of these companies were acquitted of defrauding officers of the Correctional Services Department when they represented themselves as the inmates' friends. It should be noted that the visitors in question did not have any pre-existing personal relationship with the inmates and had never met the inmates.[50] Nevertheless, the CFA determined that the 'most important purpose of any prison visit to prisoners awaiting trial is contact with persons outside the prison and the provision of moral and material support'.[51] Therefore, anyone who visits the inmate to 'provide him with some moral or material benefit consistent with the statutory purposes of visits'[52] would be a 'friend' under the prison rules. In view of this proper construction of the prison rule, the CFA held that it was unnecessary to consider the constitutional question of whether the impugned rule violated the BORO.[53]

In *HKSAR v Lai Chee Ying*, the CFA handed down its first substantive ruling on Hong Kong's National Security Law (NSL). The dispute centred on the bail requirement under the NSL as codified in Article 42(2).[54] In this decision, the CFA determined that it has 'no power to hold any provision of the NSL to be unconstitutional or invalid'.[55]

[48] ibid [108].
[49] ibid [109].
[50] (2018) 21 HKCFAR 214, [19]. See ch 6, s VI.
[51] ibid [41].
[52] ibid [45].
[53] ibid [51].
[54] Art 42(2) of the NSL reads: 'No bail shall be granted to a criminal suspect or defendant unless the judge has sufficient grounds for believing that the criminal suspect or defendant will not continue to commit acts endangering national security.'
[55] *HKSAR v Lai Chee Ying* [2021] HKCFA 3, [42].

As discussed in chapter six, it is unclear whether this is a definitive ruling on the NSL's constitutionality or it is premised on the concession by all parties – including the accused – that there was no challenge to the constitutionality of any provision of the NSL in the present case.[56] Since the NSL is constitutional, the CFA ruled that it could not use Basic Law rights to explicitly read down the legislation.[57] Notwithstanding this, the CFA also decided that 'human rights and freedoms and rule of law values' remain applicable to the NSL's interpretation because the NSL expressly affirms the continued application of those rights and values.[58] Therefore, 'as far as possible, NSL 42(2) is to be given a meaning and effect compatible with those rights, freedoms and values'.[59] In doing so, the CFA rejected the government's argument that proposed bail conditions should be presumptively excluded when a judge decides whether an accused is likely to endanger national security if granted bail.[60] The CFA's approach in this case suggests that there is potential for the court to enforce rights more robustly when interpreting the NSL in the future, by applying the ordinary rules of statutory construction and exploiting linguistic ambiguity in the statutory text.

Covert RI allows courts to spearhead constitutional changes on the stealth. Such constitutional avoidance seeks to preserve the courts' reputation and institutional capital as judges can 'effectively re-write laws while pretending to exercise restraint'.[61]

IV. SUSPENSION ORDER

In *Koo Sze Yiu v Chief Executive of the HKSAR*, the CFA held that the courts had the 'inherent jurisdiction'[62] to suspend a judicial declaration of invalidity of a law for a limited period, so that an unconstitutional law can continue to be enforced while the government is given time to enact corrective legislation. The impugned law in this case had allowed the Chief Executive of the HKSAR, whenever they considered that

[56] ibid [33].
[57] ibid [33], [36].
[58] NSL, Arts 4 and 5.
[59] *Lai Chee Ying* (n 55) [42].
[60] ibid [57].
[61] ES Fish, 'Constitutional Avoidance as Interpretation and as Remedy' (2016) 114 *Michigan Law Review* 1275, 1315.
[62] (2006) 9 HKCFAR 441, [35].

public interest so required, to order the interception or disclosure to the government of any telecommunications. If this law were invalidated with immediate effect, even legitimate covert surveillance activities would have to cease, and this would be undesirable. The Court therefore sanctioned a delay of six months in the implementation of its invalidity order.[63]

Robert Leckey has sounded a cautionary note on the courts' use of such Suspension Orders. In his view, such delayed remedies harm individual rights-bearers, as they may be victorious in court but deprived of a remedy until legislation is passed to address their situations, if at all.[64] These harms are especially accentuated when the judiciary temporarily preserves unconstitutional penal prohibitions, as it 'magnifi[es] differences amongst members of the litigant's class'[65] purely on the basis of whether the accused is convicted before or after the lapse of the Suspension Order's expiration period.

While Leckey's concerns about how delayed remedies harm individual rights-bearers are valid, in Hong Kong, the uncertainties associated with their application have been mitigated by the courts. The CFA has added significant 'bite' to the court's delayed declarations of invalidity, so that the government is incentivised to comply with the court's ruling, or judicial safeguards are put in place to mitigate any legislative or executive delinquency.

What is particularly unique about the Suspension Order in Hong Kong is as follows:

> The Government can, during that period of suspension, function pursuant to what has been declared unconstitutional, doing so without acting contrary to any declaration in operation. But despite such suspension, the Government is not shielded from legal liability for functioning pursuant to what has been declared unconstitutional.[66]

In other words, the Suspension Order in the *Koo Sze Yiu* case permitted government officials to continue engaging in interception and covert surveillance while the law was being revised, but the government is not shielded from any legal liability if they abused their authority in the interim. In compliance with the Suspension Order, the Interception of

[63] ibid [49].
[64] R Leckey, 'The Harms of Remedial Discretion' (2016) 14 *International Journal of Constitutional Law* 584, 591.
[65] ibid 592.
[66] *Koo Sze Yiu* (n 62) [50].

Communications and Surveillance Ordinance was passed by LegCo in 2006 to regulate the conduct of interception of communications and the use of surveillance devices by law enforcement authorities.

Interestingly, the CFA in *Koo Sze Yiu* drew a contrast between a Suspension Order and a Temporary Validity Order (TVO). When the latter remedy is granted, and unlike a Suspension Order, the government is shielded from legal liability during the suspension period.[67] But the CFA ruled in *Koo Sze Yiu* that it was unnecessary to decide whether the Hong Kong courts have the power to grant a TVO. Non-Permanent Judge (NPJ) Sir Anthony Mason – the overseas NPJ of the CFA in this case – in a concurring opinion opined as follows:

> Whether this Court has jurisdiction or power to make an order for temporary validity is a very large question, involving fundamental doctrinal questions relating to the separation of powers, the role of the courts, the relationship between the courts and the legislative branch of government, as well as the rule of law and considerations of justice, and of community protection and welfare.[68]

But his Lordship did suggest that the level of 'necessity' for a Suspension Order would be 'substantially lower'[69] than what is needed before the court grants a TVO.

Oddly, while the CFA has accepted that it has the power to grant a Suspension Order, it has not determined whether it has the power to prospectively overrule judicial precedents. In the CFA's view, prospective overruling is an extraordinary power and must be approached with the 'greatest circumspection'.[70] This judicial reservation over prospective overruling is particularly puzzling as the CFA has admitted that a Suspension Order or a TVO is 'even more far reaching than prospective overruling'.[71] With prospective overruling, the Court's ruling on what the law is will take effect from the date of the judgment, but with a Suspension Order or TVO, the court's judgment will take effect only after a time period specified in the judgment.

The judicial use of delayed remedies like the Suspension Order is most defensible when there is a range of constitutional options that can be implemented after the court's finding of the unconstitutionality of

[67] ibid [33].
[68] ibid [61].
[69] ibid [60].
[70] *HKSAR v Hung Chan Wa* (2006) 9 HKCFAR 614, [33].
[71] ibid [30].

a law.[72] Due deference is paid to the primacy of the legislature's law-making role when it is given the opportunity to make the initial selection on how best to comply with the court's constitutional mandates by choosing among the competing alternatives available.[73] In other words, when there is a spectrum of reasonable options for the legislature to choose from, the court should give lawmakers time and space to deliberate on the exact contours of the remedial legislation.

We see this in *Chan Kin Sum v Secretary for Justice*,[74] where the Court of First Instance granted a Suspension Order after declaring unconstitutional a blanket legislative ban on the right of all prisoners to vote.[75] The court acknowledged that the electoral disenfranchisement of prisoners prevented crime by imposing a sanction on convicted persons, and provided incentives for the citizenry to exercise civic responsibility.[76] Notwithstanding the legitimate aims that the government was seeking to pursue, the court noted that the impugned statutory ban was disproportionate as all prisoners were barred from voting regardless of the nature and severity of their offences, or even the length of their custodial sentences.[77] Even convicted persons on suspended sentences or those released on parole were barred from voting. Nevertheless, the court was willing to suspend its declaration of invalidity for about seven months as the learned judge determined that the legislature would 'legitimately require and deserve a reasonable period of time to work out a replacement arrangement, whatever it may be'.[78] On the facts, the court refused to determine what type of voting restrictions would pass constitutional muster as it is the function of the legislature and 'not the function of the courts to say what would constitute reasonable restrictions in Hong Kong'.[79] This judicial decision was therefore dialogic as the court remanded the electoral issue to the legislature, which could choose from a wide range of constitutional options available to it. After deliberation, the Legislative Council responded by repealing *all* restrictions on

[72] See K Roach, 'Remedial Consensus and Dialogue under the Charter: General Declarations and Delayed Declarations of Invalidity' (2002) 35 *UBC Law Review* 211, 212; PJ Yap, *Constitutional Dialogue in Common Law Asia* (Oxford University Press, 2015) 101.

[73] See B Ryder, 'Suspending the Charter' (2003) 21 *Supreme Court Law Review* 267, 285.

[74] [2009] HKCFI 172.

[75] [2009] 2 HKLRD 166.

[76] ibid [88].

[77] ibid [112].

[78] *Chan Kin Sum* (n 74) [79].

[79] *Chan Kin Sum* (n 75) [165].

prisoners' right to vote, thus achieving a result that actually went beyond what the court mandated in *Chan Kin Sum*.[80]

What is even more remarkable is that Hong Kong courts have coupled their use of a Suspension Order with a remedial reading-in proviso that takes effect automatically – in the event of any legislative default – upon the expiry of the suspension period.

The CFA relied on such combined remedies when it ruled in favour of transsexual marriage. In *W v Registrar of Marriages*, the Court determined that the Registrar of Marriages, in applying the existing matrimonial legislation in Hong Kong that prohibited a post-operative male-to-female transsexual from marrying in the capacity of her acquired gender, had violated her constitutional right to marriage. The CFA in the first instance issued a Suspension Order as it was deemed beneficial for the legislature to holistically address issues of law in related areas such as succession, trusts, pensions and disclosure rules that would arise from legalising transsexual marriage. The LegCo was therefore given one year to pass corrective legislation.[81] But mindful that legislation may not eventuate in the end, the Court also decided at the outset that 'it is necessary in principle that a remedial interpretation'[82] be given to the impugned matrimonial legislation so that a transsexual in W's situation – one who had undergone a full male-to-female sexual reassignment surgery – would be legally recognised as a woman within the statutory meaning of the pre-existing law. In other words, a 'woman' in the Marriage Ordinance was judicially read by the CFA to include a 'post-operative male-to-female transsexual person'.[83] The Court held that the post-operative male-to-female transsexual person would be automatically recognised as a woman for the purposes of marriage in Hong Kong upon the expiry of the 12-month suspension period if no remedial legislation was in place. Notably, in the aftermath of the Court's ruling, the Hong Kong government attempted to pass remedial legislation to allow only post-operative transsexuals to marry in their acquired gender, but chose not to address other areas of law flagged by the CFA. The proposed statutory revisions in the Marriage (Amendment) Bill 2014 were rejected

[80] See Voting by Imprisoned Persons Ordinance; AHY Chen, 'International Human Rights Law and Domestic Constitutional Law: Internationalisation of Constitutional Law in Hong Kong' (2009) 4 *National Taiwan University Law Review* 237, 255.

[81] [2013] 16 HKCFAR 112, [150].

[82] ibid [123].

[83] ibid [150].

by LegCo, but post-operative transsexuals can now marry in Hong Kong in the capacity of their acquired gender pursuant to the court's remedial reading of the pre-existing matrimonial rules.

This judicial development is precisely the two-track remedies that Kent Roach has proposed courts to use: specific relief for the successful litigants to correct the constitutional wrongs suffered by them, complemented with weaker dialogic general remedies that encourage the government to rely on its superior institutional expertise to craft a comprehensive, long-term legislation that addresses polycentric/resource allocative concerns.[84]

After the CFA in *Leung Chun Kwong v Secretary for the Civil Service* decided that it was unconstitutional for the Inland Revenue Department to bar same-sex couples legally married overseas from electing for joint tax-assessment in Hong Kong, the CFA also chose to remedially interpret the statutory phrase 'husband and wife' in the Inland Revenue Ordinance as 'a married person and his or her spouse'.[85] But at the same time, this remedial interpretation was suspended for six months so that the Inland Revenue Department could revise their computer system, tax guidelines and practice notes.[86]

Nevertheless, in *Leung Kwok Hung v Commissioner of Correctional Services*, the CFA emphasised that a Suspension Order is an exceptional remedy and should only arise for consideration 'where the Court's decision carries substantial social or public interest implications going beyond the interests of the immediate parties'.[87] The onus is on the public authority seeking the Suspension Order to justify the request by showing that it reasonably needs time to put in place changes necessary to bring itself into alignment with the Court's decision. On the facts, the CFA refused to grant a Suspension Order after ruling that it was discriminatory for the Correctional Services to require male inmates to keep a 'sufficiently close'[88] haircut while females were exempted. This was because the discriminatory policy was 'a Standing Order internally issued by the Commissioner [and] is not a piece of legislation'.[89] Therefore, any corrective measures would not involve any lengthy and

[84] K Roach, 'Polycentricity and Queue Jumping in Public Law Remedies: A Two Track Response' (2016) 66(1) *University of Toronto Law Journal* 3.
[85] *Leung Chun Kwong v Secretary for the Civil Service* (2019) 22 HKCFAR 282, [8].
[86] ibid [10]–[11].
[87] [2021] HKCFA 2, [9].
[88] Correctional Services Standing Order 41-05.
[89] *Leung Kwok Hung* (n 87) [15].

uncertain legislative processes, and the remedial haircut options available to the Correctional Services were deemed uncomplicated and had in fact been under consideration for years.

V. INVALIDATION OF CONSTITUTIONAL LAW

The most extraordinary remedy created by the CFA was the one in *Koon Wing Yee v Insider Dealing Tribunal*, where the Court recognised the power to invalidate a legislative provision that is in itself constitutional. On the facts, the CFA determined that prosecutions for insider dealing offences before the Insider Dealing Tribunal (IDT) would be viewed as criminal, and not civil, in nature because the penalty imposed was 'punitive and deterrent'.[90] This was because section 23(1)(c) of the Securities (Insider Dealing) Ordinance (SIDO) authorised the IDT to impose a penalty of an amount not exceeding 300 per cent of the amount of any profit gained or loss avoided by any person as a result of the insider dealing.

But once the proceedings before the IDT were deemed criminal in nature, it naturally followed that section 33(6) of the SIDO, which compelled persons under investigation to answer questions posed to them under the said legislation, would violate their right against self-incrimination.[91] The consequence of this judicial determination should therefore lead to the immediate invalidation of the impugned section 33(6), and the government would lose these investigatory powers under the said Ordinance.

In an extraordinary move, the CFA acceded to the government's request of invalidating section 23(1)(c) of the SIDO instead – the penalty provision that authorised the disgorgement of 300 per cent of the defendants' profits, which was in itself constitutional.[92] Had it not been for the punitive nature of section 23(1)(c), the SIDO proceedings would not have acquired a substantially criminal character, but this penalty provision was not in itself unconstitutional. The unconstitutional portion of the law was the provision that conferred concomitant powers on the government to compel testimony in the proceedings. But in an attempt to foster a dialogic compromise with the government, the CFA acceded

[90] *Koon Wing Yee v Insider Dealing Tribunal* (2008) 11 HKCFAR 170, [49]. See ch 6, s V.
[91] BORO, Art 11(2)(g).
[92] *Koon Wing Yee* (n 90) [110].

to the former's request of voiding the penalty provision instead, which was not unconstitutional in itself, so that the government would merely lose its powers of disgorgement – the government's preferred sacrifice. And the government could retain its investigatory powers to compel testimony.[93]

The CFA acknowledged that the invalidation of a statutory provision that is not unconstitutional was novel, and no case had been cited in which a court had held a statutory provision that is constitutional to be invalid. But the Court opined that section 6(1) of the BORO expressly empowers the judiciary to grant such remedy or relief 'as it considers appropriate and just in the circumstances', and the wide language of the BORO would therefore authorise this particular relief. In the Court's view, the remedial method it adopted in this case best conforms with the legislative intention; it 'give[s] the legislation as effective an operation as it can be given consistently with the BOR'[94] because it preserved the IDT's findings against the accused and other orders issued under the SIDO in this case.

VI. CONCLUSION

The invalidation of unconstitutional legislation and the judicial severance of the unconstitutional part thereof are standard practices for courts vested with powers of constitutional review. The law and practice of the HKSAR judiciary in this regard are consistent with global trends. But other delayed or expedited constitutional remedies developed by the HKSAR courts are more innovative, and invariably blur the distinction between legislation and adjudication. Nevertheless, one should note that these novel remedies were regularly issued to accommodate legislative or executive input. A Suspension Order provides time for the legislature to devise corrective legislation and avoids a legislative vacuum in the interim. And in many instances, it was the HKSAR government that requested a Remedial Interpretation – in lieu of a Suspension Order – after the law had been deemed unconstitutional, so that lawmakers did not have to spend time deliberating on a piece of remedial legislation and

[93] ibid [117]. See PJ Yap and F Chung, 'Statutory Rights and De Facto Constitutional Supremacy in Hong Kong?' (2019) 17 *International Journal of Constitutional Law* 836, 853–54.

[94] ibid [113].

the law could continue to apply under the judicially reinterpreted rules.[95] We saw the rise of such remedial measures in 2019, when LegCo was deeply divided and legislative Bills regularly stalled. The invalidation of a statutory provision that was not itself unconstitutional marked a high point in Hong Kong's judicial adventurism, but this remedy was again only used at the government's request, so that the government could retain other preferred statutory powers in lieu.

The active use of remedial discretion may pose constitutional dilemmas for legal purists. If, however, we view governance as a 'field of partnership'[96] between the judiciary and the legislature, then these innovative remedial strategies used by the HKSAR courts have the capacity to foster greater democratic deliberation and improve governmental performance, for they conjoin the very best in statecraft and adjudication.[97]

FURTHER READING

Chen, AHY, 'International Human Rights Law and Domestic Constitutional Law: Internationalisation of Constitutional Law in Hong Kong' (2009) 4 *National Taiwan University Law Review* 237.

Chung, F and Zixin, J, 'An Alternative to Annulment – Remedial Interpretation in Hong Kong' in PJ Yap (ed), *Constitutional Remedies in Asia* (Routledge, 2019).

Yap, PJ and Lin, CC, *Constitutional Convergence in East Asia* (Cambridge University Press, 2021).

Yap, PJ and Chung, F, 'Statutory Rights and De Facto Constitutional Supremacy in Hong Kong?' (2019) 17 *International Journal of Constitutional Law* 836.

Yap, PJ, 'Remedial Discretion and Dilemmas in Asia' (2019) 69 *University of Toronto Law Journal* 84.

[95] *Yeung Chu Wing v Secretary for Justice* [2019] HKCFI 1431; *HKSAR v Yu Lik Wai* [2019] HKCA1093; *Leung Chun Kwong v Secretary for the Civil Service* [2019] HKCFA 34.

[96] P Sales, 'Partnership and Challenge: The Courts' Role in Managing the Integration of Rights and Democracy' [2016] *PL* 456, 457.

[97] PJ Yap, 'Remedial Discretion and Dilemmas in Asia' (2019) 69 *University of Toronto Law Journal* 84.

8

Conclusion

One Country, Two Systems – Hong Kong Story – Free Market Constitutionalism – Economic Liberty – Xi Jinping

THE WORLD WAS transfixed by Hong Kong during the 'Occupy Central' movement (also known as the 'Umbrella revolution') of fall 2014, and again when mass protests against a proposed extradition law evolved into months of rioting in the second half of 2019. To restore law and order and political stability in the Hong Kong Special Administrative Region (HKSAR), the Chinese government foisted the National Security Law (NSL) on Hong Kong in 2020 and overhauled the political system in 2021. The reaction of Western governments to these PRC measures have been negative. In particular, the US government imposed economic sanctions on Hong Kong, and even on senior PRC and Hong Kong officials.

Nevertheless, Hong Kong's economy has proven to be resilient despite the 2019 political turmoil, the onslaught of the COVID-19 pandemic, China's tightening of control over the city and the ensuing geopolitical headwinds. As of 2021,[1] Hong Kong remains the world's third largest financial centre, third most popular destination for foreign direct investment inflows, fourth largest ship registry, sixth largest trading entity in goods, seventh largest stock market and busiest air cargo hub. In 2021, there was a record high of over 9000 overseas and mainland Chinese companies with business operations in Hong Kong, although there were reports in 2022 that some international firms were relocating their operations out of Hong Kong because of the city's strict COVID-19 protocols.[2] The HKSAR, using the name 'Hong Kong, China', has

[1] See, eg the speech of Chief Executive Carrie Lam on 16 June 2022 at a forum to celebrate the 25th anniversary of the HKSAR, www.info.gov.hk/gia/general/202206/16/P2022061600318.htm.

[2] www.bloomberg.com/news/articles/2022-03-24/nearly-50-of-foreign-firms-in-hong-kong-plan-to-relocate-staff.

signed more than 600 bilateral agreements with foreign countries on matters primarily related to trade and investments. Since the return of Hong Kong to China and the establishment of the HKSAR in 1997, Hong Kong's GDP has risen from US$176 billion to US$368 billion in 2021, with an average annual growth rate of 3.1 per cent. Hong Kong's per capita GDP increased from US$27,300 in 1997 to US$49,312 in 2021, representing an 80 per cent increase.

Despite the passage of the NSL and the rollbacks on democracy in Hong Kong, the 'One Country, Two Systems' (OCTS) constitutional project has proven to be successful in the economic domain. As originally conceived in the early 1980s, the 'Two Systems' refer to the 'socialist system' in mainland China and the 'capitalist system' in Hong Kong. China never intended the 'Two Systems' to mean the communist party system in mainland China and a Western-style democracy in the HKSAR, even though the Basic Law expressly states that universal suffrage is 'the ultimate aim'.[3]

I. A NEW NARRATIVE FOR THE 'HONG KONG STORY'

Christine Loh and Richard Cullen have examined Hong Kong's identity, status and future destiny.[4] Specifically, they propose a new 'narrative' for the 'Hong Kong story', one where Hong Kong's identity and destiny are not tied to any transition to a Western-style democracy or the realisation of the so-called 'double universal suffrage' (for the Chief Executive (CE) and all members of the Legislative Council). This is because Hong Kong is not a country but an inalienable and integral part of the Chinese state; Hong Kong cannot become an independent political entity separate from China. On the contrary, Hong Kong people must understand the role that the city can play in the country's development.

Loh and Cullen observe that while 'pan-democratic' politicians have devoted all their energy to build a Western-style democracy in Hong Kong, this goal is not in Hong Kong's destiny. Nevertheless, this does not mean that Hong Kong should become just like other big Chinese cities on the mainland. Over the course of its history, Hong Kong has been the meeting point of Chinese and Western cultures, and the confluence of both

[3] Basic Law, Arts 45 and 68.

[4] C Loh and R Cullen, *No Third Person: Rewriting the Hong Kong Story* (Abbreviated Press, 2018).

cultures has enabled Hong Kong to become a Chinese society where many modern ideas and practices originating from the West have taken root. Hong Kong's continued viability as a highly cosmopolitan global city is thus of great value to China. Under the constitutional framework of OCTS, the mainland and Hong Kong systems can coexist, collaborate and co-create a more prosperous future for the whole country.

II. 'FREE MARKET CONSTITUTIONALISM' IN HONG KONG

What, then, is the essence of the 'Hong Kong system' that constitutes one of the 'Two Systems' under OCTS? One compelling perspective on this question has been put forward by Gonzalo V Puig and Eric C Ip.[5] Puig and Ip argue that this 'Hong Kong system' may be characterised as 'free market constitutionalism'. This is a concept they have developed by drawing on classical economic thought, public choice theory and constitutional economics. In their opinion, constitutionalism constrains 'government action to certain areas', and a free market restricts 'the means government can employ in the production of public goods'. 'Free market constitutionalism' merges both concepts and underscores how the constitution can be used to guarantee a free market – for labour, land and capital – as the main mechanism for regulating economic activities.

Under this system, the government has obligations to maintain law and order, protect private property rights, provide essential public goods and ensure a minimum dignified standard of living for all. But equally, the government should refrain from a close management of the citizenry's lives and their economic activities, and from excessively intervening in the market.

Puig and Ip argue that free market constitutionalism promotes economic liberty, which they define as the twin freedoms of private ownership of property and of contract, which in turn facilitates the pursuit of individual happiness and the development of the common good. The origins of free market constitutionalism in Hong Kong can be traced back to its colonial days when Hong Kong was a free port that allowed a free flow of capital without any foreign exchange controls. This relatively small and limited government practised an economic

[5] GV Puig and EC Ip, *The Freest Market in the World: The Constitutional Logic of Economic Liberty in China's Hong Kong* (Routledge, 2023).

policy of 'positive non-intervention'. At the same time, the common law system provided for the rule of law, judicial independence and the protection of property rights, and facilitated individuals to effectively enforce private contracts.

Puig and Ip explain that it was this tradition or convention of free market constitutionalism that was codified when the Basic Law of the HKSAR was enacted by the PRC in 1990. Specifically, the Basic Law expressly enshrines various key principles of constitutional economics such as fiscal transparency, a balanced budget, a low tax rate, and the maintenance of Hong Kong as a free port and an international financial centre committed to free trade and a free flow of capital. As pointed out by the authors, even after the handover, Hong Kong has consistently been ranked as one of the freest economies in the world and remains one of the world's most competitive cities.

Interestingly and insightfully, Puig and Ip identify two paradoxes relating to the practice of OCTS. The first paradox is that with Hong Kong remaining a free market that connects China to global markets, mainland China can afford to retain its own capital controls and keep its economy partially closed.[6] The second paradox is that Hong Kong's economic liberty actually works in the mainland's broader interests, and also complements the mainland's aims of achieving self-sufficiency and preserving its socialist political institutions. Therefore, Hong Kong's future depends on the mainland's perception of the former's utility to China's overall economic development.

III. XI JINPING'S SPEECH ON 1 JULY 2022

Puig and Ip's views in this regard have been reinforced by President Xi Jinping's important speech in Hong Kong on 1 July 2022 at the ceremony to celebrate the twenty-fifth anniversary of the HKSAR's establishment.[7]

[6] In this regard, it is noteworthy that the 'policy trilemma' theory of international economics posits that it is impossible for any government or central bank to pursue all three of the following economic options simultaneously: (i) a fixed currency exchange rate; (ii) free movement of capital; and (iii) an independent monetary policy. As the options conflict, any government or central bank would have to forfeit one option if it pursues any of the other two options. See M Obstfeld et al, 'The Trilemma in History: Tradeoffs among Exchange Rates, Monetary Policies, and Capital Mobility', https://eml.berkeley.edu/~obstfeld/ost12.pdf.

[7] The English translation of the speech is at http://en.qstheory.cn/2022-07/02/c_786009.htm.

In this speech, Xi praised Hong Kong's economic success over the past 25 years in sustaining an international financial, transportation and trading centre, maintaining one of the world's freest and most open economies, and operating a common law-based legal system.

Looking to the future, Xi declared that China intends to preserve Hong Kong's unique status and advantages. The central government would support the maintenance of Hong Kong's status as an international financial, transportation and trading centre, with a conducive business environment that is free, open and well managed, and is based on the common law system. At the same time, Xi stressed that Hong Kong can make a major contribution to the construction of a modernised socialist state in China and the realisation of the project to rejuvenate the Chinese nation.

In his speech, Xi reiterated the central government's firm and unwavering commitment to the OCTS policy. He pointed out that the OCTS policy as implemented in Hong Kong and Macau is in the interests of and 'supported by all parties concerned', and it 'should be maintained in the long term'.

IV. BRIEF OVERVIEW OF 25 YEARS OF THE HKSAR

As we have discussed in this book, OCTS is an innovative constitutional arrangement designed by the late Deng Xiaoping for the purpose of reunifying Hong Kong with China. The basic principles and features of the HKSAR under OCTS were first specified in the Sino-British Joint Declaration of 1984 and later spelt out in greater detail in the Basic Law of the HKSAR enacted by the National People's Congress in 1990. The constitutional experiment of OCTS began in 1997, when the HKSAR was established.

The Basic Law was drafted on the basis of two fundamental principles – the principle of Chinese sovereignty over Hong Kong and the principle of Hong Kong's high degree of autonomy, with 'Hong Kong people ruling Hong Kong'. The Basic Law provides for the continuity of the capitalist system and the common law in Hong Kong, and guarantees the rights and freedoms of Hong Kong residents. It also establishes the organs of government of the HKSAR and defines the relationship between the HKSAR and the central authorities. It confers extensive powers on the executive, legislative and judicial organs of the HKSAR. These powers cover a wide range of subject matters, with the exclusion of defence and foreign affairs.

Even within the realm of foreign affairs, the HKSAR is nevertheless still granted considerable powers to engage in 'external affairs'. For example, using the name 'Hong Kong, China', the HKSAR can participate in the World Trade Organization and in the Olympics; it can also enter into international agreements with other foreign states on matters such as commerce, trade and investment, the reciprocal recognition and enforcement of arbitral awards, and even the conclusion of extradition agreements.

At the same time, the Basic Law stipulates the powers that the central government exercises over Hong Kong, such as the power to appoint the CE after their election by a local Election Committee, the power to apply national laws to Hong Kong on matters outside Hong Kong's autonomy and the power to interpret and amend the Basic Law.

The Basic Law contains two sets of constitutional provisions that, in retrospect, have shaped post-1997 developments in the HKSAR and posed challenges for their implementation. The first set concerns national security and it is found in Article 23, which mandates the HKSAR to enact laws to prohibit acts of treason, secession, subversion, sedition, etc.

The second set of Basic Law provisions which have far-reaching implications concerns the democratisation of the political system. Although the colonial political system was by no means democratic, the Basic Law drafters responded positively to the aspirations for democratisation expressed by many Hong Kong people during the consultative process of its drafting in the late 1980s. Although the Basic Law provides that, at the HKSAR's inception, the CE would be elected by an Election Committee and the legislature would be elected partly by functional constituencies, partly by the Election Committee and partly by universal suffrage, the Basic Law also provides that the 'ultimate aim' is for the election of the CE and all legislators by universal suffrage.

The HKSAR government's attempt to legislate and implement Article 23 failed in 2003 because of the strong public opposition led by the 'pan-democrats'. And further discussion on national security legislation became so politically toxic that none of the CEs since 2005 have taken any subsequent steps to legislate on Article 23.

Meanwhile, the Basic Law provisions on universal suffrage raised hopes for further democratisation in post-1997 Hong Kong. The 'pan-democratic' political parties, which collectively had the support of more than half of Hong Kong's voters in successive LegCo elections, lobbied for the speedy introduction of universal suffrage. But when the Chinese and Hong Kong governments finally put forward a model for the election of the CE by universal suffrage upon the candidates' nomination by a nominating committee in accordance with Article 45 of the Basic Law, the electoral reform plan was opposed by the 'Occupy Central' movement in 2014 for being insufficiently democratic. The proposal was eventually rejected by the 'pan-democrats' in the legislature in 2015.

Growing dissatisfaction with the government and increasing political polarisation in the HKSAR culminated in the anti-extradition movement of 2019, which resulted in months of rioting and civil unrest that continued after legislative proceedings on the extradition Bill were indefinitely suspended, and even after it was eventually withdrawn. Some of the protesters engaged in acts of violence on a large scale or even advocated Hong Kong's independence. The central authorities viewed the social movement as akin to those overseas 'colour revolutions' that were supported by Western states, and decided to plug the loophole in Hong Kong's legal system concerning national security. Hence the enactment of the National Security Law in 2020.

Furthermore, the central authorities in 2021 overhauled the electoral system provided for in Annexes I and II to the Basic Law. The declared purpose of this electoral revamp was to install institutional safeguards for realising the principle of 'patriots ruling Hong Kong', first enunciated by Deng Xiaoping in the late 1980s. Beijing hoped that this reform would end the political instability and conflicts, the constant filibuster in the legislature and the frequent anti-China mobilisation of the public by opposition politicians and activists, which had plagued post-1997 Hong Kong for years.

V. CONCLUSION

Critics of Beijing's policy towards Hong Kong have accused the central authorities of reneging on its promise to grant Hong Kong a high degree of autonomy and the promise to fulfil the people's aspirations for universal suffrage. They also criticised Beijing for tightening its grip over Hong Kong and eroding freedoms that Hong Kong people had enjoyed for decades.

Beijing sympathisers, on the other hand, believed that the central authorities were well intentioned, and these measures were adopted only in response to the increased political turbulence in the HKSAR and rising local challenges to the authority of the central government and the 'One Country' principle enshrined in the OCTS model.

Take, for example, the issue of national security. At the time of the Basic Law's drafting, it was considered that Chinese laws on national security, which prohibited 'counter-revolutionary activities', were not suitable for application in the HKSAR. Hence, Article 23 was inserted into the Basic Law, requiring the HKSAR to enact its own laws to protect China's national security. In 2003, the HKSAR government introduced a national security Bill for the purpose of discharging this constitutional duty to implement Article 23. Notably, Lord Pannick KC, a leading British legal expert on human rights, provided a legal opinion to the Hong Kong government to the effect that the Bill was not inconsistent with the international human rights standards codified in the International Covenant on Civil and Political Rights as applied in Hong Kong.[8] But the political opposition mobilised public opinion against it, which eventually resulted in the Bill's withdrawal.

Despite this, the central authorities stayed their hand and did not issue any directive to subsequent CEs to revive the legislative exercise on Article 23. On the contrary, Beijing agreed in 2007 to establish a timetable for realising universal suffrage in the HKSAR. The decision of the Standing Committee of the National People's Congress (NPCSC) in late 2007 stipulated 2017 as the target year for the introduction of universal suffrage in the CE election. Notably, Beijing did not require the HKSAR to discharge its constitutional obligation to legislate on Article 23 before universal suffrage was introduced. Hitherto, Beijing had exercised remarkable restraint vis-à-vis Hong Kong, and did not view Article 23 legislation as a priority at that time.

Similarly, the central authorities displayed goodwill when they in 2014 put forward an electoral model for election of the CE. The 'August 31 (2014) Decision' of the NPCSC sought to introduce a universal suffrage model pursuant to Article 45 of the Basic Law as well as the 2007 Decision of the NPCSC on the timetable for universal suffrage in the election of the CE. The model was designed to allow Hong Kong people to elect the CE by universal suffrage, after the candidates are shortlisted by a nominating committee. This was to ensure that the elected CE would be a 'patriot' whom the central government was willing to appoint as CE.

[8] See CJ Petersen, 'Hong Kong's Spring of Discontent: The Rise and Fall of the National Security Bill in 2003' in H Fu, C Petersen and S Young (eds), *National Security and Fundamental Freedoms: Hong Kong's Article 23 under Scrutiny* (Hong Kong University Press, 2005) 42.

However, opposition politicians considered that this was not in line with their idea of a genuine universal suffrage election; they firmly opposed the electoral reform on the ground that the proposed nomination procedure for the CE candidates was undemocratic. But notably, Article 45 of the Basic Law plainly provides that the CE candidates standing for election by universal suffrage have to be first nominated by a nominating committee.

The opposition to the electoral reform evolved into the 'Occupy Central' movement in autumn 2014. In 2015, the electoral reform proposed by the HKSAR government on the basis of the 'August 31 Decision' was rejected by the Legislative Council, as the reform failed to secure the requisite two-thirds majority to amend Annex I to the Basic Law. After the failure of the electoral reform, some opposition politicians and activists became more radical and began to challenge the 'One Country' principle of the OCTS model.

Events leading from the 'Occupy Central' movement in 2014 to the relentless months-long protests and riots of the anti-extradition movement in 2019 underscored the fragility of the OCTS project. Beijing believed that it had to put this derailed train back on track, and proceeded to enact the NSL in 2020 and to overhaul the electoral system in 2021. Critics were aghast and believed that Beijing's disproportionate actions eroded Hong Kong's high degree of autonomy and threatened the long-term sustainability of OCTS. Residents who agreed with this view left the city in their tens of thousands.

On the other hand, many who have stayed behind would agree that Hong Kong was better off in 2022 – the twenty-fifth anniversary of the HKSAR's establishment – than it was in late 2019, when the city was in the throes of 'civil war'. In their view, the NSL and the electoral overhaul of 2021 were necessary to restore the right balance between 'One Country' and 'Two Systems', and the OCTS project would not be sustainable otherwise.

There remain lingering fears over how the NSL and future iterations of national security-related laws would be enforced in the city, and doubts whether the Hong Kong judiciary can remain independent and vigilant in defending constitutional rights in the years to come. But many Chinese patriots and optimists believe with conviction that Beijing has gifted Hong Kong a fresh start to reclaim its standing as Asia's global city. Only time will tell which narrative will pan out in the end.

FURTHER READING

Chen, AHY, *The Changing Legal Orders in Hong Kong and Mainland China: Essays on 'One Country, Two Systems'* (City University of Hong Kong Press, 2021).

Loh, C and Cullen, R, *No Third Person: Rewriting the Hong Kong Story* (Abbreviated Press, 2018).

Puig, GV and Ip, EC, *The Freest Market in the World: The Constitutional Logic of Economic Liberty in China's Hong Kong* (Routledge, 2023).

Index

Introductory Note

References such as '178–79' indicate (not necessarily continuous) discussion of a topic across a range of pages. Wherever possible in the case of topics with many references, these have either been divided into sub-topics or only the most significant discussions of the topic are listed. Because the entire work is about 'Hong Kong' and 'constitutional law', the use of these terms (and certain others which occur constantly throughout the book) as entry points has been restricted. Information will be found under the corresponding detailed topics.

www.ingramcontent.com/pod-product-compliance
Ingram Content Group UK Ltd.
Pitfield, Milton Keynes, MK11 3LW, UK
UKHW020206290926
15470UKWH00001B/27

9 781509 956296